Acclaim for Monir Shahroudy Farmanfarmaian and Zara Houshmand's

A MIRROR GARDEN

"Splendid. . . . The memoir whisks the reader down the back roads of prerevolution Iran, but its most powerful episodes revolve around the author's creative development."
—*Time Out New York*

"[Farmanfarmaian] has not allowed the past to either trap her in nostalgia or corner her into defensive bitterness. In every world she has traveled, she has never been petty. . . . She labels one of her photographs . . . 'A Woman in Full.' The reader will come away from these pages agreeing wholeheartedly."
— *Austin American-Statesman*

"Fresh and unexpected. . . . [Farmanfarmaian's] profound appreciation for the stark beauty and culture of Iran shapes a finely patterned, richly hued, and loving portrait of a now-demonized land."
—*Booklist*

"Intriguing. . . . An admirable story of encouragement, self-sufficiency and liberty."
—*Library Journal*

"Farmanfarmaian is a bona fide artistic legend."
—*Time Out Dubai*

"Thought-provoking, heartbreaking, delightful. . . . Farmanfarmaian boldly follows her dream of becoming an artist in the West before following love back to a new Iran. Like a Persian Audrey Hepburn, she recounts her adventures among boorish fanatics, elegant spies, celebrities, and, best of all, her own eccentric family, with a combination of plainspoken pluck and grace under pressure that is inspiring and irresistible."
—Tom Reiss, author of *The Orientalist*

MONIR SHAHROUDY FARMANFARMAIAN

AND

ZARA HOUSHMAND

A MIRROR GARDEN

Monir Shahroudy Farmanfarmaian was born in 1924. She now lives and works in New York.

Zara Houshmand is an Iranian American writer and theater artist. She lives in Austin, Texas.

A MIRROR GARDEN

A

MIRROR

GARDEN

MONIR SHAHROUDY FARMANFARMAIAN

AND

ZARA HOUSHMAND

ANCHOR BOOKS

A Division of Random House, Inc.

New York

FIRST ANCHOR BOOKS EDITION, AUGUST 2008

Copyright © 2007 by Monir Farmanfarmaian and Zara Houshmand

All rights reserved. Published in the United States by Anchor Books,
a division of Random House, Inc., New York, and in Canada by
Random House of Canada Limited, Toronto. Originally published
in hardcover in the United States by Alfred A. Knopf, a division
of Random House, Inc., New York, in 2007.

Anchor Books and colophon are registered
trademarks of Random House, Inc.

A Mirror Garden is a work of nonfiction, but the names of certain
individuals, as well as potentially identifying descriptive
details concerning them, have been changed.

All photographs with the exception of the photograph by Robert Phillips
on page 231 are courtesy of Monir Shahroudy Farmanfarmaian.

The Library of Congress has cataloged the Knopf edition as follows:
Farmanfarmaian, Monir.
A mirror garden / Monir Farmanfarmaian and Zara Houshmand.
p. cm.
1. Farmanfarmaian, Monir. 2. Women—Iran—Biography.
3. Iranian American women—Biography. 4. Iranian Americans—
Biography. I. Houshmand, Zara. II. Title.
CT1888.F375A3 2007 955.05092—dc22 [B] 2006048816

Anchor ISBN: 978-0-307-27878-4

Book design by M. Kristen Bearse

www.anchorbooks.com

Printed in the United States of America
10 9 8 7 6 5 4 3 2 1

To Abol *joon*

A MIRROR GARDEN

The evening sun was melting through the stained-glass windows when my nanny spread the bedding out on the carpets. Nanny was old and, under her scarf, completely bald. I had seen her in the bathhouse, bald as an egg. She was beautiful nonetheless, with white skin and big, deep blue eyes, like the china doll my father had brought my sister all the way from Russia when the czar was still king. My grandfather had fallen in love with Nanny, the other servants whispered, but what could they know? They took turns falling in love with her themselves. But I knew that she loved her cats best of all, and everyone else would have to wait in line.

I pulled my quilt a safe distance from my brother Hassan, so he couldn't steal it after wetting his own, and stared at the ceiling to calm my excitement as I waited for Nanny's story to begin. Lines of gold and black traced nightingales and roses on wooden panels of cobalt blue, the color of the night sky. I followed the winding

WHEN I WAS SIX YEARS OLD, MY UNCLE TOOK MY PHOTOGRAPH WITH HIS RUSSIAN CAMERA—THE FIRST ONE I HAD EVER SEEN.

stems of the roses across my wooden sky and counted the nightingales one by one, until Nanny spread her skirts on the carpet beside me and began.

"Once upon a time there was, or maybe there wasn't, a girl who was just as big as you are now. She was dark-skinned and not very pretty, and oh! she was trouble, as naughty as a girl could be."

"They cut off her head," Hassan decided summarily.

"Who's telling this story? No, she kept her head, and a good thing too, because she had to be very clever to get out of all the trouble she got into after she fell down the well."

For seven nights I lived with the fear that met the trouble-prone heroine at the bottom of that dark well. Each night I followed her into another of seven dark rooms. Each room lay behind a locked door that needed its own key, and each of the keys was held by a different jinn, or worse: a bear, a giant, a tiger. The tiger was the worst of all. When I could not bear it any longer, I dashed downstairs, across the courtyard, around the pool, taking a shortcut through the flower beds and down the stairs to the toilet. The tiger waited for me to finish and pull up my pants: it crouched on top of the wall at the far end of the courtyard, ready to spring. Its muscles rippled silver in the moonlight, just like the silver circles spreading slowly over the courtyard pool. I stopped in my tracks before risking one terrified step, then another. The tiger waited still, as inscrutable as one of Nanny's cats. The moon itself was its accomplice now, stalking me, moving only when I moved. I bolted for the safety of bed and the promised reward of the story's seventh night, when tigers and bears and jinns dissolved in the glow of a treasure chest spilling jewels. My courageous double grabbed the jewels and escaped through a hole in the side of the mountain, where she was snatched up and carried home, treasure and all, on the glorious wings of the Simorgh, king of the birds.

I hid my hard-earned treasure in the basement storeroom next to the kitchen, where so many other treasures were stored. It would hardly be noticed by jealous brothers there. The jars of pickles, quinces in syrup, and petals suspended in jam captured the few dusty rays of underground light, glowing like jewels. There were huge trays of golden baklava and cookies baked in batches big enough to last for months. My mother's precious bowls of deep pink crystal stood by, ready to be filled the moment guests arrived.

The storeroom stretched under half the house. The most wonderful spot in the whole room was the floating bed where the bread was kept safe from mice and bugs. A platform as big as a boat hung from the ceiling by four thick wires, a swing beyond imagining. I balanced on the ladder and stepped across space. Swaying on the edge, I surveyed my kingdom. It was autumn, and a city of giant beehives was growing from the ground below me: ceramic rings, wide enough at the bottom for two men to stand inside, were stacked into conical towers and filled layer by layer as the harvest came in. One tower held chickpeas, another one lentils, another almonds, another pistachios. A little door in the bottom ring dispensed a day's measure onto the cook's brass tray, and each one had its own sound, from the shushing of lentils headed for soup, to the snappy clatter of pistachios. I knew that the towers of nuts were only a fraction of what our

THE BASEMENT STOREROOM.

orchards produced in the villages surrounding Qazvin. I had climbed up mountains of pistachios and rolled in avalanches while the workers rubbed off the red and green skins and sorted: this pile for roasting and that to be ground up for baklava, and sacks and sacks to be sewn up and sent off to Russia.

When I leaned and pumped to set the platform swinging, the rhythm echoed the memory of the baker bending, again and again, to slap a cushion of dough on the oven wall. She would bend again, iron rod in hand, to peel off the hot sheet of bread and send it flying to the cloth. The bread, wrapped in bundles at my feet, remembered too. When I swung too hard, it grabbed the chance to fly through the air again. The broken bundles on the basement floor betrayed me to the cook first, who gave me a familiar scolding, and then, with Hassan as eager messenger, to my mother. The second scolding from her only confirmed the hopelessness of my ever keeping out of trouble.

Hassan, just three years older than I, was my most immediate and predictable tormentor. I could compete with him, or with any of the boys, at climbing trees, racing on donkeys, or setting traps at the neighbors' doors. But Hassan's knowledge of the world at large left me a straggler. When Nanny put on her best veil and herded us through milling crowds of mourners to see the *taziyeh* performance of the martyrdom at Kerbala, I promptly fell asleep in the black silk folds of her lap. So I had to rely on Hassan's authority for a blow-by-blow description of what I had missed: the martial feats, horses racing through the crowd, chanting mourners flinging chains over their shoulders, blood dripping onto white robes.

Nor could I argue when he cast me in the villain's role. Our stage was the wooden platform in the courtyard garden, where on summer nights quilts were spread for us to sleep. Hassan found a makeshift torch, a kebab skewer wrapped with a kerosene rag that the gardener used, with a sieve on his head, to smoke out the bees' nest under the stairs. Marching solemnly at the head of our two-man procession, torch blazing aloft, Hassan proclaimed the imminent death of the evil usurper, Yazid. Yazid, of course, was me. I echoed Hassan's howling vowels in cooperative ignorance. But when he followed through, flinging the torch at my head, and the blood was suddenly real, my screams brought the house down.

The bleeding continued despite all efforts to stanch it, despite even the appearance of my father, routed from his office next door. As long as the blood flowed, I continued screaming. As a final resort, Nanny gathered spiderwebs into a small sticky blob to plug the wound. Both bleeding and screaming stopped. The novelty of this miracle cure and the superior knowledge I now held gave me a delicious sense of advantage: so much so that I could beg my father to spare Hassan a beating when he dragged the guilty actor out of his hiding place in the basement.

The other demons of my childhood were more elusive. They came at me not with fists flying as Hassan did, but in the form of a tightening feeling inside that had no name, and the only thing I knew for sure was that I fully deserved my fate. I was ugly, dark, and graceless, while all three of my sisters were almost as fair-skinned and lovely as my mother. When my mother had nursed me, her youngest, at the bathhouse, other women asked if I was indeed her own. I knew that I was, no matter how many times my eldest brother, Ali, insisted that I was adopted. Indeed, Ali might well have been a foundling my mother picked up in the street after losing her first two children. (We argued this into the ground, but I was secure in the knowledge that no one would have claimed such an ugly child as me if the burden weren't natural.) Worst of all, I had straight hair. No amount of combing or wishing would make it curl like my sisters'. Obviously I was destined to spend my life in the shadows.

The one person who ever challenged this verdict was my mother's youngest sister. She was dark like me. I called her Auntie Aziz-jan, my dearest, and she called me her little black bug. "Monir is ugly," she conceded, "but her eyes have a sparkle that comes from the heart."

I could dream of no greater compliment. Whenever she came to visit, after the flurry of greetings, the lifting of veils, the kisses all around, I would rush down to the basement to make sure that the very finest cookies filled the pink crystal bowls. Once my mother sent for grapes to be picked fresh from the vines that grew in the courtyard. How could she know that Hassan and I had already stripped all the best fruit we could reach from the ground? In collusion for once, we had not betrayed each other as yet. But even this fragile alliance would lead to trouble if Auntie Aziz-jan were denied the best. I ran up the stairs and squeezed through the balcony railing. Hugging the trunk of the old vine, I leaned for the plumpest bunch, the worthiest

gift, all the sweeter for being the hardest to reach. I pulled, but the vine pulled back, and I crashed through the leaves to the ground.

Stunned and winded, I knew that everything hurt, but I had no idea it would matter so much. The fuss and commotion were well worth the pain. The droshky was hitched up to the horses, and a blanket found to bundle me up. The doctor was serious, but his hands were surprisingly warm for such an important man. Nothing was broken, thanks be to God, said my mother, but for days I was special and lay on my quilt counting roses and nightingales. When I added them all up, it was clear: I was not so terribly unloved.

I ADORED MY AUNTIE AZIZ-JAN.

After my fall Auntie Aziz-jan claimed that I brought her good luck. From that time on she made sure that my own face was the first face she saw after sighting the sliver of the new moon in the night sky each month. She would come at other times as well, but I waited especially for her new-moon visit and watched each night as the moon shrank in anticipation. After she looked at my face, she would close her eyes and hold out her hands to receive the Qoran and the coin I would place in her palm. In this way I ensured that she would have money enough for the month, and I took this responsibility seriously. I knew her husband was stingy. He was from Isfahan, where everyone was stingy. When he came to visit, he would ask for paper to write his letters and then ask for stamps to mail them. But thanks to me, Auntie Aziz-jan would never have to stoop so low.

The geography of my world was both circumscribed and vast: its center was the courtyard of our home, where a pool some twenty meters long, surrounded by flower beds and sheltered verandas, offered a vista of cool peace in the midst of the hubbub of the household.

In one wall of the courtyard, the servants had cut a tiny door into the brick as a shortcut to my father's offices in the caravansary facing the street beyond. In those days my father was a merchant trading with Russia, in partnership with his brother. Business had been bet-

THE COURTYARD OF OUR HOME IN QAZVIN.

ter before their revolution, when the house that had served as my uncle's office and home in Moscow had been confiscated, along with all of their goods. My uncle had come home half dead from his terrible journey through the war-torn country, having crossed the Caspian Sea stowed away in the coal bin of a steamship. Now there was talk of trading with Germany instead, but our caravans still carried pistachios and wool and hides to Russia and returned with fine fabrics and objects both beautiful and strange. Our telephone was one such curiosity, the first in all of Qazvin. A wire ran through the passage that linked the courtyard to the office, so my mother and father could talk to each other as if they were miles apart.

At the far end of the courtyard was a massive, iron-studded wooden door, flanked by two small hexagonal rooms where the doorman lodged. It was his job to watch out for thieves but also to welcome the constant stream of visitors with effusively humble greetings. The door opened onto a narrow covered alley with a high arched ceiling of brick woven in patterns like basketry. A few of the bricks were loose where thieves had once stashed some jewelry, confirming my notion that treasure might be found in the least expected places. Next door was an empty lot that served well for games that required a wilderness setting or were better played clear of grown-ups. Opposite our own door was the entrance to the public bathhouse, with a painting hanging above it of the epic hero Rostam mounted on his white steed, gazing into the distance. In the daytime women came and went,

**THE ENTRANCE TO THE BATHHOUSE
ACROSS THE STREET.**

red-faced from hours of steaming and scrubbing. At night the men took their turn.

The city of Qazvin beyond the alley was unknown to me for the most part, viewed from a donkey's back or the seat of a horse-drawn droshky on the way to our outlying gardens and orchards. There was the great mosque where my father's grandfather, the Ayatollah Shahroudy, had preached Friday sermons but where I had never set foot. It was a place my father dismissed darkly—a place, he said, where the answers to questions would not be found. I didn't know what kind of questions he meant exactly, but I sensed that my own questions about these questions would not be welcome. It was not until several years later that I learned the source of my father's bitterness toward the mullahs.

The nearest of our gardens, and my most familiar playground, lay an hour's walk toward the city's edge. It was built like a small fortress: four towers marked the corners, tall enough to see bandits on horseback at a distance. The gardener lived in one of the towers; the

THE SHRINE OF THE SHI'ITE SAINT SHAHZADEH HOSSEIN,
AN IMPORTANT LANDMARK IN QAZVIN.

others housed storerooms, stables, and a carpeted room for sitting or eating or napping. The perimeter walls were topped with a loose thatch of branches to protect the sun-baked mud from eroding under melting snow.

I knew those walls well. Although fruit trees filled the entire tract— peach, apple, mulberry, almond, and walnut—the peaches that hung from the neighbor's trees over the wall were always a little bit riper and sweeter, or just a more interesting challenge. A donkey's back offered the best boost up but also the danger that I would be left hanging if the donkey walked away.

The giant walnut tree was best for climbing, and of all the brothers and sisters and cousins, I was the bravest climber. A bird's nest just out of reach was a reason to leap for the branch rather than just give up like the others. When one such attempt left me hanging helplessly in midair, I knew better than to trust the donkey that Hassan pulled under the tree to break my fall. Donkeys were much better suited to racing than to climbing. I swung for a better hold and came thrashing down through the branches as the donkey predictably backed away.

In one corner of the garden there was a spring, small and deep, no good for swimming but perfect for keeping a melon cool. In the winter, when we children abandoned the garden, that spring had another purpose. My father would make the hour-long trek from home early every morning to take a dip in the icy water. At breakfast each day we would ask him, "Was it cold?" and he would answer ritually, "Not bad, not bad."

The icy winter dip was just one of his routines. He was a fanatic for health, and just as well, because when he was sick, the whole household felt it. One winter he caught a bad cold, and I watched as he paced up and down the length of the living room in his white woolen bathrobe, kicking the wall hard each time he reached the end. He had a white scarf tied around his head, and he sang a silly Turkish song as he marched:

I'll go to the market,
Buy a scarf for my head,
And then I won't complain
About the pain in my head.

The end of the verse was punctuated with a final kick and a loud groan, and then he would turn around and start all over again. Periodically he yelled for the servants to bring a charcoal brazier with hot stones and a bowl of yogurt mixed with water. Dropping the stones into the yogurt, he would inhale the steam noisily with a towel tented over his head. I watched the show for hours and wondered just how bad a cold could be.

In the winter our outdoor world was limited to the courtyard. The grapevines were now bare, the long pool frozen solid. A mountain of snow piled up, almost as high as the second floor, where the gardener shoveled it off the flat roof to prevent it collapsing. The afternoon sun and the freezing nights gave it a slick coating of ice, ideal for sledding on a sheet of tin.

One day as I was sledding, Hassan appeared with a rifle he had found and proceeded to attack my mountain. "I'm going to conquer Turkey!" he announced as he struggled to the top. The rifle was more interesting than my scrap of tin, so I enlisted as his lieutenant. We had completed the conquest of Turkey and were gathering forces for an attack on the Caucasus when I decided that I had been taking orders for long enough: it was my turn to hold the gun.

We fought as viciously as ever. I was taking a real beating by the time my screams brought the gardener running. But he couldn't manage the icy slope and kept sliding back down as he yelled at us. Finally a voice that held real authority cut through the racket: "If you don't stop right now, I'll get a gun that's loaded and shoot you both down."

It was Uncle Dervish, standing there in his white robe, as grand as the angel Gabriel. My mother's eldest brother, his real name was Hajji Mohammad Sadeq, but everyone called him Daie Darvish— Uncle Dervish. His arrivals were always a little like magic, for he came and went on his own terms and answered to no one. He had piercing, deep-set eyes, and everything about him was long and tall: the long white robe with trailing sleeves, the long hair that curled below his shoulders, the beard that hung down to his waist. His beautiful hands had long fingers that danced when he spoke. He never wore shoes, winter or summer, and his naked feet were cracked like the desert earth.

Uncle Dervish had shown up just in time for Yalda, the solstice celebration on the fortieth and longest night of winter. I forgot my bruises soon enough in the excitement of the preparations. The best fruits of summer had been saved for an unseasonable appearance on this night. I scampered from the basement, where a watermelon had been buried in cool sand since the last days of summer, to the dark room at the top of the house, where bunches of grapes were strung together and hung from the rafters to the floor in long rows. By now they were sweeter than summer, halfway to becoming raisins.

The watermelon was always a little bit mushy, but it made a beautiful picture of red and green, echoed by deep green cucumbers and jewel-like pomegranates laid out in a lavish spread on the *korsi*. The *korsi* was the heart of our home in the winter, a low wooden table draped with quilts and surrounded by pillows propped against the walls of a small chamber off one side of the living room. You could lean back in comfort and stretch your legs toward the heat of the charcoal brazier under the table, and most nights the children curled up to sleep in a cozy nest under the trailing quilts.

But Yalda was an excuse to stay up all night, listening to stories and songs. My father asked Nanny to sing for us, and she played her

UNCLE DERVISH.

large flat drum like an oversize tambourine, making up verses that teased each one of us in turn. While I listened, I nibbled from the large bowl of *ajil,* a mixture of dried fruits and nuts. We were supposed to make a wish as we ate it, a wish for an end to a problem. I knew that tomorrow the remainder in the bowl would be added to a much bigger tray of *ajil* and given to the poor to ensure that the wishes would be answered. But the only wish that came into my mind was that I could have another handful.

In the springtime my mountain in the courtyard melted slowly to slush. The streets of Qazvin became a treacherous maze of puddles and mud. Nosrat, a servant who, like Nanny, was close as family to us—these lineages were woven together over many generations—walked me to school. It was the first year that I had such a regular appointment with the outside world. School at that age—five or six—was little more than an exercise in sitting still for a few hours each day, but the journey there and back was an adventure worth that brief confinement. Nosrat and I carefully planned our route, which skirted the bazaar. We weighed the relative hazards of puddles and mud. The mud, we discovered too late, was deep enough to suck off and gobble up my shoe. Nosrat groped for it, but it had disappeared forever into the bowels of the earth. He carried me all the way home. At any other time the piggyback ride would have been a treat, but with Nosrat's steps sinking even deeper under my weight, it only added to the indignity of losing a shoe.

Nosrat rescued me too when I was fool enough to tease a camel in heat that had parked itself in a clearing at the edge of the bazaar. The twisting and twitching lips, all bearded with foam, were just too bizarre for me to pass without comment. I mirrored the contortions of the camel's lips and made an attempt to imitate the strange braying noise that came out of them. The camel took offense and came after me, followed by Nosrat, with the camel driver far in the rear. The chase ended only when I ducked between some barrels into a shop. I stood shaking behind the startled shopkeeper, who faced the camel peering across the lucky barrier of barrels like a dissatisfied customer, while Nosrat did his best to calm us all.

"That was no way to talk to a camel. You should never tease animals," Nosrat chided me as we walked home. I was still weak at the knees and not ready to hear the finer points of his lecture; it seemed wiser to avoid any conversation with camels altogether. Nosrat rubbed his chin sagely and said it would perhaps be better if we avoided any conversation with my mother about the matter, which would land us both in trouble.

I should have listened more closely to Nosrat's lesson, for I also teased one of Nanny's cats in an escalating feud that we both ended up regretting. The hostilities began innocently enough. I had discovered her kittens, nesting on a pile of spare bedding in a storeroom. Nanny had propped a window open for the cat to come and go. When I climbed a stack of mattresses to peek at the kittens, the enraged mother came flying at me through the window with a bloodcurdling shriek and claws extended. I managed to push her off me as I slid down the mattresses, but I was badly scratched.

My revenge was a drawn-out game that went on for weeks. I followed her around the house, hiding behind first one curtain and then another, meowing pitifully in my tiniest voice. I wanted her to think that I'd stolen a kitten, and she seemed to be convinced; at any rate she searched endlessly, looking more and more confused as I led her on.

The next round came later. I had forgotten the kitten game, distracted by a new pet. One afternoon when everyone except me had

THE BAZAAR IN QAZVIN, WHERE CAMELS MIGHT BE FOUND AT REST.

dozed off, I had wandered down to the courtyard pool. I dragged a shallow copper laundry tub to the water and launched off paddling in my boat. The steering was crude, so it was a matter of fate when a baby starling fluttered to a landing on the tiled lip just within my reach. I grabbed it, and though I upset the tub and was doused, I held on. My excitement was loud enough to wake the household. I ran dripping even to my father's inner sanctum, which was strictly off limits at nap time, to announce that I'd caught a bird.

Eventually the fuss subsided and the little bird settled into the household routine. It lived in one of the empty upstairs rooms, and I would bring it down to the living room to visit. It would peck at the large Persian carpet and sing as it waddled around its woven garden. The whole family became very fond of it; I adored it and rushed upstairs to see it the moment I got home from school each day. But one day Nanny intercepted me, and I knew by her face that the news was not good.

The cat had got her revenge. I was inconsolable, sobbing so hard that I barely heard Hassan's announcement that he intended to bring the cat to justice. I was sobbing the whole time he gathered his cohorts, sobbing still as they hammered together a makeshift scaffold in the empty lot next door. I didn't realize he was serious until an ominous drumroll on a large tin can heralded the imminent execution. I ran, turning the corner just in time to witness the cat with the rope at her neck still slack. I turned again and ran screaming, "They're hanging the cat!" Nobody believed me. The day ended darkly: two deaths, many mourners, and my brother brought to some appropriate justice that was kinder than what he had served.

The freshness of spring evaporated and the green faded under a layer of dust. For a brief period we slept outdoors in the courtyard on a large platform that was covered with kilims in the daytime and spread with bedding each night. The stars replaced my ceiling of roses and nightingales. But the heat came on fast, and soon enough it was time to move to Abdolabad, the village home of our summers.

We could see Abdolabad even from our city, though it was a three-hour ride by droshky to the cool mountains. The mud-brick village melted into the brown shadows of the foothills, but we could recognize it by the huge sycamore that towered above. It was really a stand of seven trees that joined in a ring at the base; each one of the seven trunks was bigger than three men together joining hands could wrap their arms around. The giant tree was a holy shrine for the people of the village; they came there to pray and make *nazr*—a vow, usually a promise of charity, in exchange for an answer to their prayers. They would tie a strip of colored cloth to the tree as a token of their promise, and these strips danced from all the lower branches in the wind.

Beside the tree was a spring that ran down a stone-lined channel to a small lake, half natural and half built from stone, like a terrace of water on the mountainside. I taught myself how to swim in that lake, which was full of algae and frogs and water snakes. I would dive to reach the *tupak*, a huge stick wrapped with rubber and cloth that plugged the hole where the water drained into a hollowed-out log that ran down the mountain. The plug would be pulled for a few

· 18 ·

\text{\textARABIC} ١٣١٧ o ٮسٮ

MY BELOVED IRAN. I WOULD
BRAID HER HAIR, TWIST THE
PLAITS INTO BUNS, AND
SECURE THE STYLE WITH A
NEEDLE AND THREAD.

hours late each afternoon, and the water would rush down the channel, turning the wooden wheel and the great stone disks in the millhouse below, then churning into a smaller pool where pennyroyal grew fragrant around the edges. From there it flowed to the patchwork of fields surrounding the village, through a carefully governed system of gated channels that each farmer would open and close for their allotted time.

When I tired of swimming, there were endless games of hide-and-seek behind the black boulders jutting from the mountainside. I played house with a strip of old carpet spread in the hollow heart of the giant tree. There were almonds to pick from low-hanging branches and wildflowers to gather for my sister's hair. We would sit for hours side by side on two special rocks while I plaited delicate splashes of color into her long curly braids. Iran was six years older than me, and to me she was the epitome of all beauty. She was everything I wished, without much hope, that I could be, but I was proud to be skilled at making her even more beautiful.

Uncle Dervish would come often to Abdolabad in the summer, but he didn't stay at our house in the village. He pitched a tent beside the spring in the shade of the giant sycamore tree, under the dangling promises, where he kept his bedroll and a samovar and a few glasses for tea. My parents had given strict orders that the children were never to enter that tent in the evening, so it was always a little mysterious to us exactly what went on inside. Perhaps there was opium or hashish; there often seemed to be a party going on, with singing, and strangers having a good time. In any case, the servants would carry up trays of food to the tent and the food would disappear.

But many afternoons we went to the tent and called for Uncle Dervish to come out. He would walk with us under the trees or sit on a carpet spread at the edge of the lake. If we were lucky, he would tell stories: mysterious mountain adventures or tales of strange cities. One late afternoon as I sat with my sisters and a few cousins, picnicking on watermelon that had cooled in the spring by his tent, Uncle Dervish offered to tell our fortunes. A heavy book was passed from hand to hand, and turns were taken to open it blindly. Uncle Dervish read the chosen poem out loud, wrapping his tongue around drawn-out vowels in a musical chant, then revealed the message that was buried in the verse.

I wasn't paying much attention. The poetry of Hafez was opaque to me, book language that my sisters learned at school. I didn't even really expect a turn. As the voices droned, my eyes were drawn to the city of Qazvin miles below us, looking very still and small in the early evening light. Here and there a blue dome shimmered in the dun-colored huddle that melted into the sprawling plain. On either side of the city a thin straight line was etched into the plain, fading into the horizon. I knew that the road east led to Tehran; and to the west lay Hamadan, Turkey, Europe, and the world beyond.

Uncle Dervish's voice broke into my daydream: "Let's see what the future holds for Monir." He passed me the heavy book. I closed my eyes and brushed my fingers over the edges as I had seen the others do. But when I opened the book on my lap, Uncle Dervish didn't take it to read the poem out loud. Instead he held my hand on top of the page. His long thin finger traced the lines of my palm, and I thought of the roads on the plain. "Monir will be very lucky," he said, "and very beautiful. She will marry a prince and have two lovely daughters."

What nonsense, I thought.

CHAPTER TWO

One unusually quiet afternoon we found Uncle Dervish in a storytelling mood. Sitting by the lake, with the softest breeze playing in the leaves and barely a ripple on the water, he told us the story of his life.

"I was your grandfather's eldest son, the eldest of seven children, and he was a very important man in the world of men. He was the consul who represented the Ottoman emperor to the merchants of Qazvin, and Qazvin in those days was a very important city, much bigger than Tehran. One day it occurred to old Tajerbashi that there was more to life than buying and selling, and it was time to look after his soul. He decided to make a pilgrimage to Mecca, and he took me along. I must have been about eighteen years old, and I was ready for adventure. We traveled to Mecca in the consul's fancy carriage along with a caravan of hundreds of camels and horses. We were three months on the road. It was the first time I'd ever traveled, and I loved every minute. When we reached Mecca and finished our business with the rituals, and a month more of visiting merchants on Father's official business, I knew by the end of it all that I wouldn't go home. I had figured out by that time that religion was a ticket to travel, so I told my father I wanted to go to Cairo to study religious law.

"My father was thrilled that I had become so devout. He gave me the money I needed and wrote letters of introduction to all the great merchants of Cairo, and we parted ways. I lasted all of six months as a scholar, then took off for Turkey. Turkey was one step away from Russia, and Russia was an adventure like nothing I'd ever imagined.

"I discovered St. Petersburg—theater, parties, dancing, restaurants—and several fine young ladies discovered me. I was quite the Don Juan, and I dressed the part, like a wealthy young European. A year passed by, and another, and another. My father sent messages, asking when I planned to come home, and I sent messages back saying that my studies weren't finished yet. Finally, after four years, he sent an ultimatum: 'No more money until you come home.'

"So I came home, but slowly, savoring each city, via Turkey again, then through Baku and Tabriz. From Tabriz I sent a messenger ahead to let them know I was almost home. My father prepared for my arrival, brought all his sons and every merchant and dignitary he knew to welcome me. They all rode out in their carriages beyond the city gates, as if royalty were arriving. My father brought a sheep to sacrifice in my honor, and he even brought the Ayatollah, to whom he would show off his eldest son, who by now must surely have become a great scholar of religious law.

"When I stepped down from the carriage, in my trousers and frock coat and top hat, my patent leather shoes and my spats and my cane, my father took one look at me and fainted. He was out cold, flat on the ground. When he came to and got back on his feet, I gave him a kiss. He just stared as if I had come from the moon. All he could say was 'Why the hell do you look like that?' I told him that I'd become a European.

"They went ahead and killed the poor sheep anyway. What else could they do? But for days my father shouted and my mother cried, and they all kept begging me to change my clothes. When family and friends came to pay their respects to the returning scholar, I wasn't

MY GRANDFATHER IN HIS CARRIAGE LED THE PARTY THAT GREETED
UNCLE DERVISH OUTSIDE THE CITY GATES.

allowed downstairs, and they certainly wouldn't let me go out of the house.

"Finally one day I'd had enough. I put on the long *ghabah* my mother had laid out for me, and I went for a walk. I wandered the streets talking to myself, in Russian, in Persian, saying whatever came into my head. I picked up fruit in the bazaar and took a bite here and there, telling the poor surprised grocer that his fruit was quite delicious. When I ran into merchants my father knew, then I really talked nonsense. Everyone said, 'Poor Tajerbashi, his son Hajji Sadeq has gone crazy. That's what comes of spending too much time in foreign countries.'

"For a long time this was my only escape. Then it occurred to me: maybe I should become a Sufi. I had met a Sufi teacher when I was in Turkey and had spent some time at the *khanegah* where he and his followers lived, but it wasn't until I came home that the things he had told me really began to make sense. So I looked for a Sufi teacher, and I found a *khanegah* here in Qazvin.

"When word got back to my father, all hell broke loose. He thought I would be smoking hashish and going barefoot and giving his money away, so he locked me up. At night one servant slept inside my room, and another just outside the door. I learned to pick the lock and silence the latch and chain with a piece of wax so I wouldn't wake my guards. I would sneak out almost every night. I would climb across the roof and jump down onto a horse that a friend from the *khanegah* had waiting for me. We had a secret password to enter the *khanegah,* and of course what happens there remains secret too. I would come back just before dawn and sleep all day with a book draped over my face. The family thought I was tired from studying all night, and they let me be.

"But one night when the moon was especially bright, a servant spotted me up on the roof and cried thief. I ran and slipped and fell off the roof. When they found their thief, he had a broken leg and two broken arms, and a few ribs broken too. They had to kill a sheep and skin it and wrap me up in the skin, still warm, to keep all the pieces together. For three months I lay in bed like a cripple.

"My father took it into his head then that maybe a wife would help me to settle down. He forced me to marry my cousin, your aunt Massoumeh. We lived together in the same house, but I was never really a husband to her. Poor woman, it wasn't her fault. She was beautiful too. When my father died, I put an end to that game. I gave her a huge emerald ring that I had bought in Turkey. I gave her the house and the land my father had left me, and I told her, 'I'm not your husband, I never was. Forget about me.' And from that time on I was free to go where I pleased.

"I got very involved in the *khanegah* then. I wore the white robe and went barefoot and let my hair grow, and devoted my life to realizing the presence of Ali.* I even wore a *kashkul* on a chain to go begging and carried a fancy ax in case I met a leopard in the mountains. Although the one time I did meet a leopard, I didn't even need to use the ax. I just raised my arm, and that was enough to scare it away . . . see? The wind was with me."

Uncle Dervish lifted an imaginary ax, and a sudden wind off the lake caught his sleeve, billowing gently. The leaves above us rustled, and I was amazed. He finished his story in a whisper, as if telling me the most precious secret: "After a while I gave up all the praying, gave up even reading the Qoran. I have enough to do just trying to be a good human being."

*The cousin and son-in-law of the Prophet Mohammad, who succeeded him as the first Imam and who is especially revered by Shi'ite Muslims and by some Sufi schools.

CHAPTER THREE

My mother had a story too, though it was not the story of her whole life. How could a life that filled the air I breathed ever squeeze itself entirely into a story? No, it was only the story of her wedding, or rather not-a-wedding—which reminded me of Nanny's stories, which always began so equivocally: "Once upon a time, there was or maybe there wasn't . . ." My mother's story was told many times over by many people and always with pride. But the first time I heard it was the best, because that time she told it herself.

The story bubbled up by chance one winter night when my mother was arguing with Uncle Dervish as we all sat together around the *korsi*. My mother was closer than anyone else to Uncle Dervish, but she was angry because he had given away a sheep to a villager who was getting married. Uncle Dervish was always giving things away; that was why he had nothing at all of his own.

"What's one more sheep to you?" he asked. "You have hundreds of sheep." He waved it off as if a sheep didn't matter at all, which only made her angrier.

"A sheep is nothing to me! But it wasn't your sheep to give!"

"You have far too much stuff anyway. What do you need all this stuff for?" Uncle Dervish waved his arms around, the white sleeves flapping like wings as he accused the carpets, the crystal, the Russian clock . . . "You spend as much on one dress as a wedding costs in the village."

My mother indeed was very well dressed. She wore stockings and elegant dresses in the European style, though when she was younger, she had worn velvet jackets trimmed with gold, and *shaliteh,* the short, flouncy brocade skirts that were worn over pants. That too was a fashion that came from Europe a long time ago, she had told me when I peeked in the chest where they were neatly folded. The Qajar king Nasser al-Din Shah had been impressed by the ballet on a visit to Paris and commanded the ladies of his harem to wear short skirts like tutus, and naturally fashion followed. But even though my mother dressed in the Western style at home, when she went outside she always wore a veil of pleated black silk and a mesh embroidered with flowers to cover her face.

"How do you know what a dress costs?" she snapped at Uncle Dervish. "Or a wedding for that matter? You live without money— you don't know what anything costs!"

"You should talk," Uncle Dervish answered. "You threw away the grandest wedding Qazvin had ever seen. Oh, the money that was wasted! The gifts, the food—the shouting and screaming. My God, the shouting that was wasted on you!" But my uncle was laughing out loud now, and my father was laughing too. Hassan and I could sense a story coming, and we begged to hear what had happened.

"Tell them," my father said, and my mother gave up trying to look angry, conceding the argument in exchange for an eager audience.

"It's true. I was the apple of my father's eye, the first in everything, even though I was a girl, even though Uncle Dervish was really the first child. I was the first daughter after a string of five sons, and I guess he was tired of boys. Your grandfather did things his own way. In any case, he had chosen a husband for me, and he was very pleased with his choice. The man was a mullah, turban and all, very respectable, very learned. His grandfather was an ayatollah."

"Was it Baba?" I asked, confused. I knew that my father's grandfather was an ayatollah, but I couldn't picture my father himself in a turban, no matter how long ago.

"No, your baba's grandfather was a different ayatollah."

"Far too many ayatollahs buzzing around like flies on a donkey," my father grumbled.

"Save us the sermon," said Uncle Dervish. "Let my sister tell her story."

"After his family proposed to mine and my father accepted, they came for the *aqd*, the engagement ceremony, in a great procession with ten men carrying wooden trays on their heads, piled high with gorgeous fabrics and jewelry and clothes for my new life. There were tulip candlesticks and sweets and a Qoran and a great mirror, all ready for the ceremony. Musicians came with them just like a parade through the streets. So many people came, the whole garden was spread with trays of food, and outside in the street they were dishing up huge pots of rice and stew for the poor.

"But I didn't want him." She paused for effect, just as Nanny did when her story got really scary.

"Was he ugly?" I asked. "Was he mean?"

"No, he was very good looking, or so everyone said. I never even saw him. But I didn't want to marry a mullah who lived on people's charity. A beggar is a beggar, no matter how rich.

"My father wouldn't listen to me, so I went to the *abanbar*, where the water was stored underground. I unlocked the iron gate that kept animals out, crawled inside, locked the gate behind me, and put the key in my pocket. I sat there on the ledge above the water, and I told them that if they didn't call off the engagement and send the guests home, I would jump in and drown. Oh, how they shouted and screamed then. My father shouted, my mother begged, and everyone had something to say except me. I had said as much as I needed to."

"It was bad enough that the bride would die and the family would lose face, but even worse, they would have been forced to drain the whole *abanbar* and clean it out," Uncle Dervish observed.

"So I had my way and they called the wedding off. My father was so angry that he said, 'To hell with her! I wash my hands of this business. She can sit on the shelf till she's old and sour as a pickle, but I won't find a husband for her.' So I had to find one myself."

My father was clearly enjoying the dramatic entrance that my mother had set up for him. "I had heard about this remarkable pickle who had a mind of her own," he said. "I had heard she was a very beautiful pickle. So my father went to propose to her father. That went well enough, and her father invited me to visit."

"Of course everyone knew why he had come. I wanted to see for myself what he looked like, so I ran upstairs and peeked out the window just in time to see him walking out through the courtyard."

"She liked what she saw." My father winked. "Her knees started to shake, and her heart beat fast, and just like that she was head over heels in love with me."

"Oh, be quiet!" my mother laughed. "But one of the servants had seen me at the window and told my brother Kazem, who decided to take the family's honor into his own hands."

Uncle Dervish shook his head. "The nosy fool went looking for your mother with his rifle."

"What a commotion!" my mother continued. "Everyone shouting at everyone, and Kazem storming around with his rifle. I ran and hid behind the curtain that covered the fireplace in the summer. Kazem came through looking for me, but the room was empty. It was all I could do not to sneeze with my nose full of soot.

"I hid in the fireplace until the coast was clear, then sneaked to my bedroom. I threw on my veil to cover the soot, got under the quilts, and pretended that I'd been napping all afternoon. Obviously it must have been someone else at the window because I was sound asleep. Everyone agreed that there must have been a mistake, and Kazem finally calmed down." My mother couldn't have been more satisfied if Uncle Dervish had brought back her sheep. But my father had the last word:

"So of course she married me. And because her father wanted the family to look good, Khanom's second wedding was just as grand as the first."

No talk of weddings was complete without my sister Sediqeh reminding us all yet again about the drama of her own wedding celebration. Long before electricity reached Qazvin, my father had brought some small battery-run lamps from Russia. My eldest brother, Ali, had been fascinated by the contraptions. For Sediqeh's wedding he engineered a mantle of wires and bulbs to adorn the bride. Her entrance was spectacular. She stood in the doorway lit up like a chandelier and sent the frightened guests running and shouting "Fire!" All this had happened when I was still too young to remember, for she married when she was sixteen, but I had heard the story too many times. I fell asleep with the sound of Sediqeh's voice muffled under the *korsi* quilts.

CHAPTER FOUR

I did not learn my father's story until I was much older, but I will tell it now because it happened long before I was born. It came to light when I was about to enter high school. My father had registered me for the very first class to enter Anushiravan Dadgar, a new Zoroastrian school for girls. The friends I had made in grammar school were all headed for more predictable destinations, and I didn't understand why I should go to a Zoroastrian school. So I asked him.

My father's answer unlocked so much of his life for me that I will tell it not as he told it, in a few measured words, but as it has filtered into my heart, like the shafts of light piercing the dark expanse under the dome of an ancient mosque, that dance with dust and spread pools of gold across the dim, worn floor.

Besmellah ar-rahman ar-rahim
Allahu la illaha illa hu . . .

My father had lived his youth in a fortress of faith. The words that marched across the page of the holy Qoran were the soldiers of his dreams, their ranks impenetrable at first. But as he learned to guide the chiseled reed in his small hand and trace the magic shapes, the upright swords and gracefully curving shields, they would grasp his hand and pull him along with their rhythmic step. He found that he could wrap his lips around the strange sounds. He could kiss them, and they would breathe through him; he could sing them, and they would sing through him. And then he would vanish, and there was nothing but the words themselves singing.

The outer walls of his fortress were built of obedient stone, and from them rose towers of duty as tall as his father. The inner rooms smelled of rosewater, the scent of his mother's gentle refuge, the white folds of her embrace. In this fortress every small comfort of life was a blessing from God: the shoes on his feet, the food in his mouth. Every step, skip, and jump of his growing body was a molding of self to the

MY GRANDFATHER, MOHAMMAD HOSSEIN SHAHROUDY,
HAD THIS PORTRAIT PAINTED WHEN HE WAS IN RUSSIA.

great will, and from every bow of submission he rose ever so slightly taller.

His own father was a great man, a merchant who had once done his part to save the country when he received a message from his representative in Moscow saying that twenty thousand loaves of sugar were on their way to Qazvin. He had the sense to recognize that the loaves of sugar he had never ordered must be Russian soldiers. But he was also a scholar of the Qoran, the traditions of *hadith* and the Sharia, and he was much sought after in the city for his knowledge. But higher still above my father, like the moon above the minarets of the old Friday Mosque, shone the light of his grandfather, the great Ayatollah Shahroudy. The Ayatollah was more than a scholar. He was a holy man whose simple presence turned people's hearts to God. He had come to Qazvin from faraway Shahroud at the Shah's request because the great Friday Mosque was dying: the slow death of brick and cold marble unwatered by tears, the dust of many years gathering undisturbed by prayers.

It was an ancient mosque, and Shah Tahmaseb had lavished much care on it before he moved his court, and the artists that served him, from Qazvin to Isfahan. But for many years the people had avoided it. They whispered stories about unclean land, about the ghosts of an even more ancient fire temple that haunted the site, about the peculiar marble *mihrab* that attracted stone as a magnet attracts iron. The mosque's abandonment was a seal on the decline of the once-great city.

When the rivers of trade shifted again, however, Qazvin came to life once more, a thriving bazaar on the route to Russia. As the Shah played mullah against merchant on the seesaw of provincial power, he looked for a way to revive the dead mosque. So the holy man from Shahroud was invited to preach there. His calm light was so bright that the people followed, and the old mosque breathed again with prayers. And though Shahroud is a lovely town, the Ayatollah liked the people of Qazvin; so he stayed and fathered a son.

That son did his scholarly best to live up to his father's name, and when the great Ayatollah passed away, the people of the city honored his memory by paying respect to his son, Mohammad Hossein Shahroudy, who by then was a merchant and a politician. On Fridays, after the public prayers, the wiser men of the city would gather at the Shahroudy home to drink tea, eat sweets, and debate the ways of God. Poetry, history, politics, and news of the world were also shared around the circle seated on the carpet, and even what passes for gossip among men, but always the talk returned to the matter of religion. And almost always Hajji Shahroudy would call for his son and ask the boy to sing from the Qoran. Young Mohammad Baqer would enter shyly and sit among his seniors, the gray beards nodding, their veined hands swinging beads. He would sing the holy words until the voice moved out of his mouth and into his soul, and he disappeared inside the words the way the water of a pool disappears in the reflection of the sky. The old men never saw him disappear because their eyes were closed in pleasure, and their own mouths were mumbling "*Barikallah, barikallah . . .*" He was hardly aware of the old men's praise, of his father's light touch on his shoulder, hardly aware of anything until he was back in the *andarooni,* in his mother's world and the delicate smell of rosewater.

The Fridays came and went. After the first wisps of a beard appeared on the face of young Mohammad Baqer, he spent less and less time in the *andarooni,* shooed across the courtyard to exile in the company of men. He made friends among the *taleban,* students from the *madreseh* who came to call on his father. He listened carefully to their questions and to his father's answers. He was privileged, he knew, to share in these discussions beyond his years. His own lessons proceeded with exceptional speed, and the path ahead seemed straight and clear.

Until the day the fortress collapsed.

His mother had been sick, too sick to get out of bed, and for days the *andarooni* had been in a state of chaos. Strange women came and went, veiled figures scurrying across the courtyard . . . Mahdiyeh Khanom dripped tears in the soapy water, moaning as if in pain herself as she scrubbed and beat a hill of wet white cloth by the side of the pool . . . A huge block of ice had landed in the dust with heaving grunts and cries of *Ya Ali!* and was melting to mud faster than it could be hacked away to cool the fever. Mohammad Baqer felt useless in this commotion and, restless, had gone to the kitchen. He stood outside the door and coughed to announce his presence—he was a man now, full grown at eighteen years, and no longer easily welcome in the rooms where he played as a boy—but the voices inside were too loud and heated to notice him. He stood there awhile like a fool and listened in spite of himself to women's talk—of the monstrous invisible fly whose deadly wings scattered sickness, of the epidemic unleashed just five years before, of all that they had suffered then, and of how Khanom's fever was different, or not. He had walked away, stunned, but knowing somehow this confusion was contagious and not useful. Then Mahdiyeh Khanom chased him down and, wiping her tears, delivered the message: your mother is calling for you.

Her smile when she recognized him was radiant, a sun that filled the room and blinded him. He barely saw the sunken cheeks, the shadows that ringed her eyes. A white curtain hung outside the fretted window, and the midday sun dissolved through it. Another pool of white cloth encircled his mother's frail body, rippling out across the floor. Everything seemed awash in whiteness and light, and he was suddenly afraid of the unearthly glory of that smile and the place that it touched in him: afraid of the heat in the thin hand that grasped his, the heat of her cheek as he bent to kiss it, the white heat of her whisper, "Please pray for me."

And then he was running across the courtyard to the Friday gathering of men, to the cool dark circle of low voices around the carpet, and bowing low, too low to see faces, mumbling softly, too softly in answer to lengthy greetings. His voice was trapped inside him, choking him. He hoped that tea would help, but it spilled with the trembling of his hand. The old beards wagged as if nothing had reached them from the other side of the house. There was one new face, an eminent *hakim* who had come from the capital, and it seemed that his father's polite smile hung on the doctor's words, but they were few and extremely reserved. When the time came, as it must, for Mohammad Baqer to sing from the Qoran, he opened his mouth and choked as his throat tightened. He lowered his head in shame and swallowed hard, watching tears splash down on the precious pages open in his lap. But there was no shame, no censure, no hardness at all from his father, and none from the circle of men. There were hands on his shaking shoulders, and mumbled prayers, and earnest words of advice . . . You must pray, you must fast, keep a vigil, make *nazr* . . . There is a special book of prayers; if you can complete the whole cycle without sleeping, well then—God's mercy is infinite.

And so he closed himself in his room and prayed without stopping, without sleeping, without eating, with barely a sip of water, through days and nights. No one knew what promises passed between him and God, what groveling bargain, what awe-filled wrangling and wrestling with angels. Instead, in the other rooms, there was fear of a terrible race between mother and son and talk of which would reach the gardens of paradise first.

Then it was over. The women unleashed their wailing and found themselves suddenly relieved by the business at hand, the washing of the body, the preparation for a flood of visitors. In the real crush of death, the son was forgotten for a while. Or if not forgotten, then no one was so rude as to interrupt his dealings with God, or so brave as to break the bad news.

It was his father finally who opened the door. No words were needed. The undeniable smell of camphor followed him into the room. Mohammad Baqer closed his eyes on the light that spilled in from the doorway and remembered the smell of rosewater. Then he opened his eyes and closed the book, which was now just a book. He spoke: "There is no God, and no prophet, and no Qoran."

That was the first shot fired in my father's personal feud with the mullahs, but his disillusion was in the spirit of the time. A year after his mother's death, my father married my mother. At the same time—the dawning of the twentieth century—he was swept up in the *mashrutiat,* the movement to build a constitutional democracy in Iran. His travels to Russia as a merchant, at a time when that country was brewing its own revolution, opened his eyes to foreign ideals of democracy and egalitarian justice, although the disastrous loss of his business in Moscow and his brother's harrowing escape saved him from too rosy-eyed a view of communism, or of violent solutions. His weapon was the pen. He wrote passionately rational tracts on the need for modern secular education to free the people from superstition, and he was adamant that women, the most hapless victims of the mullahs' backward ways, should be included. He was no less passionate in attacking the Qajar shahs, who were selling the bankrupt country piecemeal into the hands of foreign powers to finance a corrupt and decadent court.

His writings were published in the progressive press that was sprouting across the country, and when those papers were stamped out by the censors, he continued to speak out in *Habl al Matin,* a highly respected newspaper that was published in Persian by the Zoroastrian Parsis in India.

Was it surprising that he disappeared? Were those times more innocent than ours, drunk with the newfound power to speak ideas of change through the printed word? In any case, my mother was helpless with worry at his sudden and unexplained absence. In those days a woman had no business knocking on doors, demanding explanations from the authorities. So it was all the more terrifying when one night, long past the hour of curfew, there was a loud knock at the door. A servant brought word that an officer in the uniform of the Cossack regiment—the elite Russian-trained troops who guarded the Shah—demanded to enter. "Tell him that Agha is not at home," my mother said. The servant went back and forth. The officer insisted on speaking to Khanom, regardless of whether her husband was home. She put on her veil and went to the door. She opened it a crack, and a heavy boot inserted itself, followed by an urgent but familiar whisper: "*Abji!* Sister! It's me!" She opened the door to a tall Cossack who, except for his flour-white hair and long black beard, looked just like Uncle Dervish. He had tracked down my father in jail and was doing his best, using influential connections and his own theatrical talents, to get him released.

When my father was freed several weeks later, his own hair had turned completely gray. He was only twenty-four years old. But he was not broken, and the gray hair added an aura of elderly dignity to his stature as public spokesman. He continued to write and to advocate secular education and a modern role for women.

His theories begged for tangible grassroots action, so he opened the very first school for girls in Qazvin. A handful of brave parents escorted their daughters to class each day through the jeers and taunts of the righteous men of religion and the slack-mouthed stares of loiterers who had nothing better to gape at than little girls bent on learning to read and to write. To write! Even my mother, as free-minded as she was, never learned that skill. In her youth she had attended a traditional *maktab,* a religious school, and learned to read the Qoran; but that was Arabic, sacred, and safe from any practical application. God forbid, if girls learned to write in Persian—though many people doubted that female brains could stretch so far—then what was to stop them from writing love letters? The whole moral fabric of society was threatened by such modern notions.

It was a tribute to my father's foresight and perseverance that by the time I started kindergarten, it seemed to me no big deal. Twenty-odd years had passed since that first school had opened. Although more traditional families still kept their daughters at home, there were now three or four girls' schools in Qazvin, enough to warrant inspection by the Ministry of Education. Even that had my father's stamp on it: the inspector who appeared at my school one day, welcomed with much polite *ta'arof* by the principal and teachers, was my own sister Sediqeh. She was not just grown up and married, pedestal enough in my eyes, but also honorably employed. I thought she looked ever so modern and important in her European coat fastened with a brooch, but I couldn't quite figure out why all this business of schooling mattered so much. To me it was just plain boring.

My father's involvement in the political and intellectual life of Qazvin continued in tandem with his career as a merchant all through the ups and downs of the constitutional revolution—the birth of democracy in Iran and the many betrayals that crippled it, through the Russian occupation during World War I, the chaotic final years of the Qajar reign, and the stunning rise to power of Reza Khan. There was talk again of republic, but it vanished like a mirage in the dust kicked up by the mullahs, and Reza Khan crowned himself Shah. That notwithstanding, a leader had finally appeared with strength enough to restore order and the nation's self-respect. More important, he held a vision that embraced the future—a truly modern Iran—and the promise of a government in which service could be meaningful.

MY FATHER, THE REPRESENTATIVE FROM QAZVIN.

When Mohammad Baqer Shahroudy decided to run for a seat in the Majles, he had already earned a reputation as a man of honesty and principle. Still, the election was hard work and the family was enlisted to help. My uncles loaded up ballot boxes on donkeys and trekked to the farthest villages, explaining over and over again why every man had a duty to vote, and why every vote mattered. When the votes were counted, it was clear that the name of Shahroudy was held in high respect by the people of Qazvin and that we would be moving to the capital.

CHAPTER FIVE

I t was 1932 and I was seven years old when my father was elected to parliament as the representative from Qazvin. My world was disassembled piece by piece and packed into cloth bundles for the move to Tehran. The carpets were rolled up, leaving the empty rooms suddenly loud with echoes, as if the nightingales and roses on the ceiling were straining to protest their abandonment. The saddest goodbyes, with many "one last" hugs that left tears running down his coat, were for my pet deer. He had fed from my hand for months and entertained the household by butting me around the courtyard. The last of my childhood menagerie, he had grown too big to follow us to our new home.

Even without my deer there were far too many of us, servants and children, and far too many last-minute bundles to fit in the car that my father had acquired to match his new position. I rode with the tail of our caravan in a public bus. It seemed to me monstrously huge, overwhelming in its proportions, its elevation, its noise, and the endless stream of strangers that filed aboard. Our road was that straight line stretching across the plain that I had seen from the heights of Abdolabad; but here on the ground, or rather tottering above it in the belly of the monster bus, the distant illusion of the plain's vast calm was churned into a dusty chaos of carts and camels with bells clanging, donkeys so loaded with stitched-up bales that you couldn't tell head from tail, and motorcars that were even more precariously piled with rooftop bundles than the poor donkeys.

Tehran itself was hardly as impressive as the bus ride. It announced itself prematurely with a fabulous city gate that had still no city behind it. There was an empty stretch yet to go before houses and shops appeared. All together it was not so very different from Qazvin, I decided, though there was rather more of it. There were horse-drawn trolleys and a few more cars than I'd seen on the streets of Qazvin, but just as many droshkies and about the same ratio of donkeys, camels, and mules.

We had come to Tehran for my father to be close to the seat of gov-

WE ENTERED TEHRAN THROUGH ONE
OF THE OLD CITY GATES.

ernment, and our new home in the winding *kuchehs* behind Cheragh-
bargh Street could not have been more strategically located. It was
just a few short steps to the vast cobbled expanse of Tupkhaneh
Square, where gateways like floating castles, the antique cannons and
endless arches of the Armory, and the ornately crusted frontage of the
Imperial Bank all proclaimed, in the language of brick and plaster
and iron, that history was at home here. A few blocks in the opposite
direction was the Majles building. The legislature met in this imposing mansion, a century old, that had been built for Nasser al-Din
Shah's grand vizier. Its stone walls were surrounded by cool gardens
and great wrought-iron gates, and my father went to work there
every day. The perfect snow-capped peak of Mount Damavand hung
above it in the distance, like a reminder that what happened here
affected the fate of the whole nation.

All this high seriousness and smell of history had seeped right into
the walls of our own rented house. Kings and great men of the
past paraded around our living room—Ebnesina, Ferdowsi, Ardeshir,
Khosrow, and Shapour—carved in relief in the plaster and painted

with faux marble veining. Their crowned or turbaned heads were up by the ceiling, too high to reach, but the flowering tendrils at their feet begged for my fingers to touch. I used to trace the curves endlessly and count the repeating motifs. Some afternoons Hassan and I would take naps in that room on a sheet laid out on the carpet, and I would fall asleep counting kings. I tried to imagine my father flattened and lined up with the rest of them, his top hat high among the crowns and turbans. The thought was too absurd.

More fun were the summer afternoons we spent in the *zirzamin,* a cool dark basement where a fountain played in a small pool lined with tiles and surrounded by carpets. One day my father joined us with a mysterious smile and a single egg in a bowl. We sat on the carpet and watched as he made two small holes and blew out the scrambled goop, then set the hollow shell on top of the fountain. It hovered and bounced and rolled on the burbling water, and I was absolutely delighted—not just by the egg but to have a father who knew how to do such things.

The salary of a Majles representative was modest in the extreme. Not so long before, civil servants had been paid with bricks from the bombed-out rubble of the Majles building in lieu of cash. The government was a skeleton picked clean by Qajar greed, and the oil wealth was being siphoned without challenge into the British exchequer. It was remarkable that my father refused to accept gifts or to reap his expected rewards in the game of *parti bazi.* What he lost in the way of material reward, he gained in reputation. The gifts kept coming regardless, naturally, in the way of custom or in gratitude for the new roads, hospitals, and schools that were built, for his long struggle to gain government funds for the building of a dam, and for his efforts to bring science to bear on the diseases of pistachio trees. For politeness's sake he would accept a token, a single box of pistachios or grapes, and suggest that the visitor must have many friends to call on, having traveled so far to the capital, and that certainly those friends would appreciate the taste of Qazvin's finest crops.

The real burden of my father's honesty fell on my eldest brother, Ali. He gave up his schooling to manage my father's neglected import-export business, and it was a very long time before Ali married and raised his own family. Even so, the orchards and village farmlands were sold off slowly, piece by piece. Not that we lived poorly at all or completely lost our connection with the land. When the grapes were

TUPKHANEH SQUARE WAS THE BUSTLING CENTER OF TEHRAN.

harvested each year, a load of the rare, thick-skinned black *shani*—special to Qazvin—would arrive at our home in Tehran. Our city courtyard was transformed into a village scene, and my father would personally supervise the trampling of the grapes. The frothy black fluid flowed into vats, and with no chemistry beyond that of tradition and poetry, it somehow became wine.

For all his modern stance, my father's personal pleasures—like the wine and the poetry that celebrated it—were deeply rooted in traditional culture (though they always managed to skirt the Islamic portion of that culture). The holidays that mattered to him were the ancient Zoroastrian celebrations of equinox and solstice. Noruz, the springtime new year, brought out a special zeal. It was the only time my father ever cooked. (Thank God! the servants whispered as they recovered from the operation.) No hands but his could roll out the paper-thin dough or sprinkle just the right mix of sugar and ground pistachios for the big trays of baklava that baked in a specially built oven. No matter how late in the night the new year officially started—it varied each year with the earth's course around the sun—we had to be assembled at the table dressed in brand-new clothes from head to toe, the entire house scrubbed sparkling clean. When the cannon boomed to mark the moment of the year's turning, we kissed him.

Then he handed each of us a gold coin. We sat around the table where the *haft-seen* was spread, seven symbols of springtime and good luck that each start with the letter *S*. There were other symbolic objects as well: goldfish and a mirror and painted eggs and an orange, which represented the world, suspended mysteriously in a bowl of water. We munched on sweets while my father read poems of Hafez. Finally, if it was still dark out, we were sent back to bed with far too much sugar inside of us to fall asleep.

My father had talents besides honest government, the making of wine, and the baking of baklava. He designed carpets, methodically plotting elaborate gardens in a precise hand over large sheets of graph paper, blocking the colors out in watercolors. In Qazvin he had set up a small studio next to his office with an upright loom where an old man translated the graphs into a singsong chant, and three pairs of young girls' hands twisted and pulled and beat the threads in time to the rhythm: "Three of blue, four of yellow, two of red . . ." My father obsessed about the quality of the wool. My brother Ali had to ask the workers packing up bales for export to set aside the very finest wool, and the dyer who came to our home had to double his calculations so there was no danger that a single uniform batch of color would ever run out before the carpet was finished. Later the workshop expanded and moved to another location, but my father continued to supervise and draw all the designs himself.

The summer vacation before we moved from Qazvin, I worked alongside the weavers for a few days of utter tedium. My mother had lost patience with my restlessness and my endless fights with Hassan and sent me over to my father's domain. As a novice I sat at the end of the row of girls on a wooden plank, working on one single color in the border. My nose was barely at the waterline where the slow wave of rising color and swirling patterns met the pale blank warp in a plushy foam of untrimmed yarn. I struggled to keep up. This little finger goes in between, pulls out the yarn, the other hand cuts with the knife . . . again and again and again. As the newly woven pile rose slowly up the warp, another pair of bricks would be added under our seat. The bench kept rising until it was time to roll up another section and start again at the bottom. Outside the door bumblebees, clustered around the water pump in the courtyard, called to me with their buzzing. Bored, I jiggled on one of the bricks under our seat and inched it out until the plank and all of the weavers' weight came crashing down on my fingers. I lost two nails, and the bulky bandage made it impossible for me to weave, though I still had to come to the workshop for another two weeks. I spent the rest of my time there chasing bees around the pump, swatting them with a piece of wood in my one good hand.

After that, school didn't seem so bad. In fact, as soon as I started grammar school in Tehran, I made a very interesting discovery: I could make my classmates laugh. This unexpected power was exhilarating, and I tested it every opportunity I could grab. I caught flies in my fist, which made my deskmate Leili giggle. Pretty soon I was launching the poor flies back in the air with tiny paper streamers stuck to their tail ends. Whole waves of giggles and screeches circled the class in their wake. How far could I push my audience? A grape landed square on the math teacher's forehead in mid-equation, then rolled down his nose and straight across his desk. That got me two days' suspension, which I spent remorselessly planning my next pranks. I was the chief jester and troublemaker of Madraseh No. 14, and no punishment could stop me. The only thing that ever silenced me was our field trips, and only then because my screaming on the bus at the top of my lungs left me croaking and mute by the time we got home. Somehow in all this I learned to read and write, though the possibility of penning love letters never crossed my mind.

While I was raising hell at school, the city around me was changing almost overnight. Reza Shah was determined to kick the country into the twentieth century, regardless of the mullahs' grumbling, or Britain's reluctance to pay for its oil thirst, or the tribes' resistance to giving up arms in exchange for an unwanted roof. He had recently visited Turkey and was much impressed with Atatürk's vision for a secular, modern state. If Turkey could do it, why not Iran?

I was too young to understand the deeper changes that rocked the country, but much was obvious even to a child's eyes. Whole portions of Tehran were being razed to dust and rubble and rebuilt in the image of a European city. The fanciful towers of the city gates were toppled, and brigades of men with picks and shovels cut broad avenues straight through the old neighborhoods. Lonely little saplings, watered by soldiers, lined the new avenues, their leaves heavy with dust as they waited for the streets to be paved. Camels were banned from the city, not because they were a hazard to traffic—Tehran had not yet grown to fit the new clothing that Reza Shah designed—but because they were too old-fashioned.

Women in veils were also banned from the streets, as if they were just like those embarrassing, old-fashioned camels. For many women, the unveiling law was traumatic. Many simply stayed home as much as they could, and stories were told of an old woman whose son had to lug her to the bathhouse in a gunny sack once a week. It was a challenge even for my mother, who as the wife of a member of parliament was required to set an example before the law came into effect. At home she never wore a scarf, as the servants did; they still wore long skirts over baggy pants while she wore fashionable dresses. But she had never set foot in the street without first putting on her chador—and a servant always followed a few steps behind to carry her handbag and purchases, which were awkward to hold with the veil—until the day she stepped out with my father, under orders to attend a garden party at the Majles. The party was an annual affair, but this year it was to celebrate the unveiling. My sister Sediqeh went along for moral support; she was used to taking off her veil, if not on the street then at least in the more public venue of her work as a school inspector. There was much discussion of the appropriate dress, stylish but with a high collar, and I went along when my mother shopped for a hat and gloves to match. The shopkeeper announced, haggling over the price, that these items were now specially exempt from tax to encourage their use, and it was my mother's patriotic duty to make the purchase. The party was a fashion show with very nervous models, and the talk for a long time afterward was entirely of whose wife wore what, now that they all could be seen.

I was too young then to wear a veil, so I didn't have to worry about taking it off. My first worries about fashion began when I was ten, and they were focused entirely on my hair. It was still straight. Hopelessly straight. I wanted nothing more in the world than to have curly hair like my sister, but no matter how much I combed and twisted and fussed in the mirror, the face that looked back was still framed with stubbornly straight hair. Finally one of the servants took pity on me and offered some practical magic: if I shaved my head three times against the grain, it would surely grow back curly, she counseled.

My mother dismissed the scheme with a laugh. "You're a girl! How can you shave your head?" I begged and pestered her endlessly. Summer was beginning, and I watched with envy as a street-side barber shaved one boy's head after another. Boys had lice, he explained to me; girls didn't. I swore to my mother I would wear boys' clothes. I begged and cried and pouted and refused to talk about anything else. My sisters eventually took my side, tired of my whining.

"Let her try it. It's not worth making her cry."

Finally my mother relented. We rode in silence to the hairdresser's home in the Jewish quarter. Khanom Varshoh seemed more amused than surprised by my mother's request, but she contained her smile behind lips pursed in concentration as she started the job. First she cut the long hair short with a scissors. My head was suddenly triumphantly lightened as the thick black strands fell to the floor. When she set the razor to my lathered scalp, I panicked: "Not like that! You have to do it against the grain!" God forbid that all this should go to waste. At last the operation was over, and Khanom Varshoh handed me a mirror: I saw two very big eyes under a strange white pumpkin. A scarf was procured for the ride home, and still my mother said nothing. I spent the rest of the day ignoring my brother Hassan's uncontrollable laughter and rubbing my unbelieving fingers over the smooth skin.

That night we slept on the rooftop, with the moon winking through the trees like another complicit bald head. It was summer, but I was freezing with the wind on my scalp and had to get up to fetch a scarf. The next morning I kept my promise and stretched my legs and arms into Hassan's cast-off jacket and pants. While I waited for my curls to appear, the tomboy in me took over. The servants renamed me Hooshang. It was a joke at first, but it seemed like a good enough name so I stopped answering to Monir. My mother played along, until I did something to earn a scolding, and then suddenly it was back to "Monir!" I corrected her: "Hooshang!"

I begged Hassan to accompany me on a walk through the neighborhood, and he was uncharacteristically cooperative, eager to watch the show. I didn't care if he sniggered. With the breeze on my scalp, I felt free as a boy, and tough. I put my hands in my pockets and swaggered a bit, rehearsing boyish speeches in my head. The neighborhood boys were suspicious and taunted me. "It's a girl!" they shouted as I walked by coolly, pretending their cries had nothing to do with me. Hassan dropped several steps behind me. The coward, I thought; but then he surprised me with a stroke of cleverness, calling to me, "Hooshang!" It didn't work. The boys shouted, "You're not Hooshang! You're a girl!" The taunts turned into stones, and we ran home.

Grown-ups were easier to fool. When my mother went shopping, Hooshang came along, pushing boldly ahead through the crowds on Lalezar Street. My mother was looking for fabric to sew my father a suit. The shopkeeper called to his own boy, "Bring tea for Khanom and her son!" and he chatted enthusiastically as he unrolled bolt after bolt. I was caught off guard when he grabbed me under my arms, planted a kiss on my head, and lifted me over the heap of cloth to the far side of the shop, saying, "Hooshang Khan, come look! This is the very best wool." My breasts were just beginning to bud, and they hurt in his grasp. I folded my arms over my chest as I hung there, embarrassed and confused. Just then more customers entered, and I was released from my torment as the shopkeeper turned his attention to them. My heart sank when I heard my mother greet them as friends—this was all too close for comfort. Fortunately they were not such close friends as to show any surprise when she introduced her youngest son.

After more tea and bargaining, the women concluded their business and decided to share a droshky home. We didn't all quite fit, so my mother told me, as if it were perfectly normal, to sit up front with the driver. As I clambered onto the narrow bench, the driver grumbled, "Don't push me, boy!" These adventures were too complicated, I thought. Home was a welcome relief.

It was even more of a relief when we returned to Abdolabad for a few weeks' vacation in the village. Once again I was climbing trees, scaling walls, galloping free on a horse's back, and rolling in the dust trading blows with Hassan. I had always been just as brave as the boys, and now I knew that nothing really stood between us.

By the end of summer vacation, my hair had grown back an inch or two. I had to wear a dress to school, with a beret as cover. Sadly, the hair was growing back straight, which made me all the more reluctant to return to being a girl. My breasts were achy too, which was becoming a nuisance. And now when I climbed a tree or straddled a wall or swung from a rope, my nanny would shake her head and warn me soberly, "*Dokhtaraki mirizi*"—be careful, or your girlhood will pour out. I couldn't imagine what inside me was suddenly so fragile, or how it might come pouring out, but the idea scared me.

She wouldn't explain except to say that if this terrible event should happen, I wouldn't be able to marry.

Not that I had high hopes in that department. One day the son of the *kadkhoda,* the village headman, had come from Abdolabad to our home in Tehran to deliver several boxes of grapes. My mother was thanking him and making polite conversation. I was shocked to hear her say to him, "One day I hope that you'll be my son and Monir will be your wife." I looked at the tall and clumsy young man who had outgrown the dusty suit that he wore for his trip to the big city. Was this my only prospect? No, there was another one, but no better than this: the son of my mother's cousin. Whenever they came to visit, my mother would coo, "One day Monir will be your *aroos!*" Ahmad Agha was skinny. He was a coward too: he had been too frightened to sail with me in my copper tub on the courtyard pool when we were small. Worst of all—and this my mother should have understood—his father was a mullah. Between Ahmad Agha and the *kadkhoda*'s son, I didn't see a good reason to stop climbing trees.

When I was twelve, I got my first glimpse of the vastness of Iran beyond the confines of Tehran and the familiar trek to Qazvin and the village. My eldest brother, Ali, had business in Amol and Babolsar on the Caspian Sea and offered to take me along. I was thrilled. The railway had just recently been completed: Reza Shah himself had driven the final golden stake to much fanfare, and the nation was now chugging headlong down the tracks into modernity. What a ride it was, eight or nine hours of continuous excitement. I bounced on the plush seats and imagined myself in Russia or in Europe, steaming through the Alps. But no, it was the Alborz that my window framed. The soft violet peaks on Tehran's northern horizon had solidified now into tawny browns in heaping curves that embraced us like a giant sleeping bear. In her crevices and clefts, poplars and birches shimmered in sudden patches of silver and green. A pair of hawks circled and swooped. We snacked on the boxes of nuts and sweets and fruits that my mother had packed, enough to feed an army, and passed them around to the other passengers, who reciprocated generously from their own supply of delicacies. As we climbed slowly, the soft brown curves gave way to towering rocky crags and sheer cliffs. A waterfall plummeted in what seemed like miles of frothy white down a cliff face. We swooshed into blackness, then out into blinding light, then again through tunnel after tunnel after tunnel. I gave up counting the tunnels after twenty or so, but I continued to hold my breath on the bridges that teetered over empty space. They were safe enough, Ali assured me: Reza Shah had made the German engineers stand underneath as the first locomotive passed over each bridge they had built.

The mountains gave way to forests of oak, green meadows, orchards, and patchwork fields; green, green, and more green everywhere, thousands of different greens. The villages and towns were different from anything I had ever seen. There were roofs of thatch with flowers growing on top, and others of red tile hanging over the street. When I walked underneath them, half-skipping to keep up with Ali's long stride as he led the way to our hotel, and my arms laden with the boxes of half-eaten snacks, I looked up and saw that there were flowers under the roofs as well: the eaves were painted with floral designs running down each slat of wood. I breathed the unfamiliar moist air deeply. There were Russian soldiers everywhere. It was hard to believe I was still in Iran. My brother's business partners met us at the hotel. They were foreigners too, Germans. They spoke to us in an odd stilted Persian and to each other in a choppy stream that sounded to me like the clucking of chickens.

When I awoke in the morning, I opened my window overlooking the *meidan* and watched the Russian soldiers marching in drill. The whole formation turned together, now left, now right, like a strange dance, trailing long shadows in the early morning sun. The rhythmic stomping of the boots was suddenly broken by a screeching commotion behind me. I ran to the door and out to the veranda that circled the courtyard below, where feathers were flying and wings flapping as a man lunged and lunged again after the terrified chickens. He caught one and whacked its head off, flying with a big knife. I was shocked to see the poor headless thing continue to run and flap, and I ran screaming next door to my brother's room, where the Germans had already gathered. One of them grabbed me and swept me up, kicking, and forced me back out to the railing. "*Negah kon!*" he laughed. "Look, look! It's happy to die! It's dancing!"

I kept a careful distance between me and that man for the rest of the trip: many long paces away when we stood watching bales of sheepskins and goatskins being loaded onto a truck. I could hear the poor animals bleating under the knife when I looked at his face. And why should I eat chicken when there was sturgeon kebab on the menu? I had never tasted fresh fish before. Only smoked and dried fish found its way to Tehran in those days, and then only for a special meal at new year's with heaps of *sabzi polo.*

The sea itself was the most amazing of wonders. We walked on the beach, on clean gray sand that tugged at my toes as I pondered all this water. *Where does it go? How does it end?* A ride in a rowboat provided no logical answers, just the pleasure of watching the oars dip, the wind in my face, the fresh salt smell, and the changing colors of the sea. Simplicity. Light and air and water. The horizon's steady line and nothing more.

On the shore we watched the construction of a great hotel, also under Reza Shah's orders. One day this would be our Riviera, the Germans said. I didn't know what a Riviera was, but it would be ours and it sounded quite beautiful. Away down the beach a fire burned in the distance. I ran to it, left the men behind, and ran and ran with the joy of speed and the salty wind behind me. The fire seemed to be burning magically on nothing, no wood, no pile of garbage, just fire burning out of a crack in the sand. I kicked sand over it, lifted handfuls, and threw them, but it had no effect. Ali had caught up with me by then. I asked him, "Is it a jinn? Is it angry? Should I pour water on it and say *besmellah?*"

"No, it's just something natural," he said. "It's been burning for years and years. Everyone here knows about it." That seemed to be explanation enough for him. I don't think he really knew that this jinn was natural gas, burning on our Riviera. I tossed a handful of seawater at it anyway, just in case, and whispered, *"Besmellah ar-rahman ar-rahim."*

A couple of years before I started high school, my family moved to another rented house—two houses, really, linked by a long covered hallway. It was just beyond Darvazeh Shemran, the northernmost gate of Tehran, which stood for several years after the other city gates had been torn down. Walking home from school, I passed under the immense tiled archway, then down and up the slopes of the last remaining section of dry moat that had once surrounded the city. Children sledded down the dust and pebbles on pieces of tin, skidding into the garbage that collected in the gully at the bottom. In the house at Darvazeh Shemran I learned certain skills all by myself that would serve me better than anything I ever learned at school.

One summer I was left behind in Tehran when the family went back to Qazvin for the vacation. There was a reason that made sense at the time, to do with transportation—lack of space in the car, an easier ride later perhaps. In any case, for two weeks I was left alone in that big house to care for a strange prisoner who was locked in one small room. My father was there in the evenings only, working at the Majles every day. No doubt a servant was left behind too, or checked in occasionally, but my memory is of an empty house, long silent mornings and afternoons, and solitary meals.

The prisoner was my cousin Mohammad. He was one of three sons of my mother's third brother and was about eighteen years old at the time, an exceptionally handsome young man with curly blond hair. My uncle had brought him from Qazvin to Tehran to see a doctor, and one doctor led to another, prolonging his stay after everyone else had returned. In any case, there was something not right about him, though it was nothing I could see. He was confined in a small room near the entrance to the house, with a big padlock on the door. There was nothing at all in that room but a narrow bed: no books, no games, no pen and paper. Just a bed with an intricate patchwork quilt of many-colored little triangles. The patchwork was a traditional remedy for madness, believed to make crazy people calm.

I kept the key to the lock. I opened it whenever he called to go to the bathroom and when I brought him his food. Even before the others had left, this was my job. The servants were afraid of him and said—whether it was true or not—that he would accept food only from me. I myself was afraid and at the same time not afraid. I was afraid of the room, the locked door, the empty house, the strangeness of the situation. I pushed away the fear by busying myself in the kitchen, helping to prepare simple meals for him. I learned to light the stove: first put a bit of charcoal in a wire basket and swing it around and around to catch flame, then blow on more charcoal in the stove. Slice and fry up onions and tomatoes, then break a few eggs into the pan. Then dish it up and arrange it nicely with some bread on a tray. These were things I knew how to do, and they kept the fear at bay.

But when I unlocked the door and Mohammad looked up—a simple, open face—there was nothing really to fear. My only feelings then were pity and sadness. Sometimes I would sit for a while on the crazy quilt and keep him company. We made small talk: The food was good. It was nice when they watered the garden, so cool. A letter had come from his mother. Everything was fine in Qazvin. When we ran out of things to say, I wished him goodbye or goodnight, and then I closed the door and fit the key into the heavy padlock once again. As if a key could ever lock or unlock the mystery of another person's mind.

CHAPTER SIX

Goftar nik, pendar nik, kerdar nik—right speech, right thought, right action. The words were emblazoned in colored tiles above the entrance, under the wingspan of Ahura Mazda, creator and lord of wisdom. They were difficult to argue with and no less difficult to live up to.

If I had any qualms about attending the Zoroastrian high school that my father had chosen, they vanished soon enough. There were no lessons in fire worship, no priests in white frocks, and no sign of vultures feeding on corpses. If anything, it was an institution that today might be advertised as a haven of diversity, attracting Armenian, Jewish, and Baha'i students as well as Zoroastrians, and the daughters of freethinkers of various stripes.

The school had only recently opened, in a new building on the freshly cleared expanse of dust that was now Shahreza Avenue. It was next to Alborz College, the Eton or Andover of Iran, which was founded by American missionaries, and where our male counterparts, the future leaders of the nation, were busy doing whatever it was that boys did when girls weren't watching. All that separated the two schools was an empty lot between two walls, but it might as well have been miles of desert sand. If it weren't for the fact that girls inevitably have brothers and cousins, and for the prospect of marriage that dangled obscurely before us like an inscrutable math problem or a late chapter in next year's history book, the very existence of the opposite sex might have been in doubt.

Boys existed, we knew, but as insubstantially as in a fairy tale. Now and again a cluster of boys would appear like a mirage in the no-man's-land between our camps, or drift tentatively a few yards in the direction of our gate as school was letting out. Our school day ended fifteen minutes before theirs, to minimize contact, but we always had some reason to dawdle. The boldest advance we could possibly imagine consisted solely of eye contact. But what eye contact! Query and consummation were rolled into one lightning bolt. What smoldering confessions, what eternal pledges, what mountains scaled and oceans crossed were posed in those glances of a bare moment! And what fuel for gossip! The net of brothers and cousins and second cousins and sons of cousins of wives of cousins was woven so densely that we could identify every player in our silent drama by name and kinship, even if their ambitions and their weaknesses remained mysterious.

In high school we wore uniforms for the first time, a penance cruelly timed to coincide with my newly hatched desire to look pretty. I spent a great deal of mental energy plotting the tiniest infractions, such as pinning a small piece of costume jewelry backward under my collar, until I had passed Banu Khanom's regular morning inspection. The whole school lined up in the courtyard, and then we marched in file to class when our grade was called. Banu Khanom stood in the doorway, watchful as an eagle, and examined our nails, our hair, and the length of our skirts as we filed past. She had a fierce talent for exaggeration. If I had pinned my hair, still woefully straight, and nudged it up in a modest little bank on my forehead, she would shout at me, "Khanom Shahroudy! Have you built a skyscraper?" then grab my hair and pull the clip out roughly.

I was no longer the only clown in class. There were five of us now in cahoots—though if a prank required planning, that role fell to me. I was the one who brought the *shireh,* grape molasses, to make sherbet out of the snow that piled in the courtyard and melted in a sticky mess all over the classroom floor. I was the one who collected the cash to buy fresh almonds from the vendor when he took a shortcut across the empty lot, and I was also the one left hanging from the wall when the others ran at the sight of Banu Khanom: "A thief escaping over the wall!"

"I'm just looking for our ball," I explained.

"Perhaps you'll find it in the principal's office."

All five of us were routinely marched into the principal's office, showing true solidarity, at least when jointly apprehended. Our punishment was always the same: face the wall on one leg, for an hour or two or even three, depending on the magnitude of the offense. We spent so much time there at the wall, like so many storks, that we knew every detail of the school's administration, every issue that reached the principal's desk.

Of course not all of our crimes were planned; some were completely spontaneous. Yes, it's true I had brought the *saghez* seeds that we chewed into a kind of bitter gum, but it was Khadijeh—

Mossadegh's daughter—who used the sticky lump to wax her hairy legs under the desk during class. When the fuzzy spiderlike blob came sailing at me through the air, what could I do but scream and bat it away? Was it my fault that the laws of physics sent it careening straight at the teacher? Once again we stood, a flock of storks, but Khadijeh wasn't finished. Her slip was coming undone, and we choked on our giggles as we watched it droop lower and lower. When she put her foot down for a moment, the slip fell to the floor; as she bent over to pick it up, she let out a fart. At that we all lost our balance. It cost us one more hour at the wall.

At lessons I was good at only two things. One was needlework. I had always been good with my hands, and despite a household full of servants, many odd tasks—sewing a button, mending, ironing—somehow fell to me without question from the very youngest age. When I was a child of eight, my uncle arrived from Qazvin with his suit all caked with mud from a rainstorm and handed it to me. He needed it cleaned and pressed to wear to an appointment the next day. Perhaps I was proud he had asked me; in any case, it never crossed my mind to ask someone else. I brushed the mud off and scrubbed the spots clean, lit the charcoal for the iron, pressed the suit, and delivered it back to him neatly on a hanger. Later, if I wanted lace on my collar or a shorter skirt, it seemed only natural to do the job myself. I knew how to please in this way if few others. I spent weeks knitting a sweater of red angora with white diamond patterns for my sister Iran, every stitch a little twist of adoration. At high school in my very first year I impressed the needlework teacher with an especially fine piece of embroidery, delicate flowers and butterflies on imported beige linen. But I had also learned not to waste my effort: in the second year I washed and pressed the same piece and submitted it again, to equal praise. She did catch on to me the third year.

My other knack was for drawing. Once a week we had art class. For most of my high school years, art was strictly limited to copying postcards with colored pencils. When the cards were dealt, I always hoped for a flower. I could draw a cyclamen with such precision that it seemed clipped that morning from the garden. One day in our final year the postcards were replaced by something odd: an earthen jug on a chair, the chair atop a table. The teacher called this "still life." It perplexed me at first, but still it was more fun than math. I hadn't the faintest idea then that art might hold more for me than this.

CHAPTER SEVEN

My sister Iran had been sick for a long time, though I didn't realize it was serious until the very end. I thought it was just a cold with a bad cough; I didn't know that a cough shouldn't last for two or three years. I didn't know what it meant when a visit to the doctor led to whispers that ended abruptly when I appeared, and I had never so much as heard the word *sel*—tuberculosis. Perhaps my ignorance laid a protective spell on both of us, but Iran's illness never cast the slightest shadow on her kindness to me or the delight that I took in her company. It never dimmed her beauty or my eagerness to please her.

At some point it was decided that the air in the mountains would be good for her. A small house was rented in the village of Darband in the mountains overlooking Tehran, and my mother and sister were installed there along with one of the servants. At the same time, we moved from Darvazeh Shemran to a house on Villa Avenue, increasing the distance between myself and my sister even further.

I would bicycle to visit her on weekends and drag along my nephew, Sediqeh's son Bahram, as a token chaperone for the trip. It was an hour and a half ride up the Pahlavi Road to Tajrish, pumping uphill all the way but still pleasant through the dappled shade of the sycamores watered by rushing streams on each side of the road. Then another half-hour of really steep climbing in the suddenly cool air, panting up narrow lanes where slender poplars lined up against the mud walls, and rocky outcrops of the mountain pressed into every gap. Listening to the river, invisible a hundred meters below in the ravine, the rushing sound echoed in the windy rustle of leaves. There were uneven patches where we had to walk, dragging the heavy bicycles up the exposed stone spine of the road; elsewhere we absolutely had to stop to pick mulberries. Bahram ate them shamelessly, but except for a taste, I saved all of mine to bring as a gift to Iran.

Our time together was precious, too short to tell all the things that had to be told, all the thoughts that I hoarded through the week, all the little random occurrences that, even as they were happening, I rehearsed in my mind as stories to offer her. Yes, because the time was short I stretched the pleasure of it with anticipation. The return trip was always mercifully swift, downhill all the way; the city was spread out like a map of itself below us as we raced against the coming of darkness, the deepening sapphire blues that swept down like a curtain across the high desert sky.

Then one day I was packed off to Sediqeh's home with no explanation for the sudden holiday or the anxiety that edged my mother's voice. Three days later a messenger came to the door. My sister relayed the news.

I cried for days, for weeks, for months. I cried inconsolably, uncontrollably. I cried at the doorway, unable to move, unwilling to get in the car when the caravan left for the burial in Qom. I cried in the company of many weeping women at the recitation of the *rozehkhan,* at the *hafteh* that marked the end of the first miserable week, and the *chelleh* that marked the end of forty miserable days. I cried every night in my bed, exhausted and deeply, utterly, terribly alone. When my mother brought the Qoran and begged my father, please oh please, to recite just one page, he conceded with a strange, sad grace. I listened transfixed to the music of his voice, the melisma rising like waves of grief released to the sky, like the purified sobs of an angel, the cry to unlock all cries.

At Abdolabad that summer, I haunted the two special rocks where Iran and I had sat so often. I remembered the silky feel of her hair as I wove it in braids. I remembered the nights we had sat there, the moonlight casting shadows on the rocks and washing the plains below, the lilt of her voice as she recited poems to me, the poems she was learning as a student at college. The red-winged locusts buzzed at my feet, the grasshoppers bounded away unmolested. There was no reason now to catch them, no one to present them to proudly, all tied up in a stocking. I watched the wind toss the dangling rags that hung from the *nazr* tree. They looked forlorn, unanswered and pointless. There was no vow I could make that would bring her back to me. I sat on the rocks and cried, my tears drying in the wind with a tiny chill almost as fast as their trails could run down my face.

A year later my second sister Mehri died. It happened very suddenly. We had gone for a picnic in Abdolabad and stuffed ourselves on grapes cooled in the pond. When Mehri got sick, everyone knew that she had eaten more grapes than anyone else, and everyone had a remedy to recommend. It wasn't till she got much worse that my father called for a doctor to come from Tehran. By the time he arrived and informed us that her appendicitis had nothing to do with eating too many grapes, it was too late to save her.

Mehri was older than Iran, and we were not close at all. If anything, I had avoided her. She would order me around and hit me if I didn't do things just as she expected, though she was kinder to me after Iran died. Perhaps she was jealous. She was talented also, played the piano and the clarinet and drew fine portraits in pencil. But in the dark illogic of my wrung-out heart, Mehri's death was a travesty, a betrayal. If, in my overwhelming loss at Iran's death, I could cling to any consolation or tragic justice, it was that she was too precious to live. Iran was an angel; Mehri had no rightful claim to share a similar fate. If both could die, if just anyone could, then the world was a flat and hollow place.

MEHRI.

CHAPTER EIGHT

The summer after Mehri's death we had gone to the village as always, though with my two sisters gone the usual crowd of cousins seemed drastically reduced. My mother barely had the strength to pack. She wept constantly and kept to her bed much of the time. Sediqeh helped, but she had her own home and family to mind, and without much thought I took on responsibility for most of the household management.

No newspapers reached us at Abdolabad; there were no phone lines and no electricity for a radio. For news of the outside world we relied on my brother Ali, who came up once a week from Qazvin. The Nazis had invaded Russia, he told us, and my father had confided that there were rumors at the Majles that Iran might be drawn into the war. Our oil was needed now more than ever, to fuel the ships and planes and tanks of whichever side could claim it. And the railway that had been the source of so much national pride was now a prime target, a vital supply route linking the Persian Gulf to the Caspian Sea—the only route left by which the Allies could reach into Russia.

Technically, we were neutral, but that wasn't much of a defense. The British had demanded that all German nationals be expelled from Iran, and Reza Shah had refused, much to the relief of Ali. For a long time our export business had gone entirely to Germany, and he feared for the safety of his partners. Hassan loved the Germans. It wasn't that he cared for Nazi ideology—such things were beyond the scope of our thinking. But the Germans had the best technology, he said, and were the most intelligent. He had hopes of going there to study engineering as soon as the war was over. In any case, they were better than the British. We knew all too well what the British were: high-handed, stiff-necked, and two-faced.

My own experience with Germans and their cruel disdain for chickens had not endeared them to me at all. As far as I could see, the Germans were no better or worse than the Russians or British. The only side I was rooting for was Iran. And if war broke out, I was ready and eager to do my part. I announced my decision boldly: I would be a nurse and help the soldiers. I would go to Tehran for training, then off to the front. I wasn't entirely sure what a front was, but that's where nurses were needed.

"Oh, shut up," said Sediqeh.

My mother shook her head in despair: "This isn't even our war." I thought she might start weeping again, but I was too charged up by my fantasy to hold back.

"Why not?" I said. "Our army is strong. Reza Shah is a good king, and he's surely a great commander." So I believed.

One afternoon in August we were sitting on the terrace discussing these matters for the umpteenth time when suddenly the war became no longer a theoretical prospect. A distant buzz in the sky became two black dots that grew like malevolent flies. They were airplanes, small ones, black with red marks that we could soon make out as stars: Russian planes. They circled wide above us, then headed for Qazvin, a pale urban cluster of sun-baked blocks on the plain below. My heart was beating wildly as I watched the explosions, dwarfed in the distance. There was no sound, no flame, just sudden plumes of billowing dust, then columns of smoke rising high. We watched and waited, trying to decide exactly where the bombs had hit. Two hours later Ali arrived on horseback. My father had telephoned from the capital: Abdolabad was too close to the city for safety. We had to leave as quickly as possible. Our destination was Rudbar Alamut.

Alamut! I had no idea what it was, but Hassan filled me in. He was thrilled at the prospect of holing up in the ancient fortress of the Hashashin in a hidden valley of the high mountains that stood between us and the Caspian Sea. I thought we had quite enough adventure on our hands as it was without worrying about hashish-crazed assassins in the service of a magical cult, but perhaps his fantasy was no more far-fetched than my own Florence Nightingale scenario.

Ali went into the village to find the *kadkhoda* and arrange for him to bring horses and mules. I threw myself into the job of packing, gathering up bedding and quilts. If need be, I could tear up sheets for bandages, I thought, still half-dreaming patriotic daydreams. I tied up bread in cloth, boiled eggs, packed fruit, and wrapped up cheese. I gathered cooking pots and shifted sacks of rice and beans. Enough food for such a crowd would be hard to come by in remote mountain villages at the best of times. I had heard the servants talking: for those who could remember World War I, wartime brought the specter of starvation. We continued packing late into the night. We slept a brief spell, or tried to, then awoke in darkness to eat a hurried breakfast. As soon as there was enough light in the dawn sky to see the path through the mountains, we set off: a long caravan of horses and pack mules, many of us on foot, and a few straggling goats and sheep.

We had no maps and could piece together only a sketch of the route from the villagers. Nobody from Abdolabad had ever trekked all the way to Rudbar Alamut, but the *kadkhoda* had a general idea and was confident that at each village on the way we would surely find guidance to the next.

The path was steep and winding, in places just a narrow ledge between towering rock and deep ravine, in other places treacherous with a slippery carpet of broken shale. Little seemed to grow here, and nothing at all to offer shade, just a few handfuls of parched grass as tough as rope. The only signs of life were eagles careening above us and lizards scampering off the path. The sun was relentless and unforgiving in the thin mountain air. After a few hours even the rocks were blinding in its glare. I was terribly afraid for my mother. She was weak from grief and exhaustion, and several times she fainted. I walked alongside the mule she was riding, talking to her constantly to keep her alert, holding tight to her leg in fear she would lose her mount and fall.

Just as the sun was threatening an even worse vengeance, abandoning us slowly to darkness and a whole new set of fears, we reached a village. I blessed the *kadkhoda* in my grateful heart, blessed the reliable lore of the villagers who knew these mountain paths, and blessed the ageless logic that had placed such villages exactly a day's march apart. It didn't matter that it was a pitifully poor village with skinny sheep and half-feathered chickens and a few scraggly almond trees, or that we came unannounced and didn't know a soul. The rules of hospitality still held. In any case we were well equipped and didn't need to burden our hosts too much. Luckily it was summer, so they could offer us a place to sleep on the roof.

We were too tired to cook and made a meal of bread and cheese and hard-boiled eggs for the third time that day. The servants untied the bedding that was stacked high on one of the mules. I passed out quilts and blankets to each of our party and spread a bed for my mother. By the time everyone else was accounted for, there was only an old kilim left for me. I curled up on the edge of my mother's quilt and used the kilim as cover.

I awoke in the middle of the night, struggling to breathe. The kilim was heavy on my chest. I pushed it aside, but that didn't help. I was gasping silently for air, but each breath seemed empty, sucking on nothing. It was very dark. Just a thin, curved sliver of moon jutted like a dagger from the mountaintop into the near-black sky. I could barely sense the sleeping shapes surrounding me, but I heard a very soft step. A long moment, then another slow crunch. Then I could see him, almost, a half-crouched form that was just a hint blacker than the sky. When he moved again, I was sure. Somewhere deep in my paralyzed lungs I found the breath to scream.

He ran, stumbled on a blanket or a leg, and almost fell, then leaped to a second, lower rooftop and disappeared in the night. The whole party was awake by then. The people of the house came up with lanterns, and neighbors came out too. There was much loud discussion, most of it in a Turkish dialect that I couldn't follow. Finally, when they kept asking me what I had seen and I had no breath to answer, my brother Ali realized that I posed a more serious problem than the burglar.

In the morning I could hardly move. If I tried to sit up, I choked, and I certainly couldn't stand. Ali said it was altitude sickness. He carried me down from the roof, and they laid out quilts on the floor for me inside the house. Sediqeh brought me a chamber pot and joked a little unkindly about how the brave nurse needed a nurse herself. I was flat on my back for three days. My mother sat in the corner and cried, which only made me feel even more helpless. Hassan scouted the path, eager to be off to Alamut. Ali took the more prudent step of discussing our route at great length with the men of the village.

By late afternoon of the third day I could sit up, and each breath followed more easily. A consensus was reached that we would leave in the morning, and I could ride one of the mules. The path from here into the Rudbar valley was easier, they said, than what we had already covered. As all this was being settled, we heard shouts of greeting outside. The *kadkhoda*'s son from Abdolabad had arrived. He had hiked alone the whole way (we had taken the last of the animals) to bring us the news: the war had ended.

Ended how? So quickly? Who had won? He didn't know. He only

knew that it was over and that my father wanted us to return. We were to take a different route, not back to Abdolabad but to another village on the road to Tehran. A car would meet us there. He knew the way; he would lead us and then bring the animals back to Abdolabad.

And so the next morning our caravan set off down the mountain again, not without a certain sense of anticlimax, but with too little information for any real sense of relief. We had no idea what had happened or what awaited us. The news, when we sat down finally with my father over our first hot meal in days, was not good: the British and the Soviets had simultaneously invaded Iran, utterly rejecting our neutrality. The British had sent mostly Indian soldiers to do their dirty work, across the border from Iraq and up the Gulf. The Russians had come from the northwest; there was fighting on the ground in Tabriz but very little elsewhere. For the most part, the army had been confined to barracks lest even defense be taken as a break of neutrality and a pretext for war. Those units that had fought so bravely had mutinied to do so. It remained to be seen what the day-to-day reality of our double occupation would be.

My fantasy had dissolved. The war was over, and it wasn't. Life went on. School started. A few days later Reza Shah stepped down, choosing to abdicate the throne rather than bend to the will of foreign masters. In his place the masters crowned his son.

Reza Shah's abdication caused much noise in the press. Now that it was safe to speak out, everybody had an opinion on the fallen patriarch's flaws. Suddenly our great king was a crook and a coward. His statues toppled, nose to earth and boots in the air, in small, dusty dramas of self-righteous vindication. His portraits burned in bonfires on the street, flames licking his grizzled mustache and fierce gaze, black holes eating into the broad chest and epaulettes. Meanwhile the man himself sailed off under the unrefusable hospitality of the British navy to Africa and ignominious oblivion as a political prisoner of the highest order.

My father's sense of justice and historical veracity was deeply offended by all the exuberant rancor in the press and on the streets. He penned a long article pleading for balance and recognition of Reza Shah's accomplishments. Yes, he had made some heavy-handed mistakes and some genuinely aggrieved enemies in the process. But hadn't he also pulled the nation out of the pit of Qajar corruption and into the twentieth century? He had reformed an antique bureaucracy and judicial system. He had loosened the foreign stranglehold on our finances. He had brought order and stability to the lawless reaches of the tribal regions and built roads and a railroad—the last so valuable that it had been his downfall, the pivot that would turn the tide of a war that otherwise had little to do with us. And dearest to my father's heart, Reza Shah had brought schooling, free and compulsory, to the whole country, girls included, with the new university as the crowning jewel. Why should we dwell on his failings, however real, when he had accomplished so much? And at such a critical time, when his son needed confidence to stand up for Iranian interests in the face of occupying armies?

The article caused quite a stir when it appeared, and the shock waves reverberated in our home. Stones were lobbed through the windows and telephoned threats were made on my father's life. He was publicly accused of being a thief or, worse, a monarchist. True to form, he was convinced that the mullahs were behind all the nastiness. At home, we were most impressed that the young Shah was moved to send him a personal message of thanks. " 'You were the only one, the only one who spoke up!' " my father intoned, interpreting the royal message with his own dramatic flourishes. His plaintive tones conjured the image of an uncertain twenty-two-year-old king, now fatherless and thrust rudely, scripted but unrehearsed, into a charade of royal power in which Britain and Russia pulled the strings.

Among the many crimes attributed to the suddenly monstrous ex-king was a spurious rumor that he had absconded with the crown jewels. It was a matter of serious consequence, as the country's currency was backed by the jewels. A commission was appointed to investigate the alleged theft. Three men of standing, chosen for their integrity, were to take an inventory and determine what, if anything, was missing from the legendary stash that had accumulated over centuries, following various armies back and forth between India, Afghanistan, and Iran.

My father was named as one of the three, but he demurred. "What do I know about jewels? I wouldn't know a diamond from a lump of glass or a carat from a carrot." Finally he accepted on condition that he could bring along an expert consultant, Hajji Mohammad Javaheri. As his name indicated, Javaheri was a jeweler. He was one of the most respected men of the bazaar, for his knowledge of gemstones and precious metals and even more for his adamantine word of honor. True to his title of Hajji, he was also a very religious man who, over the many years that I would later visit his shop, never once looked at me when we spoke.

Every morning my father and Hajji Javaheri would go off to work together. They were an unlikely pair, my father dressed impeccably in suit and tie, Hajji with his grizzled beard and a tall Pahlavi hat that remained forever firmly on his head, indoors or out. They would descend into the basement of the Central Bank as guards with machine guns unlocked one massive steel door after another. The same guards politely ferried many glasses of tea down into the vault as the counting, weighing, and checking of lists continued. They would have brought lunch as well, but my father, being very particular about his food, preferred to come home for the midday meal. So each day over lunch we were treated to amazing tales of the unimaginable wealth that had been measured that morning.

"Khanom, you would not believe your eyes!" my father said to my mother, shaking his head. "There were large burlap sacks full of pearls from the Gulf, not strung or even pierced, just heaped into sacks. It was impossible to count them, so we had to weigh the whole sack. I asked the guard to put down his gun and lift the sack onto the scale, but he couldn't budge it. So he called a second guard, but even two strong young men together couldn't lift it!"

Hajji Javaheri brought a connoisseur's appreciation to the job, and so we learned about the diamond mines of Golconda in India and those in Colombia, and about the difference between rubies from Burma and those from Afghanistan. He told us stories of how Nader Shah had captured the Peacock Throne and the Darya-e Noor, the huge diamond called the Sea of Light—"I held it in my hand," my father said with an exaggerated shrug—and how he had tricked the Maharaja into exchanging turbans with him, knowing that the even huger Kuh-e Noor was hidden in its folds. This Mountain of Light, however, was cursed, and no man who owned it escaped a bloody fate. Logically enough, it had come to rest in the hands of the Queen of England, who, being a woman, was untouched by the curse and, being British, was to blame for any loss that Iran had ever suffered.

These magical bodies of light could never have glowed so brilliantly as they did in my imagination. But even more impressive, at least to my mind's eye, were the heaps of uncut stones that my father described—trays of rubies like plates of pomegranate seeds, emeralds piled like candy—so many gems that a hundred jewelers could not have cut them all in one lifetime. They lay in the vault as smooth and round as pebbles in history's river.

It took a whole month to reckon the entire collection. When every item was listed and appraised, measured and weighed, it turned out that not so much as a single bracelet was missing. The young Shah, no doubt, was relieved. Once again he expressed his pleasure that my father had helped to vindicate his father.

The royal pleasure had consequences. Some years later another commission was assigned to investigate corruption in the government, and my father was again tapped. The task was to identify members of the government whom he deemed dishonest, ranking them from A to J. (An A identified the most serious level of corruption, while those in group J were relatively minor offenders.) It was a good way to make enemies. Some never forgot the insult of being named on that list, no matter how quickly they bounced back into active public life. Perhaps it was the double insult of a grade J that stung one offender, so that even decades later I would feel his enmity in my own encounters with him.

The war continued as a backdrop to our more immediate dramas. The propaganda on the radio had a new flavor, but we had learned not to place too much faith in anything coming over the airwaves. There was talk of a threat of famine and riots over bread in other cities. Tehran did not see the worst of it, but long lines stretched impatiently from the bakeries, and anger sparked at the gritty slabs full of chaff and stones that passed for bread. We were spared even this discomfort as we could get flour sent to us from our farmland, milled by the great stone under the pool at Abdolabad. Each morning at the crack of dawn, avoiding the neighbor's stares, our cook took a discreetly wrapped lump of dough to the bakery and paid a small fee for the use of the oven.

But the occupation had relatively little impact on our daily life. Our three foreign guests—the Americans by now had joined the British and Russians—were concerned only with oil and railroads. Iran was just a thoroughfare for moving supplies and equipment as quickly as possible from the Persian Gulf ports to the Russian front. There was an American camp some distance outside Tehran, but we rarely saw a soldier on the street.

Not even a world war could interrupt the relentless machine of education. We never lost a day of school over it, much as we tried. A car backfiring in the street was all the excuse I needed to stand up in class and scream, "The Germans are coming! Or maybe the Russians! Or even the English!"

My patriotic daydreams had transformed. I was no longer the ministering angel with bandages but a heroic pilot soaring freely above mountains and deserts, defending my homeland with shiny metal and fearless skill. My new bicycle had something to do with this. I flew missions down the long inclines of Tehran's avenues, dodging enemy vehicles. As well as the exhilaration of speed, I enjoyed the mastery of a machine. I could take the whole bicycle apart and put it back together again, absorbed in the satisfaction of a neatly fitting puzzle and the way metal responds to grease or to the heft of a wrench.

Hassan meanwhile had graduated to a motorcycle. With the help of our cousin Hossein—who was actually training to be a pilot—Hassan would spend days breaking down the motorcycle, cleaning it, and putting it all back together. I stood by, waiting eagerly for the smallest opportunity to help, watching with eagle eyes, memorizing the assembly and the names of parts. I was practicing for the day when I would have to learn the innards of an airplane. Hossein encouraged me, happy enough to have a dedicated disciple. When I begged him for some keepsake from a real airplane, he brought me a screw. I kept it in a matchbox and vowed that one day I would know exactly where it fit.

My fascination with flying stretched far beyond the mechanics of it. I watched birds, not as a bird-watcher would to sight interesting species, but simply imagining their point of view. I longed to see aerial landscapes. I longed to escape from this gravity-bound earth and travel for the sheer joy of movement.

One of my closest friends was the daughter of General Nakhjavan, commander of the air force. Once while visiting at Pouran's house, I was bold enough to announce my ambitions to her father. "We don't accept girls," he said, shattering my dream with military bluntness.

"Then I want to be the first girl in the whole universe to be a pilot," I said, bouncing back instantly.

"You're too late," he said, unimpressed. "An American girl did it first. But it's different there. The Imperial Iranian Air Force does not accept girls."

Coming from the general himself, that seemed pretty final. I moped over my disappointment and the unfairness of it all, but only briefly. A new preoccupation soon distracted me, one that would survive many more setbacks than this.

CHAPTER NINE

I sit erect at the dining room table. Mr. Mosavari sits beside me, and beyond him are six empty stiff-backed chairs dressed in red velvet flowers. Mr. Mosavari is middle-aged and a little chubby, with a gentle voice and warm smile. When he hands me another pencil, his fingers rest on mine for a moment.

On the postcard propped against a book, a bowl of glossy apples overflows in two-dimensional abundance. There are shadowy curves of deep red and highlights of pale green. Between them are many colors that I cannot name. Some remind me of fall leaves. Is this how green ripens into red? Is this fruit, or is it light? My pencil rubs ever so gently on the page, spreading a small patch of pale green. There—I have set a trap to catch the light.

The sound of my breathing. The slow, hollow ticking of the Russian clock. The soft scratching of pencil on paper.

It is summer in the city, the last summer of high school, the first summer of my life that I am not tearing through the orchards and scrambling over rocks at Abdolabad. Two mornings a week Mr. Mosavari comes, an hour each time, to teach me how to draw. He has studied art in Europe. He used to teach at the Fine Arts College, where my cousin Parvin is a student, and she had arranged for my sister Mehri to take private lessons with him. Now Mehri is gone and our village summers are suspended, too painful for my mother to want to return yet. A beautiful landscape that Mehri did in pastels hangs on the wall, a record of sister and summer. I couldn't possibly have as much talent as Mehri, my mother says, but Mr. Mosavari will help to fill the long idle days and keep me out of trouble.

When he looks at my drawing and exclaims, "Excellent!" at first I hear sarcasm. He must be making fun of me. But no, the smile is genuine. "You have a fine hand, an observant eye." Such compliments from a teacher are strange to me. Until now, no teacher has ever seen in me anything but a stubborn adversary. Stranger still, the compliments keep coming. Their regularity does not dim their warmth. Their predictability makes them no less precious. I copy postcard after postcard: apples and pears, roses, lilacs, hyacinths, lilies, plum blossoms—"Lovely! You have captured it perfectly . . . an elegant line . . . a subtle sense of color." Each phrase echoes long in my mind, over and over. I am hungry to grasp every possible nuance of those words. But I can't look at the words, and it would be wrong to stare at Mr. Mosavari. So instead I look more closely at the postcard.

One day he brings me a very different postcard. This is to look at only, not to copy: a picture of a woman in calm composure, but with a strange, shadowy, ambiguous expression. "This is Mona Lisa," he says, as if introducing me to an old friend. "You know, your smile is exactly like hers. See how the lips turn at the corner, and this little depression here?"

When he gathers his pencils and cards at the end of our hour, says his goodbyes, and closes the door behind him, I head straight for the mirror. I tense the corners of my mouth into a smile, just a little smile, and look hard for the mysterious shadow to appear. What does he mean by a little depression? Who is this Mona Lisa? Will I be a better artist if I look like her?

From Mr. Mosavari and the constrained exercise of copying post-cards, I learned that art was not just something that happened at school, filling an hour more pleasantly than math or grammar. Art was something that I, Monir Shahroudy, could *do,* and much to my surprise, I could do it well. It was within reach, as close as the tip of my pencil—much closer than nursing wounded soldiers or steering heavy metal through the sky. Fortunately, I was far too ignorant of the world to replace my nurse or my pilot with any bohemian carica-ture of an artist. It wasn't so much that I wanted to be an artist. Art was simply the doing: simply, innocently, the dance of my pencil over the page.

CHAPTER TEN

One two three four . . . smoothly! Pouran, don't wiggle your shoulders like that. It's a foxtrot, not *baba karam!*" I interrupted the lesson to crank up the gramophone one more time, and the beguine began again. Of all my friends, I was the best dancer. That, plus possession of the coveted gramophone, made me the teacher. It would have been nice to have more than two songs to choose from, but I loved those two songs. When it wasn't "Begin the Beguine" over and over, it was "Night and Day"—day and night, day after day, night after night.

My brother Ahmad had recently returned from London with the gramophone, a degree in engineering, and an English wife. Pamela was gorgeous: tall, thin, and blond, with a calm reserve that I now recognize as British but at the time identified with Mona Lisa. Her wardrobe was straight out of the pages of a foreign fashion magazine, and she shared it freely with me. Her dresses didn't fit me, but a belt, a purse, a scarf, or a piece of costume jewelry was fair game.

Ahmad and Pamela had created their own apartment on the top floor of our house on Villa Avenue. The void left by my sisters' deaths was suddenly filled with music, laughter, and chatter in two languages. There were grown-up visitors much younger than my parents, endless card games, and real parties where people danced. I watched carefully, memorizing the steps to practice later when I could get my hands on the gramophone alone.

At one of those instant, informal parties, amid all the greetings and kissing of familiar cheeks, there was one new introduction. Changiz was studying mathematics at the university. He looked like Tyrone Power.

As the cards were being dealt, a few of us drifted back to the gramophone. Changiz directed small talk at me, and I found myself suddenly, stupidly, self-conscious. I was still wearing black for my sisters—how dull! I thought—though black is not a hopeless state when you have a tiny waist and skill with a needle. I had added dark red velvet trim around the sleeves and collar of my dress, and the effect

I AM FLANKED BY MY SISTER-IN-LAW PAMELA
AND SEDIQEH, WHO WORE ELECTRIC LIGHTS
TO HER WEDDING.

was far from mournful. But my face, my hair—now there was something to cry over! I could hardly hear what Changiz was saying for all the voices arguing in my head, and I certainly couldn't believe my ears when he asked me to dance. *Right here? Now?*

There was no more doubting it when he took my hand. My first dance with an actual boy! All the hours I had spent rehearsing for this moment did not prepare me for what happened next. It's true, my feet knew what to do. But why were my knees shaking? Why was the room suddenly so hot? His hand rested lightly on my back, and then he pressed a little bit. My heart pounded against my ribs. A warm tingling crept up my spine, and down too.

I had no idea what was going on. Boys were nothing special to me. Couldn't I run faster, climb higher, and ride better than any boy in Abdolabad? I lay awake that night and stared at the ceiling. I replayed every moment, every step, every word, over and over, trying to understand. Finally I rolled over and gave myself up to sleep, satisfied at last that there was only one possible explanation. I was in love.

Dancing with boys soon became much more manageable. In my own circle were a dozen or so girls and boys of the same age whose families were close, practically interwoven. Every few weeks a party would be arranged at somebody's house, and I could dance to my heart's content. A foxtrot, a tango, a waltz—it was all child's play, all a good romp. But other parties, a bit more grown-up and special, drew from a bigger circle or from Ahmad's friends. At these there was always a chance that Changiz would appear.

Until he appeared, I could think about nothing else, and the instant I spotted him in the crowd, I had nothing else to think about. He was always elusive at first, smiling across the room but then looking away quickly, caught in a conversation. Meanwhile I was floating, so eager to dance that my every movement—lifting a teacup, biting into a cookie—seemed to fall on the beat. *Why doesn't he ask me to dance?* A turn to greet a cousin became an unconscious pirouette, my skirt swirling. *Why doesn't he ask me?* And finally he always did.

There were picnics too. These were even more of an ordeal than the parties. Without dancing, one had to make conversation. Sitting on a carpet on the grass, with a soft breeze shimmering through the birches and friends taking turns at reciting poetry—how could one not feel romantic? But sitting on a carpet on the grass is a very fixed and conspicuous position. (The dozen or so friends and family who surrounded us were all expertly attuned to even the subtlest expressions of romantic interest.) I puzzled over how to drift casually in Changiz's direction without attracting undue attention. I puzzled even harder over whether he might be thinking the same thing about me.

One evening Ahmad and Pamela were going to his cousin's home to play cards. I couldn't help hovering as they were getting ready. "Monir, why don't you come along?" Pamela asked, with a slant to her voice that wasn't entirely innocent.

Changiz was there: a tall, slim lightning bolt in the center of the room, laughing with a group of friends. He broke away and made a beeline for us. "Monir, come out on the terrace and see the moon!"

It was a beautiful night, the summer just beginning to cool, the moon in full glory. Before I knew what was happening, his arms were around me, his face buried in my hair. I was shocked—he was kissing my hair! I stammered and fussed, "You shouldn't do that!" I was confused. Wasn't this what prostitutes did? Is that what he thought of me? Would I be condemned for life now that this had happened? It had never crossed my mind that a kiss—not the polite cheek-brushing kiss of a normal greeting, but a real kiss, a movie kiss, even if just a kiss on the hair—might be a natural step for two young people in our situation.

Sadly, our story came to an abrupt end before I could gain any more experience of kisses. One afternoon, in the quiet time when most of the city sleeps, he came to our door and invited me to go for a walk. It was an event as rare as a rain shower in the desert, and as irresistible. Without saying a word to anyone, my heart pounding, I slipped out the door. We fell into step.

We had barely gone a block when he stopped in his tracks, faced me, and said, "Monir *joon,* my dear . . ." (He called me *joon*! I could feel the warm blush creeping over my cheeks and neck, and my head buzzed with a sweet dizziness.) "You and I can't be together. It would be better if we didn't see each other anymore."

It was as if I had been thrown from a horse and landed flat on my back—all the breath was knocked out of me. I could barely gasp, "Why?"

"Because Einstein said that the energy of a body is equal to its mass multiplied by the speed of light squared." He said this with his eyes fixed on the ground. The horse had now kicked me in the head. Was this how a person goes insane? Was he insane, or was it me? I didn't have the courage to ask. I didn't even have the presence of mind to ask who this Einstein was and what authority he had to make mysterious pronouncements that turned my life upside down, though I wondered for many long nights.

Much later I learned that our glances and dances and moon-gazing had not gone unobserved. A cousin of his—who called himself a friend of mine—had thought enough of the goings-on to mention it to Changiz's parents, who for whatever reason didn't approve of their son's involvement with this Shahroudy girl. Perhaps they had plans for another match; perhaps it was politics or money. I never had the comfort of an explanation, and I never grasped the meaning of the inscrutable formula. (I did eventually figure out who Einstein was and absolve him of any blame in the matter.)

After that Changiz stopped coming to the parties. We had one encounter at a picnic. The wistful longing in his look might have told me a story if I was ready to hear it, but I was too steeped in the pain of rejection to consider his side.

That pain stayed with me for a long time, outweighing the evidence offered by other eager suitors that I might be considered attractive. I never confided my disappointment to anyone. I never experienced that same intensity of longing for another person. And I never stopped dancing.

I danced as if nothing had happened, at party after party. I danced spectacularly at my brother Ali's wedding. Ali had married well. His bride was from a very prominent family that was much involved at the Shah's court when they weren't heading up various embassies in Europe and America. She was intelligent, charming, and beautiful, and she spoke French. If she had been a bit younger, her family would probably not have accepted Ali's offer, but they did. (All his life my brother would harbor an inflated notion of what it meant to be counted among the elite, and an equally inflated notion of his own standing within that category. Nothing I ever said or did could burst his bubble.)

I was still in black, but it was black taffeta with a wide skirt bordered with colorful ribbons, and it swirled with a life of its own when I waltzed. That night my partner was a very good dancer too, and an exceptionally handsome young man. We took the center of the dance floor; couples circled around us like a carousel until they stopped to watch, and we went on and on, finishing to grand applause. It was a picture-perfect fantasy, as the orchestra played in the gardens of the Darband Hotel. If not for an error in casting, I would have been as happy as I looked.

I was feeling very grown-up. I had finished high school, much to the relief of all my teachers, and was accepted to the Fine Arts College at Tehran University. As soon as I walked through the campus gates, the gravity of the situation struck me. The monumental architecture carried the weight of Reza Shah's nation-building dream, and the students—at least on first impression—walked purposefully, as if to announce this was serious business. I could no longer clown my way through classes. I had wanted to become an artist, and now I would really have to do it.

Most of my fellow students in the Fine Arts College—some twenty young men and half a dozen women—were aspiring architects. They were in good hands. Our dean was André Godard, the famous French archaeologist and architect who had established Iran Bastan, the national museum, and also designed much of the university campus. There was a definite French slant to our tuition. It was classically rigorous, with no hint of any emphasis on expression. We did a lot of still life, including an omnipresent watering can and many apples—not the postcard variety, but real ones. We did many, many drawings of Greek and Roman statues, particularly a copy of the Winged Victory. I knew every curve, every angle, every fold of her drapery. On very rare occasions we did life studies with a male model who was wearing only shorts.

Our paper and charcoal for drawing class were supplied by the university, but we had to sign for them to ensure we were not wasteful. The first time I went to the hole-in-the-wall dispensary, I was surprised to see that the supplies were guarded by a familiar triangular face, with a tiny mustache and vague eyes staring out of round spectacles. I recognized him as the eccentric friend of one of my grade-school teachers. As a child, I had teased him, grabbing any excuse to speak to him when I discovered that he had a quirk of repeating his last words over and over.

"Mr. Hedayat, look! There's a dog passing by!"

"Let him pass. Let him pass. Let him pass. Let him pass. Let him pass . . ."

"Would you like an apple, sir?"

"No thank you. No thank you. No thank you. No thank you. No thank you . . ." He was no less obsessive about tracking our use of paper and charcoal, never failing to check in his ledger how long it was since the last request. Years later I would recognize that face again on the cover of a book. When I finally read Sadegh Hedayat's writing, I regretted having childishly tormented this already tormented genius.

The teacher who made the most lasting impression on me was Madame Aminfar, a French woman who was married to an Iranian. (She was rumored to be having an affair with her driver, a notion so preposterous that it transcended censure and made her seem to me a character from a foreign novel.) She looked like a china doll, with very curly blond hair, a double chin, and deep-set blue eyes. She was from Paris, where she had known Van Gogh, Cézanne, Gauguin . . .

They were just names to me at that point. We had no art books then, even at the university; my only exposure to the images attached to these names was through a handful of postcards. I remember looking at my first Van Gogh—my first glimpse of any modern painting—on a postcard. It was as if I were looking through a tiny window into another universe, where color and light played loose and free with reality. I had a shock of recognition, as one might feel in a dream, glimpsing a passing stranger whose familiar eyes could see your innermost secrets.

Madame Aminfar made a sincere effort to get us to draw more freely. It was an important lesson but an isolated one. So much of the time we were striving for exactness. I was humbled to find that there were many aspects of art that I simply wasn't very good at. My portraits seemed always just shy of a real likeness. Perspective was a nightmare. My lines fell on the paper like pick-up sticks at odd angles, refusing to recede into the distance toward the vanishing point.

The worst was when Madame Aminfar gave us assignments to draw the bazaar. Not only was there perspective every which way, but no picture of a bazaar is complete without a donkey. I know what a donkey looks like, I thought. I know what it looks like sideways, backways, nose to nose, from up a tree or flat on my back in the dust. But for all my intimate knowledge of real donkeys, I could not draw one convincingly. Fortunately one of the older students was an expert at donkeys.

"Mr. Javadipour, can you help me? I need another donkey."

"Where do you want it? In front of the bazaar or inside?" Before my very eyes, a donkey would materialize in all its scruffy, sad-eyed, charcoal reality.

Many of the older students were also extremely knowledgeable about perspective, thanks to their training in architecture. I assumed that they were simply being kind in their eagerness to help me. I was still so stung by Changiz's rejection that I couldn't imagine any reason other than sympathy for all the ready rulers, all the available experts leaning over my drawings.

Little by little it became clear that not everyone shared my low opinion of myself. There was simply too much evidence to ignore—too many shy smiles, too many conversations on the flimsiest pretext. There were way too many offers to walk me home. This especially made me uncomfortable. To be seen walking on the street with a boy was to make a brash statement, far more inviting of gossip than my feelings for any of them warranted.

The most steadily, patiently persistent was Manoucher. After weeks of smiles and hellos, further weeks of small talk, and a few nervous walks, he mentioned that he wrote poetry. A few days later he brought me a newspaper that had printed one of his poems. It was about a woman who looked like me—or no, it really was me, though he named his creation Thaïs, after the Greek courtesan who rode on the shoulders of Alexander the Great to throw the torch that burned Persepolis to the ground. What a metaphor! The fire and drama seemed quite delicious, though it dawned on me much later that I was cast as the enemy camp follower and Manoucher as the great Iranian capital. But I was spared that insight at the time.

Manoucher was always followed close behind by Assad. Assad was as short as Manoucher was tall, a Laurel and Hardy pair. Assad wrote poems too, though they didn't make it into the newspapers. In addition to being a Greek courtesan, I was now a blue morning glory.

Manoucher became bolder, making the trek up to my brother's summer home in Darband to visit me there. He brought me another poem. We sat on the terrace, and I read it in the shimmering light that filtered through the birch leaves. In that light it was hard to deny how very handsome he was. Moments after he left, Assad showed up. I quickly folded the poem and tucked it away, wondering if they had bumped into each other on the bridge. Whatever they felt privately about this rivalry, it didn't seem to affect their friendship. When the second visit had run its course and we said goodbye, I tidied up. There was a huge gardenia lying on the chair where Assad had been sitting.

I wasn't in love, not a bit, not with either of them. I knew what love was, or so I thought. It wasn't this.

CHAPTER ELEVEN

I don't remember how or when Manoucher proposed to me, or even if he ever really did. He certainly never came to ask my father for my hand; nor did I meet his family. But somehow, through creeping circumstance and the way that one vague thing leads to another, as I approached the age of twenty, he acquired the label of my "fiancé."

I didn't think of marriage as an imminent reality. I didn't really think about it at all. But having a so-called fiancé offered certain conveniences that I was not above accepting. In any case, Manoucher's presence needed some sort of explanation, and "fiancé" was the only available category. (Boyfriends existed only in movies and gossip.) It seemed that the only thing this arrangement required of me was to tolerate his vise-grip on my hand at picnics. For the record, this heavy hand-holding was the full extent of our physical relations at that time, and he dared that much only in the privacy of a picnic spread among trees, bushes, rocks, and a few close friends.

The convenience of a fiancé became especially clear when I decided to go to America. In fact, I ended up with not just one protector but a trio whom I called my bodyguards.

America was not my original destination. Madame Aminfar had planted a seed in my mind with her stories of Parisian artists, and I had watered it with pure fantasy. I got as far as the French consulate.

"So, you want to go to France."

"Yes, sir. To study art."

"I see. Mademoiselle, are you aware that France is at war?"

"Yes, sir."

"Then I'm sure you will understand that you cannot possibly travel to France at this time. It is impossible."

This called for an instant adjustment. "Well, I will go to Morocco and wait there until the war ends. As soon as the war is over, I'll go to Paris." I don't know why I thought of Morocco. The notion just slipped off my tongue and perched on the edge of his desk, swinging its legs and winking at me with an invitation to adventure. The consul waved it away.

"Mademoiselle, the Germans are attacking in North Africa also. You cannot even find bread to eat in Morocco, or thread to mend your clothes."

"That doesn't matter. I'll bring everything I need with me."

"How big is your suitcase, mademoiselle?"

Having failed utterly in my direct assault on the French consulate, I constructed a more complicated plan of attack. I would first go to America to wait out the war, and from there I would go to Paris. Did I really have such a vague picture of the world's

READY TO FACE THE WORLD.

geography that I thought any two places so far from Iran must surely be close to each other? Or was it the influence of Uncle Dervish's tales? All you had to do was start traveling, step out through that door, cross that magical border, and the whole world would open its arms to you. Either way, my plan hinged on the fact that America was reachable while Paris was not.

Opportunity had presented itself in the form of Mr. Donald Wilber, an archaeologist and scholar of Iranian architecture. More to the point, he was American, and he was willing to sponsor me.

I was introduced to Wilber through a friend who worked at the American embassy, and afterward I ran into him again and again, often at the British Council, which offered English classes, a library, and occasional lectures or films, among the more benign expressions of empire. I had signed up for a weekly drawing class. Naturally, Manoucher decided to take the class too, and of course Assad came trailing behind. After these classes we would often run into Wilber, who would be hovering about with nothing special to do, eager to chat. These chance encounters might end with the group at a nearby café and a couple of times with an invitation to dinner at his home.

Wilber's home fascinated me. It was situated in my own neighborhood, a second-floor apartment off Villa Avenue, but encompassed a very different world. On his shelves were objects that he had excavated or otherwise collected on his travels around Iran. Some were beautiful; some were awe-inspiring for their antiquity. Some were simple objects, ceramic or metal, that I would not have remarked if I had seen them in a village home or in the bazaar—but by setting them in a place of honor on a shelf or table, Wilber had drawn attention to their graceful lines, the elegant balance of volumes, the luster of tradition. It was a lesson that made a profound impression on me.

Most delightful of all were the dishes on which our dinner was served. They were of coarse earthenware glazed in a deep blue, somewhere between cobalt and turquoise—a blue that sang as simply as a folk song of water and big sky. I had often seen a similar blue-glazed pottery in use where yogurt was sold; but no villager I knew ever ate from such a matching dinner set, with water goblets, soup bowls, and plates all in that same blue. It was a brilliant marriage of the ordinary and the unthinkable.

Over dinner on the blue plates our conversation turned to travel. I was surprised to find that Mr. Wilber had an intimate knowledge of my hometown, Qazvin. He had spent much time there in the 1930s doing detailed surveys of some of the older mosques. When he learned that I had set my heart on studying art abroad, he offered to be my sponsor to the United States. Not only would he sponsor me—a critical step in obtaining a visa—but he had connections at the War Shipping Administration and could help to arrange passage on a ship to America.

At the time, though his offer seemed to me an amazing stroke of serendipity, I was too naïve to appreciate fully how extraordinary it was, or how difficult—no, impossible—it would have been to make that journey in the middle of the war without such help. Although we remained friends and kept in touch off and on till the end of his life, I was naïve about Donald Wilber in other ways too. If it hadn't been trumpeted in *The New York Times* half a century after the events, I would never have learned that he was more than an archaeologist and an art historian. He was also moonlighting for the CIA. Nor was he any garden-variety spy—they grew thick as weeds in Tehran, or so our national obsession with conspiracy would have us believe. Indeed, he masterminded the coup that toppled Mossadegh in 1953. It is especially painful to realize that Iran's infant democracy was betrayed by a man with such a deep knowledge of the country and a passion for Iran's ancient culture and arts.

I will never know what motivated this "specialist in psychological warfare and political action" to help a young art student realize a wild dream—was it a whim or part of some more sinister design?—but help he did. He wrote an eloquent sponsorship letter, vouching for the good character of myself and my family, and guided me through the forest of paperwork. There were forms to fill out in triplicate, lines to stand in, affidavits to obtain, and school records to be translated, all duly notarized and stamped.

Not long after I declared my intention to go to America, Manoucher suddenly got the same idea. Oh well, I thought, why not? And since I had the benefit of experience, it fell to me to steer his papers through the bureaucratic maze.

As the fantasy began to take on dimensions of reality and our conversations turned constantly to the theme of America and how to get there, Assad became quieter and his smile sagged. One day Manoucher took me aside.

"You know, Assad wants to come too, but he hasn't got the money," Manoucher said, knowing well enough that I did. My father had divided up his business interests into shares for each of his children. I planned to use the dividends that had accumulated to pay for the trip, assuming I could get my father's permission, but there was more than enough for a second fare. How could I not offer to pay Assad's way? And of course I took care of his paperwork too.

I was working the pieces of my plan into place one by one, postponing as long as possible the moment when I would have to tell my parents. Every time I had tried to broach the subject, they dismissed it with a laugh. My strategy was to present them with a fait accompli. I knew they would never let me go alone, and I didn't take the fiancé business seriously enough to present Manoucher as my escort or impending marriage as an argument. The only solution I could see was to recruit a chaperone who would be acceptable to my parents. Hassan was the most likely candidate.

"America? Why would I want to go to America? If I go anywhere, it's to Germany."

"You can't go to Germany now, and when they've lost the war, you won't want to. Anyway, I don't want to go to America either. I want to go to Paris. But once we get to America, we can go anywhere we like as soon as the war ends." I knew him well enough to know that sooner or later he would sway if I kept talking. He did. And of course if I hadn't helped him with his paperwork, it would never have gotten done.

Eventually all the papers were in order. All that was missing was my father's signature on a document at the American consulate. It was time for my endgame. I concocted a reason to be in the car with my father on a route that happened to pass the consulate. I asked the driver to stop for a moment, then said to my father, "Do you mind? I have a quick errand here. Why don't you come in with me?"

I introduced my father to the consular official, who greeted him with a warm American handshake. "Mr. Shahroudy, your daughter's papers are all in order. We just need your signature here on this document to give your permission."

My father turned to me. His eyebrows brushed the ceiling, and his expression was blaring, "What on earth?!" But just as clearly he was determined not to embarrass himself in front of this emissary from a foreign government.

I answered as casually as I could, "Please, Father, sign it. It's just a formality. We'll talk later. If you don't give me the money, I won't be able to go anyway, and we can forget about it." He signed.

At home the debate began in earnest and continued for about two months. What had so recently been laughable, another of Monir's ambitious fantasies, was now cause for all manner of fear and apprehension. I was too young. I didn't speak English. (I was young enough to learn a new language easily!) Why America? It was too far. We knew nothing about America or the Americans. (But they had never done us any harm, unlike the British or the Russians.) The family had already lost two daughters. How could they let a third one go?

The logic of this last argument, the loss of my sisters, was too emotionally charged to answer. And yet, oddly enough, my victory ultimately hinged on this point. I used to have occasional fainting spells, a problem with pressure on my diaphragm that was exacerbated by anxiety or tension. Once after I had fainted, I surfaced into consciousness for a moment to hear my mother saying to my father, "Let her go. Indulge her. If we make her stay, *degh mikoneh.*" *Degh mikoneh!* It means: she will die of sorrow, of thwarted desire, expire from a broken heart. Through my half-conscious fog I was a little surprised that my haphazard travel plans were perceived as a passion so deep that to thwart it would be life-threatening. But it was hardly for me to argue.

———

MY PARENTS SAT FOR THIS PHOTO SHORTLY BEFORE I LEFT FOR AMERICA,
AND I WOULD REMEMBER THEM BY IT FOR MANY YEARS.

I was to go with my parents' grudging blessing and Hassan's protection. There was much visiting with friends and family to say goodbye, culminating in a big luncheon party at our house. A hundred different items, small and large, had to be bought, cleaned, sewn, polished, or otherwise prepared and finally packed into the growing pile of luggage. Finally the Qoran was pulled from the bookshelf, dusted off for the occasion, and held high over our heads as we passed through the gate and off into the unknown. Like the old custom of seeing a traveler off on their way by accompanying them on the first day's journey, my mother's younger brother and his wife were to go with us by train as far as Abadan. There at the port I was to meet a Mr. Anderson, a friend of Donald Wilber, at the War Shipping Administration. He would find us a ship.

The train journey was a party. I was so full of anticipation and the triumph of our actual departure that I hardly noticed the last long views of the Iranian landscape as we headed for the Gulf. What I did notice was evidence of the occupying armies that Tehran had by and large been spared. Soldiers—Americans mostly, and Indians standing in for the British—were present on every station platform we passed. Endless trains of freight cars and caravans of trucks headed north; many fewer returned south empty. These arteries were desperately pumping supplies to Russia's open wounds. We played cards, not entirely certain how seriously to frame the scenes rushing past our windows. It wasn't really our war—but it was exciting! Sooner or later these guests would leave, as all guests do.

We stopped at Khorramshahr, just shy of Abadan across the river. My father had a friend there, a respected merchant, and we stayed with him for the week or so that it took to arrange passage on a ship. We thought nothing at all of descending on his home en masse and took it for granted that we would be fed and well taken care of for as long as our business kept us there. It would be my last taste from the deep wells of Iranian hospitality for a very long time. So little was I aware of what I was leaving behind that I didn't even think to write a thank-you note or offer a gift.

No bridge yet spanned the Karoun River then. Small rowboats ferried passengers across to Abadan. We made the trip many times, and each time it felt like crossing into a foreign country. Abadan looked very English to me, or rather what I assumed England must look like. The British employees of the Anglo-Iranian Oil Company were housed in rows of bungalows, each set apart by a neatly trimmed lawn and hedge. I thought they looked strangely exposed, both vulnerable and shamelessly naked without the high garden walls that veiled most homes in Iran from sight. Over all this tidy, alien order hung a sulfurous pall from the oil refinery. Like an evil family secret, that smell was always present but unremarked.

I found Mr. Anderson at the offices of the War Shipping Administration. This short, bow-legged man with a big nose was in charge of all the matériel, from weapons to wheat, that was inching its way northward to Russia across the map that papered his office wall. I stated my business—a ride to America, please, for four, on the soonest available ship—and handed him Donald Wilber's letter of introduction. As he read the letter, the blank freeze of his features relaxed, and a fraction of a smile appeared.

"I see from Mr. Wilber's letter here that you're a nurse, Miss Shahroudy. That will make it much easier. Medical professionals have priority."

"But—" I faltered, caught off guard. I thought I had discarded my Florence Nightingale fantasy. What was she doing poking her nose in here? "I'm going to study art."

Mr. Anderson raised one eyebrow. "Hopefully peace will soon

allow us all to follow our true vocation. In the meantime, we do what we have to, don't we, Nurse Shahroudy?"

Thankfully, the persona of Nurse Shahroudy was deposited in a filing cabinet in this remote outpost of the War Shipping Administration and apparently forgotten. In any case, I was never called upon to practice my medical skills. Mr. Anderson told me to come back the next day.

He had found a British ship that could take us, leaving for Bombay in a few days. He would write a letter of introduction, which I would deliver to his colleague at the Bombay office of the War Shipping Administration. We would have to wait there until another ship was found for the next leg of the journey.

We had to pay a fee, of course, and discussed the best way to exchange rials, rupees, and dollars. I must have pulled out a wad of cash that caused him some alarm. My father had given us a substantial supply of Iranian rials, as well as several crisp thousand-dollar bills. (Hassan and I each carried half of the bills. Hassan put them in his shoes, which annoyed me. It probably wouldn't have seemed so unsavory or so silly if I had thought of it first myself.) I didn't tell Mr. Anderson about Hassan's shoes, but he was appalled that we were carrying so much cash. He offered to buy us dollars and have them sent to New York, where we could pick up the money when we reached our final destination. I handed over a good portion of our funds, and in exchange he gave me a name and address in New York. I thought nothing of the fact that business was handled like this, with trust as the only safeguard.

Our ship turned out to be hardly more than a boat. It had two first-class passenger cabins, one occupied by a young British officer bound for duty in India, and a second that I shared with a middle-aged Indian woman, the wife of a merchant who traded from Abadan. She was the only other female aboard, as far as I knew. Hassan, Manoucher, and Assad were sent down, along with my cabin-mate's husband, into the bowels of the ship. They disappeared into the dark crowd, a human cargo of Indians and Arabs. So much for my protection.

The captain and the handful of officers aboard were very eager to introduce themselves. I knew that sooner or later I would have to face up to the effort of practicing my little English. The simple conversations of new acquaintance would be a good opportunity, I thought.

"I go New York . . . I vaant estudy art."

"Oh, I say, you're an artist!"

I blushed red as a beet, horrified at the misunderstanding. In Persian, *artist* means "actress." Rita Hayworth was an artist, Alice Faye was an artist. With all due respect to the great talents of the silver screen, an artist was also by definition a loose woman. I had never felt so insulted!

"No, no, no, I am not artist. I will go to art school . . . to study art!"

My cabin was tiny and dark, the one porthole permanently covered for the wartime blackout. I awoke from the first night's sleep aboard to pitch black and a strange slapping sound that continued for about a quarter of an hour. The same thing happened the next morning, and the next. Finally my curiosity got the better of me. I switched the light on to find the Indian woman sitting up in her bunk, a jar of coconut oil in one hand and the other slapping away at the crown of her head. She explained that this technique prevented baldness. I closed my eyes again, glad that the mystery was solved but a little worried that I obviously had so much to learn about the ways of the world.

Day after day the sea was very rough, huge waves breaking around us. Everyone aboard seemed to be sick except for me. For meals I was invited to the captain's little dining room along with the handful of officers. At each lunch and dinner the captain, green around the gills, would look at me and ask with genuine surprise, "Monir, you're not sick?"

"I am fine." I was, but only just. Between my poor English and the general nausea, conversation was limited. I sat politely, ate my meal, and postponed as long as possible returning to my cabin. My roommate's husband brought meals up from belowdecks on a tray, filling the small chamber with a heavy smell of grease and spices that was much harder for me to bear than the rolling seas.

Hassan and the other boys fared as badly for meals as they did for their berth. Every so often a sheep would appear on the deck, bleating furiously, until the cook put a knife to its throat. The carcass was skinned in a matter of moments and the mess thrown into a pot to stew. That much I saw myself. For the rest of the story—the crowding, the filth, the smells, and the sickness—I took their complaints on faith and never saw what lay below the deck.

It was their good luck that the young English officer fell in love

with me. One night he asked me to go for a walk on the deck: it was
off-limits to passengers, but as an officer he had special privileges. We
walked in the pitch dark. "Can I hold your arm?" he asked. "I can't
see where I'm going." He pressed my arm tightly, and I enjoyed the
game, both of us pretending that we didn't know what he was doing.
It all seemed very romantic in spite of the pitch and roll of the metal
beneath us, the smell of machinery, of fuel and old fish.

Thereafter my officer followed me around like a shy but loyal
puppy, looking for any opportunity to offer a hand, to do any favor
I might think of. I told him how miserable my companions were
belowdecks. Soon enough he offered Hassan the empty bunk in his
cabin. A few days later Manoucher won a spot on his floor. Assad was
the last to be rescued. They couldn't squeeze him into the same cabin,
but the officer leaned on one of the crew to make room for him.

We stopped at Dubai to unload cargo. Ships—even as small as
ours—could not enter the shallow port, and cargo had to be unloaded
crate by crate onto small boats that ferried back and forth to the
dock. But the sea was too rough, and we waited offshore for four days
until it was calm enough to unload. Twenty-two days after we had
left Abadan, we reached Karachi. We spent one night in the port
without going ashore, and then went on toward Bombay, still a week
away.

Bombay seemed like paradise to me, so lush and green after the
high desert air of Iran. I was amazed at the birds perched in the trees,
at the colors and shapes of fruit I had never seen before. And I
had thought the orchards of Qazvin were so magnificent! Indeed,
I had been forewarned about the fruit by my cabin-mate. My first
encounter with a banana had occurred on board the ship, and she
laughed at my surprise. "Just wait till we reach India—then you will
see fruit! Many, many kinds! Very, very sweet! But don't think they
are all just like your banana here. No, they have seeds—*tokhme-dar*!"
The expression she used could equally mean "They have balls!" I
thought it was hilarious and repeated the joke with each new fruit I
encountered. Hassan was appalled at my rudeness and scolded me,
red-faced with embarrassment, every time I said it.

My English officer had helped us to find a hotel, and he invited me
to a movie in the evening. I was thrilled at the idea, but a date alone
was unthinkable. And so began a refrain that I would repeat many,
many times over the next weeks: "I am with my brother, my fiancé,

and my friend. If I come, they have to come along." My three body-guards trailed behind me wherever I went.

Our outing to the cinema was as splendid as a night at the opera, thanks to the privilege of the British army. Men in any kind of uniform snapped to attention and saluted as we passed. We sat in a private booth, deep in brocade cushions on velvet-covered chairs, and were served sweet iced *sharbat*. I had never seen a movie house so luxurious, and I've never seen anything quite like it since. The next evening he took us—all four of us, of course—to the Taj Mahal Hotel, the grandest establishment in Bombay, for dinner. I was eager to try Indian food and ever so sorry that I couldn't help coughing and choking on every bite. The heat was new to me and just too much to swallow. In the end, I ate nothing that night but plain rice.

There were other invitations: a dance at an English club, where women swirled in saris to waltzes and foxtrots; visits to temples; and a lunch at the home of the Iranian ambassador, who was a friend of my father's from many years back. Somehow in all the social whirl, in the dazzle of heat and color, the pungent-fragrant-nasty confusion of smells, the strange flavors and accents and many languages—somehow I remembered to find my way to the War Shipping Administration office.

My three bodyguards came along. Assad spoke the best English of the group, limited as that was, so he had started to take on a more assertive role, ordering for us in restaurants and asking strangers for directions, instead of always trailing behind. Hassan also was eager to push himself forward. He had begun to play the watchdog with me in a most unpleasant way. I don't believe that he really cared if I got myself into trouble; more likely he resented the attention I drew so easily and enjoyed lording some brotherly authority over me.

But when I marched up the steps of the War Shipping Administration building and announced that I needed to see the general, all three of my bodyguards shrank into the shadows and waited for me to take care of business. The guard seemed dubious. Did young girls never come calling on the general with such self-confidence? I wondered. I waved my letter from Mr. Anderson. The envelope was examined closely, front and back, and passed around for consultations. Finally I was escorted into the building and, after a brief wait in the antechamber, into the general's office. I introduced myself, stated my request just as I had in Abadan, and handed him the letter.

"Impossible. The only ships departing Bombay for the Pacific now are warships. You'll find that some of your compatriots have been waiting here for months, hoping to find a way to America. The son of the Iranian minister of war is one of them. Perhaps you would like me to introduce you to him?"

I had no such desire and no intention of giving up so easily. "I don't mind traveling on a warship. Mr. Anderson said you could find us a ship. He also said you would help me change some money. I would like to break this bill." I placed a thousand-dollar bill on his desk. He seemed surprised, though looking back I can't say whether it was caused by my naïve insistence or by the odd request that a general should serve as a money changer. In any case, he opened the letter from Mr. Anderson and read it. Then he looked me straight in the eye.

"Let me look into this. I'll let you know in a few days how we can arrange to get you as close to your destination as possible." He called an officer and told him to take me to the bursar to change the money. That caused no small commotion. Nobody had ever seen a thousand-dollar bill. It was passed from one officer to another and held up to a light and then under a magnifying glass. Finally they gave me change for it. I thought, *These American soldiers are so poor and stingy, they don't even know what a thousand-dollar bill looks like. How special can it be? After all, it's been in Hassan's shoe all this time.*

A few days later an American officer called at the hotel. He told us to be packed and ready the day after next, a time, a place—"There's a boat leaving for San Pedro that can take you." Our last "ship" had turned out to be such a sad little boat that I didn't have high hopes if this vessel was called a boat to begin with. I still had much to learn about American English.

Our "boat" was a huge warship, surrounded by a convoy of five other ships to protect it from Japanese submarines. The distortion of the loudspeakers that blared out orders was the next challenge to my poor English. Every time they barked, I ran to Assad for translation. "They are saying that we have to wear the life jacket at all times. It must be in your hand or on your body, no matter what you are doing." If Assad wasn't around, I had to decipher my duty by watching what others did, terrified I would make a wrong move. It was obvious I wasn't cut out for the military. It was far too deadly serious for someone who had made such a career out of challenging authority at school.

I slept with forty other women in a single room with bunk beds stacked four tiers high. My bunk was at the very top, right underneath a pipe that bruised my shoulder if I rolled over without taking care. My roommates were refugees from China, rescued somehow from the Japanese. I would never learn their story: not one of them spoke English as far as I could tell. But obviously they had much to say to one another. I awoke in the early morning to the sound of two or three voices talking. Within half an hour the chatter had reached a roiling boil—it seemed like all forty were talking at once, and I was the only one listening.

I dressed quickly to beat the bathroom rush. It was like running a gauntlet: I queued up with towel and soap to sprint through the shower; the toilet seat barely vacated by the previous visitor was always still warm. Then I stood in line once again for breakfast. We had two meals a day, but we could take as much food as we wanted and bring a stash back to the cabin. I surmised that my bunkmates had not so long ago suffered from near-starvation and was glad that the ship seemed to be free of vermin. All in all, I had a new appreciation for the luxuries of the last boat and the company of the head-slapping, fruit-loving matron.

I saw little of my bodyguards. They bunked in the soldiers' quarters, and every once in a while they were allowed to come to an upper deck where we could visit briefly. Other than that, the men and women were not allowed to mix. It was just as well, I thought. Whenever I appeared on the upper deck, a number of sailors would shout and toss their hats up in the air, six or seven decks below us. I assumed the segregation was to minimize the unnecessary loss of hats.

I did find a friend on board, another young Iranian woman who had been waiting for passage from Bombay for several months. (Her husband was traveling with her and turned out to be the son of yet another old friend of my father's. I wondered if there was a spot on the earth where I wouldn't find a family connection.) One day as we were chatting, an officer came up to us. He said there was a hospital on board, and our help was needed. I was suddenly terrified that Nurse Shahroudy had been identified and would have to perform. But the real story was simpler. Would we be willing to visit with the wounded soldiers, chat with them and cheer them up, and hand out candies?

Why not? I didn't imagine there would be any harm in providing such a simple service. I had nothing special to wear, so I went as I was. As we entered the ward, I was completely unprepared for the shock of American familiarity. Men whistled and catcalled, reached out to me and called me "honey" and "darling" and asked to kiss me. I was appalled and insulted. Who did these strangers think I was? I walked up and down the line of a hundred or so beds, skirting the most aggressive. I handed them chocolates and chewing gum and gingerly made conversation.

"Who are you?"

"I am a painter." I now knew better than to say artist, but my care with words made little difference under the circumstances. Thank goodness the ordeal was over quickly.

The journey had little other drama, though one particular week had two Wednesdays, a strangeness I never figured out. One day sirens gave warning of an attacking Japanese submarine. We all trooped out to our assigned places on deck, wearing our life jackets as always, much as in a fire drill at school. The lifeboats were lowered in readiness, but half an hour later the inscrutable loudspeakers let it be known that the danger had passed.

We made a stop at Sydney, and I watched from the deck as hundreds and hundreds of men in handcuffs were lined up and marched off the ship while soldiers walked up and down waving machine guns. Until that moment I had no idea we were delivering German prisoners of war.

Thirty days after we had set off from Bombay we reached the harbor at San Pedro. Hassan, Manoucher, and Assad had made friends among the soldiers, one of whom was also headed for New York. He helped us to find a hotel in Los Angeles and offered to show us around. After so long at sea, my bodyguards were eager to taste America and immediately made plans to go sightseeing in Hollywood. I would have none of it. As far as I was concerned, we were headed for New York, and there was no point dawdling on the way. We argued—and the huge argument, fed by sea weariness and frayed nerves, seemed to drag in every film star who ever looked at a camera, every movie they had ever seen.

"To hell with Hollywood!" I shouted finally. Assad and Manoucher went off to see the sights, and Hassan stayed behind to guard my virtue.

When we recovered from our fight, we faced the final hurdle. In wartime America, seats on trains were hardly easier to find than passage from Bombay. A sleeper was out of the question. We rode for four days and three nights, eating on the train and sleeping upright in our seats, a jacket rolled up for a pillow on one shoulder. We passed a name I recognized, Chicago, and many more that I didn't, but we never once got off the train. We passed drab towns, shabby fences, and little homes on little plots. I saw nothing to match the drama and grandeur of the landscapes of Iran. I could only hope that New York would have more to offer.

CHAPTER TWELVE

New York did indeed have much to offer, but discovering it took some time. With my expectations set by Hollywood—the *real* Hollywood that lived on a gleaming screen in a darkened cinema in Tehran, not the one in some suburb of Los Angeles—my first impressions were disappointing.

For the sheer scale of big-city bustle and the impact of the strange and exotic, New York could hardly compete with Bombay. Beyond that it seemed to me only marginally cleaner and more modern. It doesn't matter, I told myself: Paris is waiting.

Indeed, the only place in New York that really impressed me was Rockefeller Center, where we went searching for the Iranian consulate immediately after our arrival. Now this is America, I thought. Modern, expansive, and soaring—beautiful! That first impression has not faded in the more than half a century that I have known New York intimately; Rockefeller Center remains unrivaled in my mind by any other architecture in Manhattan.

Aside from my reluctance to be impressed, in every other way I was fresh off the boat. My sketchy knowledge of English led to frequent faux pas. Especially treacherous were the words that Persian has borrowed from French and that I expected to serve the same purpose in English. The *artiste* problem should have alerted me, but other words were equally slippery. When I asked the bellboy who carried our suitcases where I could find the *douche,* he denied its existence. The thought that we were spending ten dollars a night for a hotel room that offered no shower was outrageous to me, and I took the opportunity to practice my English expressions for annoyance and disbelief. I was so immersed in the exercise that Hassan finally had to intercede: "Monir! Don't shout at the poor guy—the shower is right in front of you!" I covered my embarrassment and relief with a gushing stream of "Thank you! Very good! Goodbye! Never mind!" as the bellboy escaped.

We had reached New York only days before the Iranian new year at the spring equinox. It was my first Noruz without the rituals of family visits or my father's celebrated baklava, without the fragile promise of buds unfolding in the high desert air as the snowcaps inched their way up the mountains. It didn't matter; the sense of new beginnings and springtime awakening was palpable anyway, like a secret hidden in the slick browns and grays of Manhattan, in the smell of rain-soaked pavement, and in the blossom-laden trees fenced with iron. It is not the familiar holidays that make a foreigner homesick in America, I learned—no, these become private treasures held close, unmarked by crowds but celebrated incognito with a newly-chosen family of friends. Rather, the alien bustle of unfamiliar holidays is what brings on the newcomer's loneliness, the glossy surface of Christmas empty of childhood memories. In any case, we celebrated Noruz that year more grandly than I ever had in Tehran. The Iranian consulate hosted a big party at the Waldorf-Astoria, and I danced as happily as if I were in the gardens at Darband.

Soon after we arrived, I had to locate a certain Mr. Jackson and collect the funds that Mr. Anderson at the War Shipping Administration office in Abadan had transferred for me. The Fifth Avenue address inscribed on the envelope, a little bedraggled after its long journey, had once seemed inscrutably foreign. But Fifth Avenue was quickly becoming a familiar landmark in my new geography, and it was Abadan that now seemed a universe away. The letter, when finally open in Mr. Jackson's hand, described me as Mr. Anderson's "adopted daughter" to whom he should give the money that had been wired earlier. I had no clue that financial transactions were not usually conducted so informally, or with such easy trust between strangers. For his part, Mr. Jackson seemed surprised only that I expected him to hand over all of the several thousand dollars in cash. I had neither a bank account nor any experience with checks. He tried to explain to me how banks could keep money safe, but I didn't see the point. I figured that between Hassan's shoes, the kindness of the War Shipping Administration, and my own wits, I had managed quite well without a bank so far, and I saw no reason to entrust my money to any institution at this late date. And so, in spite of his concern, he gave me the cash.

I in turn dutifully handed it over to Hassan, who maintained tenacious vigilance as my official chaperone and watchdog for this remote outpost of the Shahroudy family honor. It didn't matter that I was perfectly capable of managing my own affairs, usually at least one step, if not a few miles, ahead of Hassan in any practical matter. Still, he insisted on holding the purse strings even after we had moved from the hotel to separate accommodations—myself to the YWCA and my trio of bodyguards to a boardinghouse. If we went to a restaurant, Hassan paid. If I wanted cash for shopping or for a taxi, I had to ask him.

The real issue, of course, was not practical but a need to flex the muscles of masculine power. It made no difference when Hassan went off to the University of Iowa and worked the summers picking peaches on a farm, learning the value of one's own hard-earned cash like any American boy. Even later, when I was earning my own salary, he acted as if what was mine was naturally his. More than once he helped himself to some piece of jewelry or a trinket I had bought for myself when he thought it would make a nice gift for his girlfriend. My small consolation at such times was that, for once, he wasn't turning up his nose at my taste.

Doors continued to open for me at Donald Wilber's bidding, even from the far side of the world. Beyond all his help with arrangements for visas, the sea voyage, and transferring money, he had written a letter of introduction to his friend and colleague Arthur Upham Pope, the famous historian of Iranian art and architecture. As in so many previous errands, my three bodyguards filed behind me up the steps of the East Side brownstone and into Pope's office. The room was huge and imposing; the man himself was seated behind a desk the size of a Central Asian plateau. When he stood up to shake hands, he towered above me. He was exuberant, a volcano of knowledge spewing stories, ideas, and emphatic opinions.

I could barely keep up with the rush of words. Manoucher and Hassan were no better off; we all looked to Assad to speak for the team. Pope quickly turned the conversation to politics and grilled us on recent events in Tehran. The Shah, in an effort to impose his authority on the Majles, had instituted a new Senate chamber in which a number of seats were appointed by the crown rather than elected. Assad was explaining how this related to my father—as far as I knew, not at all. Yes, the Shah had honored him on several occasions, but he had been rightfully elected by the people of Qazvin. Hobbled by my limited knowledge of the situation in Tehran and by my even more limited English, I was infuriated by the aspersions that Assad seemed to be casting on my father's democratic credentials.

I refused to speak to Assad for weeks after the imagined insult. He hardly noticed. He was very busy cementing his friendship with Pope, who gave him a job looking after his research library and a room in his home. Although I was obviously too naïve to be much use as a political informant, Pope nevertheless took good care of me too, introducing me to his connections in the art world and in particular to a circle of art historians and curators at the Metropolitan Museum.

In a gallery of the museum that had been transformed into a formal dining room for the opening of an exhibition, I was seated at a long table with several very distinguished gentlemen. In my immediate vicinity were my host, the curator Benjamin Knot; the archaeologist Charles Wilkinson; the curator of Islamic art, Maurice Dimand; and the director of the museum, Francis Henry Taylor. I felt like a rock in the middle of a rapid stream, conversations rushing past me like paper boats folded out of newsprint—I could follow a few phrases, even a paragraph here and there, but only so far before they rounded a bend just beyond range of my comprehension or sank in an eddy of scholarly shoptalk and academic gossip.

"Tell us, Monir, what does Persian sound like?" All eyes were on me, forks suspended in midair. It did not occur to me how odd it was that these stellar scholars of Iranian art should pretend to be unfamiliar with the sound of the Persian language. I simply assumed they were extending me some kindness out of pity, a generous excuse to include me in their conversation. The sound of Persian—what should I say? No elegant verses of Hafez popped into my mind. Instead I picked up a strawberry from my plate and asked, enunciating clearly, if anyone could tell me whether it had seeds. No answer was forthcoming, but the nodding heads seemed to approve of my performance and wanted more.

Someone held up a roll. "How do you say 'bread'?"

"*Nan,*" I answered. Big smiles all around.

"And 'water'?"

"*Ab,*" I said. More smiles, knowing nods. If this was a test, it was easy enough.

"How do you say 'sun'?"

"*Khorshid,*" I responded in all innocence. For some reason this was funny, funny enough to make dignified men laugh out loud, and even louder when Mr. Knot confirmed what was obvious to everyone except me: "Didn't I hear you say 'horseshit'?" The joke was lost on me, which was just as well. I was having quite enough trouble with English without being mocked for my Persian.

Although they toyed with me, they balanced it with much kindness. They steered me through galleries and museums as if they had nothing more pressing to do than offer private docent tours to a young student. They showered me with invitations to dinners, openings, parties, lectures . . . They were determined that I should meet the right people in the art world—each of whom in turn knew somebody else to whom they absolutely must introduce me. In short, they took me under their illustrious wings.

It hadn't dawned on me yet that such kindness might be motivated by anything other than pity—that I might be an exotic novelty, an object of curiosity, or God forbid, a blank screen for the projection of some silk-and-sequin fantasy out of a Hollywood harem. If I was aware at all that I stood out in a crowd, I felt it awkwardly—I was dark, all black hair and eyebrows, and I felt my difference as a darkness, a little cloud that shadowed me in brighter company. By the time I figured out that I was supposed to be exotic and even, in some unforeseen way, beautiful, I also had plenty of evidence that these qualities opened doors. So be it. Once a door had opened and I stepped inside, there I was. Whatever luck had launched a friendship, it would survive—or not—on its own merits.

Pope also introduced me to Barbara, who was in charge of the art section at the public library on Fifth Avenue. Barbara was the epitome of kindness, and she became a good friend and mentor to me. It was Barbara who planned the grand strategy of my education.

"First we've got to fix your English," she said, looking at me through narrowed eyes and cocking her head to one side, as if she were recommending a new hairdo and some fresh makeup. She sent me off to Anglewood, a small private high school in New Jersey. For three months I listened to the babble of American girls in the dormitory every night and forced myself to stay awake, attentive, and polite in class all day. In my free moments I walked in the woods, picking wildflowers and mushrooms. I came out with the fundamentals of English, at least sufficient for an artist. My English would never be perfect. Decades of daily use would improve only minimally on what I learned at Anglewood, and nothing would ever straighten out my accent. But neither would I ever be kept from expressing myself by the technicalities of grammar.

After Anglewood, Barbara decided that I should attend summer classes in the art department at Cornell University. The brightest moments of my summer at Cornell were spent in the company of a newfound friend, Azizeh. Young Iranian women were a rare species on campus, and Azizeh and I could not help but find each other. But it was more than a common language that made us the closest of friends for many years to come. Azizeh was smart. She was more

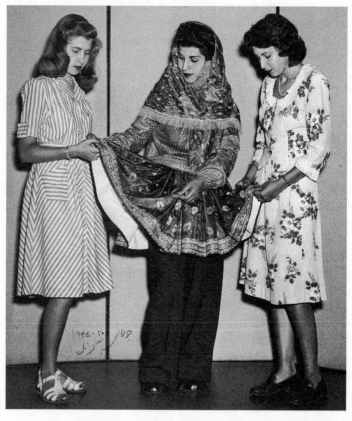

IN JULY 1945 THE CORNELL STUDENT NEWSPAPER ASKED ME TO POSE IN "NATIVE DRESS." I PUT ON ONE OF MY MOTHER'S *SHALITEH*S, THE TUTU-INSPIRED SKIRTS THAT THE QAJAR KING NASSER AL-DIN SHAH HAD REQUIRED HIS HAREM TO WEAR AFTER HE SAW THE BALLET IN PARIS.

than smart; she was brilliant. I suppose it ran in the family, as she was descended from some of the shrewdest statesmen who had steered Iran through the last hundred years. She had grown up in Europe, where her father was ambassador to Germany, and she spoke many languages. She knew opera, especially Wagner, which impressed me; and she was at the top of the advanced math class, which humbled several young men. But the body that housed all this brilliance was sadly misshapen. Polio had left her with a heavy limp, and her face was partially eaten away by leishmaniasis. As if this weren't enough, she suffered the burden of looking after a

AT CORNELL I WAS ALWAYS MOST COMFORTABLE WITH A PENCIL IN MY HAND.

younger sister who was very demanding, pampered, and wild. I had a great admiration for Azizeh's courage, her kindness, and her sharp wit. I loved her dearly, and we were inseparable.

Having parted ways with my trio of bodyguards, I was now responsible for protecting my own virtue. Time and again, on campus or off, boys would approach me. An opening line, the inevitable questions—Where was I from? Why was I here?—were followed, just as inevitably, by a request for a date. It never crossed my mind to accept these invitations. After all, I was engaged to Manoucher, sort of. More important, I wouldn't dream of leaving Azizeh alone of an evening. So I made up stories, the more exotic the better.

"I am a gypsy from Hungary" . . . "I am a refugee from Madagascar."

"*Bi haya!* You are shameless!" Azizeh scolded me from the sidelines under her breath. I would remind her to add this latest invention to her running tally of which lie I had told to whom. She had a prodigious memory, and if she cooperated, I could pick up the story and embroider it further when we ran into the same boy again.

Receiving the attention of strangers, however flattering, was only one small step removed from enduring the discomfort of sticking out like a sore thumb. So many times in that first year in America I found myself out of place, embarrassed, and awkward. An invitation to go riding ended with me galloping off across a beautiful green meadow and discovering the ritual of golf. An opportunity to join Martha Graham's dance class exposed me as a short, dark molehill in a forest of slender, long-legged, graceful blondes. It was only with Azizeh that I felt truly at home. Her company alone was a safe haven.

CHAPTER THIRTEEN

That summer saw the end of the war with Japan, an event that we celebrated at Cornell with a hayride. Strangers were kissing strangers, all of them apparently drunk, and a chaos of dusty straw and noise filled the air. It seemed to me a very strange way to welcome peace.

When the summer ended and it was time to return to New York, Azizeh came back with me and enrolled at Columbia. She never got her degree: she simply couldn't be bothered. She studied for the joy of learning and nothing more. My own situation was far more complicated. The end of the war stirred my dream of Paris again. But around this time Manoucher decided that his own destiny was to become a truly great artist, right up there with Picasso and Van Gogh. My role as his prospective wife was to help that destiny along by providing financial support, unending praise, and gracious entertainment for any gallery owners and wielders of influence who might cross our path. I went down to the public library to ask Barbara's advice.

"Two artists can't live together in New York," she said. "Forget it! One of you has to earn some money." If any aspirations for my own art had survived Manoucher's condescension, they were shot down by Barbara's ultimatum. On her recommendation I enrolled at Parsons School of Design to study fashion illustration. Whatever skill I had would be put to practical and profitable use.

Parsons subjected its students to a rigorous training. If I was missing out on anything that a more rarefied fine arts curriculum would have provided, I was too engrossed in the challenges at hand to notice.

The life drawing classes scheduled three times a week were a major hurdle. The first time I faced a nude model—without even shorts, as in my few such experiences at Tehran University—I was deeply shocked.

With this pale specimen of American manhood before me, I found it very hard to look up from the safety of my sketch pad. It turned out that drawing was very difficult if you didn't look at your subject. I tried to face my dilemma logically: Why should I be embarrassed? He was the one standing there with no clothes on, not me! Eventually, after a few sessions, I got used to it. The quiet concentration of the other students, all engrossed in their own drawings, made the situation seem natural.

I was deep in my drawing just like everyone else, the charcoal hushing other thoughts as it rubbed. The line of a shoulder, a shadowed neck, the edge of a jaw leading my hand . . . where next? I glanced up, looking for the planes of the face, bone, and muscle . . . and the face winked at me. I could not have been more surprised if I had just witnessed the Winged Victory flapping her wings and taking flight. I stared blankly, and he winked again. My eyes plummeted back to the paper. The rest of that session was torture. Every time I looked up, he winked, and every time he winked, I became more flustered. I made a few tentative strokes on the paper, but it was impossible to focus on the lines and even more dreadful to look up.

Finally the teacher called, "Change the pose!" I picked up my sketch pad and moved to another easel at the far side of the room. When I settled myself and looked up to begin drawing, I found that the model had also reoriented himself and once again was facing me. As I looked, he winked. Now I was not only confused and embarrassed but also annoyed. That at least gave me the will to keep focused for a while, but every time I looked up, he winked again. And every time the teacher called for a break or a change of pose, I would move, and he would reposition himself to face me.

I had that same model for as many as ten classes in one year, and every time it was a struggle. I started deliberately coming a few minutes late to class, waiting till everyone else was seated and the pose assumed before I chose my station. But after the first twenty minutes of peace, as soon as the teacher called, "Change the pose!" he would find me.

As future fashion illustrators, we were often assigned to draw models fully clothed or else to work from memory or imagination, visualizing the ways that fabric wraps the human form. I enjoyed these exercises, usually choosing a very fine-point pen and ink. I was rewarded with my first compliment from the teacher—"a very sensitive, refined line." It was as if I had received a postcard in the mail from Mr. Mosavari, all warm and glowing apples of praise; as if my pen had stitched that sketchy blouse as a gift for my sister Iran, and her smile were shining right through the teacher's words.

Such moments were rare. Most of the time I struggled with my own sense of inadequacy and with the casual disdain of my nearest and dearest critic. Manoucher had a way of killing my confidence with a carefully aimed and brutally qualified compliment: "This section here in the corner is really quite nice."

Color was a cause for particular anxiety. It was clear as day to me that my own sense of color was inferior. I wrestled with the arcane science of the color chart that we were assigned to build—mixing each color with more and more black and white, twelve equidistant shades painted, dried, cut, and pasted. Why would anyone want to take these pure, clean hues and poison them with black and white, let alone measure this slow death in precisely

I AM POSING IN AN OUTFIT I CREATED FOR PARSONS GRADUATION. I MADE THE TOP FROM MY MOTHER'S *SHALITEH*.

tortured steps? I envied the other students their sophisticated shades of brown, beige, gray, and black. My turquoise, purple, emerald green, shocking pink, and poppy red were evidence of immaturity, childish splashing on the shore of the dark ocean of the subconscious where the others plumbed the depths. I didn't know how to swim in those stormy grays.

Finally, overwhelmed by despair and shame at the rainbows that I could not shake from my brush, I confessed my misery to the teacher. I scraped the floor with apologies and begged for her mercy. At first she didn't understand what I was talking about, but language was not the problem. Finally my desperation registered.

"You really believe that? You believe that you don't paint well?"

"Just look at my colors! They are different from everybody else's colors!" I was on the edge of tears. My trembling lower lip was proof, if any proof beyond my garish canvases were needed, that I was infantile and incapable of meeting the challenges of Parsons School of Design.

"Monir, listen to me," she said. "Do you know how many times the teachers have shown your work to each other? Do you know what we say? We say, 'Look how different her colors are! How happy! How beautiful! You can see that her color sense comes from a different culture.' "

"You're joking."

"No, I'm serious. These are *your* colors. If you give me a painting in beiges and grays, I will fail you." She sounded genuinely angry at my stupidity, but that was better than being angry at my colors. I thought long and hard about her words. *A different culture.* It was the first inkling I had that Iran had something to do with my art, or that I had something unusual to offer.

Soon afterward we had an assignment to do a rendering of fireworks. I threw myself into it with abandon, my colors exploding, liberated, on the deep blue night. In my final year the task of designing a set for a hypothetical ballet was another chance to indulge my colors shamelessly. I had just seen *South Pacific,* and I loved the image of girls in pink and red and white jumping up and down against a brilliant background. I also found the gay hues of my idol, Marie Laurencin, seeping into my dancers. The teacher made a fuss over the work and talked again about my foreign color sense. I was proud, but I also sensed that what she said was only partly true. Right here in America I was finding rainbows enough that spoke to me in their own language. If my eyes wore the stained-glass windows of my childhood, the jeweled jams and pink crystal dishes, and the deep pure colors of a carpet garden, they could see the lights of Manhattan just as clearly. Later I would learn that the brilliant colors that are native to me are not necessarily the colors of happiness; even in the saddest, most despairing times, my colors refuse to darken or fade.

Many of our classes at Parsons were excursions: museum visits, trips to the zoo to sketch animals—any place where there was a piece of life to be captured on paper or some interesting example of antique art to be studied by copying. One day I found myself drawing faithful copies of Indian artifacts at the Museum of Natural History. Thirty of us were scattered throughout the museum halls, each a little encampment staked out on a plastic dropcloth with paints and water and brushes arrayed around us. We were absorbed in our work, hardly more animated than our subjects. Tourists drifted past, children straggling to stare at us, a few GIs in uniform hovering conspicuously. One young soldier passed by me again and again. He would disappear for a while and then return. Finally he sat down beside me, apparently fascinated by the angular birds hopping around the belly of the pot I was drawing. I tried to ignore him.

"What are you doing?"

"I'm drawing." This was obvious enough to give him pause. After a moment he tried a completely novel approach.

"Where are you from?"

"Look, I'm very busy. I have to do an assignment for school. Please don't talk to me."

He kept quiet for hardly three seconds. "Can I take you out for lunch? Somewhere we can talk alone."

"I can't. I'm engaged to someone else." He excused himself and left, but half an hour later he was back.

I BOUGHT MY FIRST WINTER COAT IN NEW YORK WHILE I WAS LIVING AT INTERNATIONAL HOUSE.

"I have to take you out! Please?"

"No, I'm engaged. I don't go out with anybody."

"How about the three of us go to dinner together tonight? You, me, and your fiancé."

The evening was predictably awkward. Manoucher was stiff at the best of times—I used to tell him that he looked like he had swallowed a *choob-qalyon,* the long wooden mouthpiece of a hubble-bubble pipe. That night all three of us went through the motions of dinner like robots, except for a brief moment when Manoucher's attention was diverted and my soldier whispered with terrible urgency that he really had to see me alone. "Absolutely not," I said.

Looking back, I find it hard to believe my own stupidity. The sheer number of invitations I turned down should have alerted me to the fact that dating was a perfectly normal activity for young people in America and not a slippery slope to prostitution and debauchery. Given the ambivalence of my feelings for Manoucher, a little exposure to other options would have been healthy. But my head was still deep in the sand.

Soon enough Manoucher decided that he needed more than New York had to offer if he was going to realize his extraordinary artistic destiny. While I was at Cornell and Parsons, he had been studying with the French Purist painter Amédée Ozenfant at his studio in Greenwich Village. Paris was the obvious, the logical, and the absolutely necessary next step for him. Naturally, I would stay behind and wait for him, not to mention helping to support him while he was there.

The possibility of refusing or even putting up a fight never crossed my mind. I was eager to do the right thing, and his expectations were not unreasonable for an Iranian man of his generation. Whatever resentment I felt was buried so deep that I didn't even recognize it. Naturally it would come back to haunt me later: thoroughly undead. In the meantime I continued at Parsons, and Manoucher flew off to Paris. As a parting shot, he asked me to promise that I wouldn't date anyone else while he was gone. I didn't ask the same of him, but he volunteered it anyway.

While I was at Parsons, I lived at International House, a residence for foreign students on Riverside Drive. Azizeh, who was at Columbia, also had a room there. That was enough to make it genuinely feel like home.

I did make another close friend at International House. Katja was a very beautiful Swedish woman, tall and blond, who had been a model in Europe, then married a radio personality and had a son; when her marriage fell apart, she came to New York to study art. She was also taking classes at Parsons, so we made the long trek together daily. It was seventy blocks by bus and then a comedy for the final stretch: Katja's stride was impossibly long, and I raced behind her like a panting puppy, dropping notebooks and brushes. Our classmate, dear Emmet, who was charmingly gay—a new concept for me—dubbed us "Night and Day."

Katja was always short of cash. I helped with her tuition and rent and offered an unquestioning open hand for spending money. One summer Katja went off to Hollywood. She phoned me from there. She had found a rich boyfriend and had enough cash in hand to pay me back. "Don't worry about it," I said. "Wait till you're married. Who knows what will happen before then." I wasn't entirely the innocent fool, just partly. I also came from a culture that takes pride in its readiness to sacrifice at the altar of friendship. Katja did in fact get married and came back to New York a couple of years later. Our story, when it continued, was very different.

KATJA AND MONIR, DAY AND NIGHT.

By the time I finished at Parsons, the money I had originally brought from Iran was long gone. My parents were sending me a small sum each month, but it didn't go far. I needed to find a job. One summer I had worked as a babysitter for a family in Connecticut. Room and board were included, but the mistress of the house borrowed more from me than she paid, and I had to fend off her husband's advances to boot. No, I needed a real job.

The opportunity arrived, like a Christmas present, at a holiday dinner at a classmate's home. Her father happened to own Stern Brothers' department store. A few days later I was dressing mannequins in the windows on 42nd Street. Because I was visible to the public as I worked in my goldfish bowl, I was required to dress as if I were going to a tea party, white gloves and all. Every day my coworkers, all of them young gay men, would appraise my outfit, critique my sense of fashion, and express the most earnest concern if I gained a pound or two. I didn't mind the attention at all. It was like having a whole family of shrewd and caring sisters, and I didn't have to worry about dodging would-be suitors.

The salary, however, was barely enough to subsist on. Technically I had to remain a student so that my parents could continue sending money from home, as foreign exchange was severely restricted in Iran at that time. I registered at the Art Students League and took a couple of classes there in the evenings.

Azizeh and I moved out of International House and rented a basement apartment at Riverside Drive and West 103rd Street from an old German couple who lived upstairs. The wallpaper looked as if it were vomiting roses, and we hated it with a passion that we voiced loudly and frequently. We took turns sleeping on the narrow couch or in the big double bed, or sometimes even together in the big double bed on the nights we fell asleep talking. It was my first home away from my parents that actually had a kitchen instead of a dining hall. Azizeh didn't know the first thing about cooking, and she wasn't interested in learning, so it was up to me to figure it out. I started off with Jell-O in multicolored layers and made gorgeous arrangements of incongruous ingredients until Azizeh complained about too much art in the kitchen. She asked wistfully for some real Iranian rice and *khoresh.* That was a challenge that could be met only with a true labor of love. I conjured memories from home with every sense: the complex perfume of herbs, the sizzle of eggplants in oil, the texture of ground walnuts, the logic of the many-stepped ritual that arrives at saffron-gilded and perfectly crusted rice . . . with a lot of trial and a few yucky errors, I taught myself to cook Iranian food. If a traditional ingredient was not available in the market, I improvised or foraged. A sunny day might find me sitting in the grass in Central Park with a shopping bag and scissors, cutting wild chives. If a curious passerby stopped to ask what I was up to, I made up a story about feeding my pet rabbit.

One night I went out with some friends to hear Toscanini conducting Beethoven's Ninth Symphony with the NBC Symphony Orchestra. We had excellent seats at the front, and I was awestruck at the intensity of the performance, amazed to hear the great conductor shouting in the fervor of the moment. I was still riding the swell of the music, surging with free-flowing, abstract emotion, when I got home to find that a telegram had arrived. In the moment it took to rip open the envelope and unfold the paper, all my worst fears were spinning through my mind, or so I thought. I was wrong. The message—from Manoucher, announcing his imminent return to New York—blindsided me with a heart-clenching dread. In the few days remaining before the threatened event, I found myself grasping at thin hope: *Maybe he'll change his mind.* Worse thoughts bubbled up from the mud at the bottom of my consciousness, surprising me with their viciousness: *Maybe his plane will be hijacked. Maybe it will crash.* It was the only time in my life that blind desperation led me to wish harm to another person.

IN THE APARTMENT I SHARED WITH AZIZEH AT WEST 103RD STREET AND RIVERSIDE DRIVE. YOU CAN JUST MAKE OUT THE TUMULT OF ROSES IN THE UPPER-RIGHT-HAND CORNER.

The plane didn't crash, and no hijackers rose to my defense. Manoucher returned and moved in with friends. He talked of marriage, and a strange paralysis came over me. Nothing I did could escape his relentless judgment: nothing I did was quite good enough, from painting, to cooking a meal, to even a matter as simple as choosing the left or right fork of a path on a walk through the park. But it didn't matter—I simply didn't have the nerve to speak my mind.

Meanwhile Azizeh was suffering her own crisis. Some spark of romance in her life had misfired. She refused to speak of it, even to me, and I could only guess at the shattered hope that made her despair, or the betrayal of her poor, twisted body. But the emotion was clear. We cried together through one long night, with no explanations asked for or needed. Not long afterward she packed up and left for London. The apartment was barren without her, and the roses more nauseating than ever. My last line of defense against Manoucher was gone, and he moved in very quickly.

He asked me again and again to marry him. I kept saying, "Why? We don't have to," but I didn't have the courage of my convictions. I wasn't even pinning my hopes on some half-baked notion of bohemian cohabitation—it was 1949, and that was far beyond my known horizon. I was simply treading water to put off drowning. The tide, however, was rising: the inevitable happened, and sex was no longer a mystery. With that initiation I started to sink.

Sadly of a piece with the way our relationship had started, marriage felt more like a matter of inexorable convenience—his more than mine—than anything related to genuine affection. I still puzzle over why I did it. In my skewed "good girl" logic, it was as if by consenting to sex, I had relinquished any right to refuse marriage. I had made my bed, and now I had to lie in it.

For a wedding that was planned without a lot of enthusiasm or cash, we created quite an impressive display. I sewed my own wedding dress, not a frothy white thing but a perfectly elegant blue-gray silk satin with three-quarter-length sleeves, a rolled collar, and a flared skirt that set off my narrow waist. Lacking a sewing machine, I took my bag of basted pieces on the bus back and forth to the Singer shop, where you could rent a machine by the hour, then home, to try it on in front of the mirror. I made a hat, covering a milliner's frame in satin and adding an ostrich feather and two pompoms, each bit of trim the fruit of hours of scouring the garment district. Finally I splurged on a pair of gray shoes.

The morning of the wedding we took the subway to Brooklyn, where we had located a mullah who could perform the Muslim marriage ceremony. He was Arab, not Iranian, a distinction lost in the melting pot of America. I knew little enough of Islam in any flavor; he might as well have been speaking Greek for all the sense his gobbledygook made to me. Still, the deed was done, and we were Mr. and Mrs. when we rode the subway back to Manhattan.

That evening the Iranian consul hosted a cocktail party for us at his home. I invited a few classmates and my colleagues from Stern Brothers. My brother Ahmad and Pamela, who were living now at Lake Mahopac, represented my family. Manoucher carried me over a threshold that was no threshold, really, just a moment staged for the blinding pop of a flashbulb.

The illusion was capped and captured by the wedding present that my friend Emmet gave us. My classmate at Parsons, he had gone on to start his own public relations firm and was doing very well for himself. At the party he announced with much coy mystery that his gift would arrive the following morning. And indeed it did: a mention in *The New York Times* and a full-page write-up in the *Daily News*,

**AFTER OUR WEDDING, AT THE IRANIAN CONSUL'S HOUSE.
ON THE FAR LEFT IS MY THIRD CHAPERONE, ASSAD.**

with the photo of Manoucher carrying me aloft. But that wasn't all. It wasn't till I got back to work at Stern Brothers after our honeymoon that the second part of Emmet's gift was unwrapped.

"Monir, didn't you hear it?" The boys were prancing with excitement. "Walter Winchell himself announced your marriage!" I had no idea who Walter Winchell was, but now of course I had to tune in to his show. What a nasty, snide little voice, I thought, feeling horridly exposed as I imagined him describing our nuptials to the whole of New York.

CHAPTER FOURTEEN

For our honeymoon we rented a room in Woodstock—what today would be advertised as a bed and breakfast but in those days was not so far removed from a boardinghouse. Honeymoon or no, I still had a trio of bodyguards: Assad tagged along as usual, along with another friend of Manoucher's who had recently arrived from Tehran.

That first encounter with the village nestled in the Catskills is hard to make out beneath the history that followed. The darkly wooded mountain slopes and shady paths, the canopies of maple and hemlock silent on a windless day, the smell of sun-warmed sidings and the faint mustiness of rooms that are empty for several months of the year—these recall for me the unraveling of our marriage, not its inception.

From the beginning we were lost, Manoucher and I walking alone in the woods, not knowing which way led back to the village, and arguing as usual about which path held more promise. An army jeep rumbled by, then stopped as we waved and shouted. No soldier sat inside, but a kind-faced gentleman.

"You're headed in completely the wrong direction. It's a long way to the village. I'll give you a ride." By the time he dropped us off, he had extracted the much-rehearsed story of who we were and where we were from and had invited us to his home. And so began a friendship of many years with Alf Evers, a writer of children's books—which were illustrated by his wife—and a historian, keeper of the collective memory of Woodstock. We couldn't have asked for a better guide to the curious soul of the place.

The seat of that soul was Byrdcliffe, an artists' colony of some thirty cottages scattered over the mountain. Its guardian angel was Peter Whitehead—son of the English textile magnate Ralph Whitehead who with his American wife had founded the colony at the turn of the century. Peter himself told us the story of his parents' romance with this land and with each other, their utopian vision and the journey of many false starts that led them here, and how, when they arrived in New York, his father had set fire to the yacht that carried them here so that the memory of their sea-marriage would not be defiled by time.

Much inspired by John Ruskin and William Morris, his father had shaped the settlement as a socialist utopia with an Arts and Crafts aesthetic. His vision had faded to sepia and curled a bit around the edges in the years since his passing, and by now it was subject as much to Peter's whim as to any political principles. The artists, musicians, and writers who inhabited the scattered cottages were no longer obliged to support the commune by tilling the soil and crafting furniture, although the rent they paid was still a token. Above the artists' colony, at the top of the mountain, stood the fire-scarred shell of the Overlook Mountain House Hotel, where the Communist Party of America was born. Together with Maverick, a nearby offshoot artists' colony with competing revelry, it stood as a reminder that Byrdcliffe in its heyday was no isolated, eccentric folly but a piece of the living patchwork of American counterculture.

Peter himself never married, as if the perfection of his parents' marriage had rendered that state unapproachable, but he acted as father and presiding magician for the prodigal herd that populated his domain. The whole mountain was a bohemian hideaway where normal rules were seemingly suspended, and Peter's mansion—with its library, auditorium, swimming pool, badminton courts, and Ping-Pong room, its imperturbable long views, and the dark nooks and moody cast of Craftsman detail—was the center of the colony's social scene. Most of the artists lived on the mountain only in the summer, returning to the city for the long, harsh winters. An even more transient influx arrived from the city each weekend, making for especially lively parties.

Manoucher and I were both completely charmed by Woodstock, though it would reward each of us very differently as our paths diverged. In any case, after the honeymoon we decided to return as soon as we could manage it.

Back in the city we moved out of the basement apartment of the nauseous roses and into a fifth-floor walk-up on West 85th Street. I found Manoucher a job matching colors at Grumbacher, the paint manufacturer. It didn't pay much, just twenty-one dollars a week, which barely covered our rent of eighty dollars a month. It did, however, offer the substantial perk of an unlimited supply of free oil paint. With my tiny salary from Stern Brothers and the occasional bonus from my parents, we managed.

To outside eyes we did much more than manage. With a good deal of frugal planning behind the scenes, we entertained with a generous extravagance that belied our tiny budget. However reluctantly, I had accepted the responsibility of marrying a great artist, or at least a great-artist-to-be. As naïve as I was in so many other ways, it was perfectly clear to me that an important part of my job description as artist's wife was to cement the social connections that would further Manoucher's career.

While I was still at Parsons, I had stumbled into another lucky friendship that opened many doors. I was wandering the Museum of Modern Art one day and found myself on the fringes of a group listening to a fascinating speaker, a chubby middle-aged man with that rumpled, distracted, and bespectacled look that shouts New York Jewish intellectual. When the crowd dispersed at the end of the tour, the speaker approached me. He introduced himself as Abe Channen and asked if I was an art student. We chatted a bit: he was intrigued, as so many people were, that an Iranian girl in that day and age had come to America to study art. He kindly arranged a student pass for me so I could get into the museum for free. So I went often, we ran into each other again, dinner invitations were exchanged, and soon, with Manoucher and Abe's wife, Marguerite, the four of us were spending a good deal of time together. Marguerite was Abe's precise antithesis and complement: a German he had met while stationed there in the war, extremely attractive, pencil slim, and dressed impeccably with an eye to detail and effect. Together they were a social dynamo, wired into every corner of the New York art scene. They took genuine pleasure in mixing and matching people.

It was Abe and Marguerite who introduced us to the Tenth Street Club, a monthly affair in Greenwich Village organized by a circle of artists. Folding chairs were set out in rows in a big room. Two or three artists sat at a table at the head of the room, and the audience, mostly other artists, listened in on their conversation. Big words boomed over my head, words as abstract as the art in question, code names for different camps and troop movements in wars I hadn't known were being fought until that moment. Critics sniped articulately at styles, standards, and standard-bearers, leaving the dead and the wounded bleeding on the field with their isms buzzing around them like flies.

When a cease-fire was called, the survivors would adjourn to the Cedar Tavern on University Place and continue in the same vein without the formal constraint that keeps an audience mostly quiet, and now with personal gossip also unleashed from the armory. I didn't drink at that time, but the alcohol flowed freely around me, and the air was thick with smoke and voices loud in judgment.

Abe went out of his way to make introductions and steer us toward conversations. Jackson Pollock, Willem de Kooning, Mark Rothko, Philip Johnson, Joan Mitchell, Frederick Kiesler, Larry Rivers—they were all at home in the club. If I was impressed, it was only because they were real artists and interesting people who could speak with passion and intelligence about their own work and others'. Fame had not yet opened its hall of mirrors to them (or perhaps it had only just cracked open for a glimpse); nor had it tested their integrity with huge sums of money. If I was intimidated at all, it was by my own ignorance of the high philosophical matters under discussion and the diminutive aspirations of my own art. Once, at the Cedar Tavern, Jackson Pollock asked me gruffly what kind of art I was studying. "Fashion," I said. The word hung there in the smoky air between us, an ism-less orphan, a silly child made up like a whore. I wished I could open my mouth and suck it back in, but the smile on my face refused to budge. Manoucher's strategy for coping in such company was to assume an air of icy aloofness and hope that it would be read as intriguing mystery. The business of actually talking to people and sparking some human connection fell to me.

After the Tenth Street Club and the Cedar Tavern, we would often wind up the evening over a snack or dinner with Abe and Marguerite. Abe would clear some of the accumulated smoke of the evening's debate, explaining in plain English and adding footnotes on everything from art history and aesthetic theory to personal rivalries and who was sleeping with whom. Little by little through these conversations an education in contemporary art managed to seep into my head.

Of course, where so many artists congregated, there were bound to be collectors and gallery owners. This was the real target as far as Manoucher was concerned, and Abe was not above helping with strategic maneuvers. He phoned one day to say he was invited to a dinner party at the home of a Very Important Collector. Would we like to come along?

Bernard and Becky Rice lived in a spectacular East Side townhouse overflowing with Picassos, Matisses, Duchamps, and much more. "That's Duchamp himself," Abe whispered in my ear, lifting an eyebrow in the direction of a man hunched over a chessboard in one corner. I couldn't keep up with all the names that I was obviously supposed to recognize, though I do remember meeting Alex Liberman, the imperial editorial director of Condé Nast. To judge by the attention he commanded, fashion was not such a terribly poor cousin of the arts after all.

As I drifted through the crowd, passing through one masterpiece-laden room after another, I became aware that I was being followed by a heavy-set, white-haired man clutching a whiskey glass. Finally I caught up with Abe, at which moment my stalker chose to pounce.

"Damn it, Abe! I'm tired of following this young lady. Introduce me to her." It was Alexander Calder. Not that I had a clue then who Alexander Calder was. In fact, I felt just a little sorry for him at first, if he thought that I was somebody worth meeting here where everybody else really was Somebody. He asked the old familiar questions, and I played my broken record: Iran . . . art student . . . no way to get to Paris . . . months at sea on a warship . . . I was bored stiff with my story by now, but it was fresh to Calder. He invited me to an exhibition of his and later, with Abe, to his home and studio in Connecticut, where he capped a lovely evening with a gift of a tiny carving he had made of a seal.

The party led to other invitations as well, though none so delightful as Calder's. In fact, the invitations seemed an endless chain, from one party to the next to the next. It became obvious to me that Manoucher and I were exotic flowers to decorate a dinner table. I sewed for these evening deadlines, picking apart and recycling many times over the dresses I had brought from Iran to appear at parties where the hostess wore haute couture. I reciprocated religiously and extended dinner invitations to every gallery owner, curator, art critic, and wielder of influence who crossed my path. Sidney Janis, Leo Castelli, Robert Hill, Sam Kootz, Frederick Kiesler—I fed them all. And if they expected the exotic, who was I to disappoint them? I offered them the elaborate, labor-intensive feasts that are the showcase of Iranian hospitality: golden-crusted rice, stews aromatic with herbs, saffron, pomegranate . . . and all in abundance. In the spirit of that same hospitality that abhors an empty serving dish even at the end of a meal, I spent freely on a good cut of meat or a respectable wine while I counted pennies for groceries the rest of the week.

All my efforts came to nothing. No gallery signed Manoucher, not a single painting was sold, and no offer of help arrived in any form whatsoever; just more invitations to dinner parties, running in endless circles.

We consoled ourselves and took a break by heading back to Woodstock in the summer. I had made a close friend there, a young woman named Dora who had artistic aspirations but no training. Her husband, Arnie, was an advertising executive who made very good money. Together we rented a large cottage at Byrdcliffe, an arrangement that continued for two summers. Arnie had a car, and he and Manoucher would drive out for the weekends and return to the city on Sunday nights. Dora and I stayed on the mountain through the summer, along with her daughter, just a toddler then.

In half of the living room we set up a studio where Manoucher worked on weekends. During the week I coached Dora in her painting as best I could, echoing the phrases I had heard from my teachers at Parsons. In the quiet of the long afternoons while her child was napping, Dora would pose for me in the nude. Her body had a swanlike beauty, with a long neck and a loving grace that I never tired of drawing. When Dora tired of posing, I did small sketches of the landscape in pen and ink, or drew the flowers that grew wild beside the mountain pathways: dogs and lilies, irises, buttercups, and daisies.

It was the beginning of an easy habit that would follow me the rest of my life, like a loyal seeing-eye dog: a sketchbook, a bottle of ink, three pens, and sometimes a brush. I could look at a flower very carefully and trust my hand to follow a spontaneous line from the top of the page to the bottom. When I looked at the drawing—complete even as I saw it for the first time—usually I was pleased to see that somehow it had worked. The anatomy was true. The dance of thin lines and thicker lines captured the tissue of petals, the tease and flounce and swirl of their skirts, and the certainty of deep rhythms in the shape of all plants. If I was successful, the flower traced in ink on my pad was latif: no single word in English fulfills the sense of the Persian, hovering between *delicate, sensitive, graceful,* and *precise.*

Always there were flowers, but not only flowers. I might dwell for a while with the honest trunk of a tree, the map of runneled bark and the knobby knees of knots, or exposed roots like the fingers of an old woman. Leaves conforming and unique, as much alike and unalike as human faces. The sleek, side-eyed arcs and angles of a bird's body, the sweep of wings. The way a squirrel's tail listens with a taut curl.

The gentle peace of these days was punctuated by frequent visits with our neighbors on the mountain. Peter Whitehead descended from his mansion almost daily on one excuse or another. "Mo-nayr!" he would shout at the top of his lungs as his car pulled up to our door. "I have come to have tea with you!" Often he brought along an artist, a writer, or a musician who was eager to meet us. I don't know what stories he told them that so piqued their curiosity, but he was not above whipping up a fantasy simply because it pleased him. Once at the Woodstock Harvest Festival he asked me to pose for a photo with him as we trotted around the grounds in a horse and buggy. The next day the photo appeared in the local paper with a caption identifying me as "Princess Monir."

I was a little weary of women hiding behind veils; the last thing I had expected was to find camels and scimitars chasing me up to my mountain refuge. Peter had only the vaguest awareness of the source of my own discomfort, and I, for lack of a postcolonialist vocabulary, had merely the vaguest awareness of threatened innocence.

I got pregnant the first year after Manoucher and I were married. I had tried to avoid it—the contraceptive methods available were clumsy and unreliable. My first reaction was despair. The prospect of anything that rendered me even more dependent on Manoucher was terrifying. Manoucher himself did nothing to reassure me and expressed no interest at all in our child-to-be. During my first trimester I spent time with Ahmad and Pamela at Lake Mahopac, where they were building a new home that Frank Lloyd Wright had designed for the island in the lake. While Ahmad charged up and down the lake in an amphibian vehicle that he used to move construction supplies to the island, I went through the motions of making myself useful, lifting big stones from one spot to another.

At the back of my mind was a vague hope of losing the baby, but nature was on its inexorable track. Even if I had known such a thing was possible, an outright abortion would have been unthinkable.

With motherhood a dark cloud on the horizon, I was very anxious about our financial situation. This was the moment when Katja, my Swedish friend from the days at International House, chose to reappear. The husband she had found in Hollywood was Rod Geiger. They had been lying low in London after he was blacklisted in the McCarthy witch hunt for producing *Christ in Concrete*. Now they were back in New York, with a baby as well as her older son, and the four of them were living with Rod's parents.

Katja complained bitterly about her penny-pinching in-laws. I bit my tongue and swallowed the memory of her debts. "You're so talented, and I'm not stupid," she said, starting a clean page. "Why don't we figure this out together?" And so Day and Night hatched *Designs by Katja and Monir.*

In fact, it was Rod who was not stupid. He had a very shrewd business sense and quickly managed to set up a partnership with some people in the knitting industry to produce our designs. Katja and I worked out of their Seventh Avenue offices. We showed our first pieces to a friend of mine at Saks Fifth Avenue. He liked them, and so did every buyer we showed them to. We were off and running.

Within weeks Rod had cut out the Seventh Avenue middlemen, and we were working directly with the manufacturers in Queens. I took the subway to Queens daily and measured the progress of my pregnancy by how much tighter the turnstile seemed each day. By this time Rod and Katja were living in our apartment rent free, though the children stayed with his parents, and we were paying for their food and their phone calls to London. But somehow, as my belly and the bills got bigger, my share of the design work was shrinking. Then new labels appeared: *Katja of Sweden.* The old name was too long, Rod said; this was much catchier. Finally one day I was giving the sample-maker some instructions when Rod walked in and started shouting at me. "You have no right to tell her what to do! Katja has to tell her."

"I designed this," I said. That was all. I walked out and took care of some errands, and by the time I got home they were gone. I never saw them again.

During the time when things were unraveling with Katja, my friendship with Marko Markovich was a special blessing. Marko was the Yugoslav consul general and a central figure in a tight circle of Yugoslav intellectuals and artists living in New York. He introduced me to the painter Boris Bogdanovich (whose son Peter was ten or eleven at the time) and to Zinka Milanov, then diva soprano of the Metropolitan Opera. Marko and Boris both took an interest in my drawings. I was touched by their support, a little bit light-headed to find myself taken seriously, and buoyed to be among friends who were too happily alien themselves to notice anything exotic about me. We got together often, especially with Marko, who lived just a block away. I cooked Iranian feasts, adding a bit more love to the recipes when I cut back on some of the extravagance.

One evening during my pregnancy Zinka was invited to sing at a special performance of *The Marriage of Figaro* in Greenwich, Connecticut. Marko insisted that I come too and arranged for a car and driver from the consulate. Zinka's performance was heavenly, as always. After the show I followed Marko backstage as he parted the crowd of fans waiting outside Zinka's dressing room. Somehow the fans mistook me for one of the singers, thrusting autograph books in my face. The crowd and the confusion did not yield, until finally Zinka appeared at the door. "Just sign them!" she laughed, and so I did, writing "Monir" in Persian for each of them.

After the opera the entourage moved to a very elegant Greenwich mansion for a party in Zinka's honor. It was almost three in the morning when we finally said our goodbyes and started back for New York. A thick fog had descended, painting the windshield a blind white. The driver hunched over the wheel, straining to see. He pulled over several times to wait for a clearing, then inched on again. Conversation was suspended, as if we were collectively willing the driver's concentration. I sat in the back between Zinka and her brother, exhausted and queasy. "Don't look at the road," Zinka said to me. "Put your head on my shoulder and take a nap." I nestled down, and Zinka began to hum a beautiful melody. My head floated on the pillow of her rising and falling breast, lapped by angelic vibrations, as the car moved slowly through the layered blankets of fog. What a beautiful way to die, I thought, suspended by this heavenly voice in a cloud between heaven and earth.

CHAPTER FIFTEEN

The pains came on as I was standing in the shower one afternoon. Still dripping, I phoned the obstetrician. "Zis is it!" he confirmed in his Viennese English. I stumbled down the five flights of stairs, thanking God that I would never have to climb back up them again pregnant. Manoucher hailed a cab, and we headed for the hospital. Six hours later the pain was unbearable. The doctor poked and prodded, determining that I would as feared need a cesarean section, but it was too late to operate that night as the approval of two additional doctors was needed. Manoucher felt sleepy and went home. At four in the morning, waiting for the doctors' convenience was no longer an option. Despite the protests of my obstetrician, who was firmly of the old European school, they gave me a spinal injection, newly in fashion. I had no complaints and was only too happy to be conscious through what happened next.

They pulled a curtain around me, and I found that I could watch the mystery of a body's interior exposed, reflected in miniature in the lamp above me. Framing the lamp, the white tile ceiling of the operating room shimmered with an unclinical beauty. The anesthesiologist's palm on my forehead radiated with a gentle warmth. Instruments tinkled like clear bells above the cello of the surgeon's voice, an exquisite music. All this a prelude merely to the incredible beauty of the creature, wet with life and shiny with love, whom hands lifted high: the curve of her cheek and her chin, her slippery shoulders, the heaving vigor of her rib cage, the roundness of her thighs, her miraculous miniature fingers and toes, and most surprising of all, the brilliant lightning of her lash-swept, storm-dark eyes. Nima had arrived.

I stayed in the hospital for two painful weeks and came home at the beginning of October, still barely able to walk. The stairs were an Everest, each landing a hard-won camp I was reluctant to leave for the next ascent.

The very first weekend I was home, Manoucher announced that he was off to Woodstock to see the fall colors in the Catskills. I couldn't muster the energy to argue, no heat of anger to fight the

NIMA AND HER MOTHER.

bone-deep chill that I felt at his words. I just exuded a terrifying calm. I still could not manage even to lift Nima from her crib. I quietly—almost in a whisper—pointed out to Manoucher that I would be alone with the baby on the fifth floor.

"You'll be okay. You have enough food." The door closed behind him. Nima was asleep. The silence stretched like a desert to the horizon at the walls of my skull, the possible futures, until the phone broke through my trance. It was Dora. I told her what had happened. She was appropriately outraged and came over with Arnie to spend the weekend.

Manoucher came home on Monday, and life went on as if nothing had happened. I realized that he had no intention of finding a better job or supporting us in any way that would distract from his ambitions as a painter. Handling diapers and bottles was far beneath the artist's dignity. So far as he was concerned, the baby was entirely my responsibility. As Nima grew, as she learned to smile, to crawl, to speak her first words, and to toddle across the room—nothing changed. If she was entirely my problem, she was also entirely my joy.

When Nima was nine months old, we went to Woodstock with Dora and Arnie again for the summer. Many of our neighbors in the cottages at Byrdcliffe had small children, including Leon Barzin, conductor of the National Orchestra, and his wife, Mina, who became very close to me. It was wonderful to be surrounded by friends who didn't consider babies and art to be like oil and water.

Milton Avery and his wife, Sally Michel, were also neighbors and became lifelong friends. Every day at eleven in the morning precisely, Milton would walk down from his cottage with sketchbook in hand and stay for exactly two hours. I was usually walking with Nima ensconced in my arms or draped over a shoulder as I did one-handed chores. Milton would settle down to his drawing, saying, "Never mind me, Monir. I'm just sitting here watching nature." Nature in this case was mother and child. We spent many other good times together, shared many dinners at the cottage as well as back in the city, and made many trips into the village for shopping, as I had no car or telephone at the cottage and relied much on Milton and Sally for simple matters of survival. But those peaceful mornings in the cottage were a special time. The love in his quiet attention was content to flow through pencil or brush and demanded no further acknowledgment.

Thanks to Milton and Sally, the problem of finding a gallery for Manoucher was finally solved. One afternoon at the cottage I was resting for a moment, stretched out exhausted on a low bench that happened to have a velvet blanket tossed over it. A knock came at the door. A young man introduced himself as Philip, the manager for Grace Borgenicht Gallery. He had come up to see Milton, whom he represented, and Milton—bless him—had suggested that there might be something worth looking at in the cottage below. Manoucher showed him the paintings he had been working on that summer, while I did my best to throw together a presentable meal with what I could find in the cupboard. Before the evening was over Manoucher had a gallery to represent him. A year and a half later they gave him his first solo exhibition. It was as simple as that. But when I compared notes with Sally the next day, I had to laugh. In fact we both laughed ourselves silly. Philip had reported back to Milton and Sally that on his arrival at our cottage he had found "a stunningly beautiful woman lying on the couch like a tigress." *Whatever works,* I thought.

Tigress or no tigress, it was a tremendous relief to me that Manoucher had found some success. At that time his style had taken a new turn, thanks at least in part to the generosity of the Grumbacher paint company. He was painting abstracts as well as still lifes and landscapes, all using a lot of white space behind the subject and laying the paint on very thick with a palette knife, much in the manner of Solange. As the work progressed, he would ask me at frequent intervals how I liked it. The ritual belied the scant stock he put in my opinion. I would answer as kindly as I could, but also honestly, giving myself up to the question and the painting in front of me without straining for much diplomacy. And sometimes I would make suggestions: "Perhaps this should be a little bigger" . . . "Do you think it would help if that blue was repeated over here?" He would look at the

YEARS LATER I RETURNED TO WOODSTOCK AND FOUND THAT
ONE OF OUR ARTIST FRIENDS WAS STILL USING A PORTRAIT
HE HAD MADE OF ME TO DRUM UP BUSINESS. HE WOULDN'T
PART WITH IT, SO NIMA POSED BESIDE IT.

painting askance, brows knit as if he were actually considering the sense of my words, then shake his head and mumble, "No, no, no."

But often the next morning I would see a change. If I asked, "Manou, did you change it? It looks better now," he would feign innocence.

"No, I didn't touch it. I didn't have time." And I would bite my tongue, amazed less at how the paint had magically laid itself on the canvas than at how anyone could be twisted so tight with complexity. Sometimes the competition he imagined between us played out with a childishness that would have made me laugh if I had seen through my own dismay and embarrassment. When Marko came to our home, as he so often did, he would always ask, "Monir, what have you done recently?"

"Not much. Just a couple of sketches."

"Bring them out. Let me see them." Even before I could dig out my sketchbook, Manoucher would be setting a painting in front of him.

"Mr. Markovich, you haven't seen this one."

"Yes, I saw it last time I was here."

"No, no, no—I changed this part. You haven't noticed it."

It was Dora who finally opened my eyes to the dim possibility that marriage to Manoucher was not a life sentence. The previous summer at Woodstock, Dora had met Bernie. It had happened over the Ping-Pong table at Peter Whitehead's mansion. The game was long and close; paddle-smashing, ball-thrashing, net-ripping passion blazed from their eyes, and they flamboyantly, orgasmically moaned and groaned over each lost point. By the end of the set they were soul mates, and the rest of the world could go to hell.

I was appalled. "Dora, you have a husband! How can you do this?"

"It's no big deal, Monir. Don't worry. Arnie will never find out."

Bernie was a violinist studying chamber music with William Kroll, who was staying at one of the cottages. During the weeks when Arnie and Manoucher were in the city, Bernie spent every night at our cottage. Dora and Bernie would retire upstairs to my bedroom, and I would shift to the downstairs bedroom with Dora's young daughter. The wooden ceiling above us would shake and shudder all night. Sleep was impossible. I stared in the dark at the ceiling, praying that the child would not wake up and pondering the meaning of marriage.

Arnie was handsome, wealthy, good-natured, and a caring father; he was in love with Dora. Their life seemed perfectly happy, and I knew them well enough to know that not much was hidden from me. Very slowly it dawned on me that if Dora could have all this and then some, what kind of fool was I to put up with Manoucher?

The eye-opening I experienced under Dora's bedsprings was only underlined by the general carryings-on at Byrdcliffe, where the woodsy isolation was a perfect cover for many affairs. The absence of a telephone at our cottage was an attractive feature to the lovers, and it was even more appealing to me. Too many times in the city I would be assigned to lie to Arnie: "She's just gone out to buy cigarettes. I'll ask her to call you back."

The third summer at Woodstock I was alone in the cottage with Nima. We had given up the apartment in the city, thinking to save on rent and find another place at the end of the summer. In the meantime Manoucher stayed with friends while he worked at Grumbacher during the week, then joined us on weekends.

As the season turned and the night chill hung in the air late into each morning, our neighbors vacated the cottages one by one. They had been built for the summers only and were too drafty to heat through a Catskills winter. Each weekend when Manoucher came up, I would beg him to look for an apartment in the city.

"Wait till next week. I just need to finish this painting first." But Sunday night would come, and the painting wasn't finished. Another week would pass, and no apartment was found.

With Milton and Sally gone, I had no easy ride to the village, which was an hour's walk down the mountain. The nearest phone was miles away. At dusk shadows raced over the mountain, gripping the woods earlier each night, and I could hear branches breaking as bears foraged nearby. Days of anger faded into nights of fear. Each night I fixed a bottle, placed it within Nima's reach, and curled up to sleep at the foot of her crib. If a bear came, I reasoned, I would be the first serving and hopefully enough of a meal. Nima would have milk to drink until someone discovered her.

A few times Alf Evers came by to check on me, though he lived on the far side of the mountain. The sight of his khaki-green jeep tearing up the dirt road was as welcome as the sight of a liberating army. One day he climbed out of the jeep with a huge rifle.

"Monir, you have to protect yourself."

"What should I do? Hit the bear on the head with it? No thank you!" My cousin Hossein, the aspiring pilot, had once tried to teach me to shoot. I had managed by beginner's luck to down a bird in a flurry of feathers, and such was my remorse at my very first shot that I never touched a gun again. But I knew that if a soul as gentle as Alf was urging me to take up arms, it was time to get the hell out of there.

With Alf's help, I got to a phone and called a friend in the city. Fred Shoren was a lawyer, so I figured he could cope with a problem like finding an apartment in New York. Of all the friends I could think of to call, he stood solidly at the farthest, coolest remove from the insanity fueled by art.

Fred did his best, but I think he was shocked to discover the limits of our budget. He located a place on Third Avenue at 21st Street. I informed Manoucher that the deed was done. He agreed to forgo his weekend painting at the cottage, and I took the bus back to the city with Nima. Dora and Arnie insisted we come to their home for the weekend, but I was embarrassed to burden them any longer than necessary. With the chaos of two young children and more marital tension than any one family has a right to inflict on another, it all seemed too much. On Saturday we went to see the apartment.

When I opened the door, my heart sank. Fred had described it as a railroad apartment, but he didn't say it was a cattle car. The place was filthy, the walls caked with grime and dust and the linoleum on the floor torn to tatters. A stinking toilet sat right in the kitchen, and a rusty bathtub with a plank on top served for a kitchen table. No doors separated the chain of tiny rooms, and you could see right through from one end of the pathetic mess to the other.

Nima was not yet walking at that point, and I couldn't put her down for a moment. This was unsafe territory for a crawling baby. "Manou, I think we have to clean the place first," I said. He didn't say a word. We went back to Dora's, and the next day we packed the sum total of our belongings—plus a mattress that Dora gave us—into one taxi. We had barely unloaded when Manoucher exploded and walked out in response to the suggestion that he should help me clean before we spread the mattress down. I took Nima and went shopping for a broom.

Over the next few days I swept and scrubbed and bleached. I ripped up the shreds of linoleum and laid a new roll down. Elbow grease is an excellent antidepressant, but exhaustion has nasty side effects. I put some water on to heat a bottle for Nima on the electric hotplate sitting on my brand-new floor. When she crawled over and knocked the pot off—mercifully, the spill missed her—I fell apart. I dripped tears all over her face as I tucked her into her crib and then cried myself to sleep.

I stayed in that apartment alone with Nima for a couple of months. My most urgent problem was how to find work with a baby on my hands. I swallowed my pride and phoned Manoucher to ask if he would look after Nima while I looked for work. He refused flatly. I dug out the diamond ring my father had given me when I finished high school, and I pawned it. I had never liked it anyway, regardless of Hajji Javaheri's claims for the quality of the gem. It had traveled with me across the Pacific buried in a jar of face cream. Now was the time for it to shine.

Relief came finally through a couple who were close friends of Manoucher. Alia and Majid had a large apartment in Jackson Heights. Alia was expecting a baby of her own, and she wasn't working. She suggested that I move in with them; she would take care of Nima while I looked for work. I was confident that I could make money doing freelance illustration if only I could show my portfolio.

I took the subway into Manhattan every morning and pounded the pavement. I visited agencies, magazines, newspapers, and department stores. Each editor admired the pages I spread on the table, and each one thought the work belonged elsewhere. "This is magazine quality—you don't belong with a newspaper." "This is more uptown." "This is more downtown." "This is actually fine art. You need some commercial experience."

Finally I screwed up my courage and called Alex Liberman at Condé Nast. I had nothing to lose. Whether he remembered me from our brief encounter at the Rices' party, or whether the Russian immigrant artist recognized my predicament, or whether he simply liked my portfolio, I'll never know. He gave me an assignment to do pen-and-ink drawings of six brassieres for *Glamour* magazine. I couldn't have been happier if he had asked me to pose for the cover. And when I picked up my check for a hundred and fifty gloriously independent dollars, I could have danced all the way home to Jackson Heights.

At that point not even Manoucher could shake my confidence. He came to apologize and begged me to come back. *Back to where?* I thought. It was easy enough to say no to the first few appeals, but he kept it up relentlessly. When I retreated into my room and shut the door on him, he poured himself out to Alia and Majid late into the night, pitifully leaning on them to intercede.

As if evidence of the sad state of their marriage were lacking, Dora and Arnie chose that moment for their own crisis. It was after midnight when the phone rang. Dora's mother was in hysterics. "Monir, where are you? You have to come! Dora has committed suicide!" I went at once, of course, but when I got to their apartment, I didn't know whether to laugh or cry. Dora was out cold, lying in bed like a corpse laid out for viewing, the empty bottle of sleeping pills prominently displayed on the bedside table. Her violin—Bernie had started giving her lessons—lay in wire-tangled fragments on the floor, along with several dozen roses and a broken vase, as a puddle of water seeped into the carpet. Dora's mother stood in the middle of the mess and squawked at me, "Who is this Bernie? Arnie's not good enough? What kind of money does a violinist make? Arnie's got money! Arnie can afford a detective!" She continued squawking while I dragged Dora to the bathroom and forced her to throw up.

Arnie's contribution to the farce came several days later when he announced that Dora could go to hell and it was me that he loved. I insisted that I would never dream of having an affair with my best friend's husband and said he was like a brother to me. No way was I going to step into the middle of that mess. The melodrama continued, with Arnie kidnapping their daughter and running off to Florida, and more detectives snooping around . . .

After a few months the dust settled, and Dora moved in with Bernie. That left their huge apartment on the corner of Columbus and West 85th Street available. The whole affair must have addled my brain, because it seemed like a good idea at the time to sublet the place and share it with Alia, Majid, and Manoucher. My luck in chasing freelance work continued to improve steadily, and I even bought a few simple pieces of furniture. Manoucher behaved himself, at least as far as I could see, but then I wasn't paying much attention. Strange symptoms of discord kept surfacing in our day-to-day relations with Alia and Majid. By the time I found an incriminating note in Manoucher's hand at the bottom of a wastebasket, it was too late. Alia and Majid moved out under a dark cloud of anger. I was left alone with Manoucher and Nima, three empty bedrooms, and no help with the rent.

I put up ads on the bulletin boards at NYU and Columbia and rented the rooms to students. It might have been a very nice arrangement, except that I could not entirely convince myself that New York landladies are exempt from the rules of Iranian hospitality. I knew that I wasn't expected to cook for them, but it was hard not to ask them to join us when there was food enough on the table. And I didn't know that I wasn't required to clean their rooms for them.

Things got easier when I managed to get a scholarship for Nima to attend preschool at the Ethical Culture School on Central Park West. It was a very exclusive and snobbish place, to judge by the parents who dropped their children off in the mornings. But it was also extremely progressive and unencumbered by religious baggage, and I felt that Nima was in good hands.

The denouement with Manoucher was sparked by my brother Hassan's graduation from Johns Hopkins University. Ahmad and

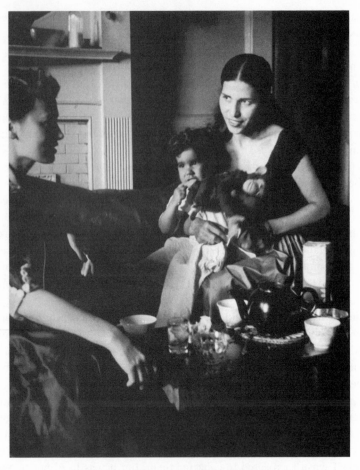

WITH NIMA IN DORA AND ARNIE'S APARTMENT AT
WEST 85TH STREET AND COLUMBUS.

Pamela planned to drive down from Lake Mahopac to Baltimore
for the graduation, and they invited me to come along. I begged
Manoucher to look after Nima for just that one weekend. We were
leaving Friday night, and I would be back Sunday evening. He said
no—he had to finish a painting, of course—but for once I insisted.
Hadn't my family supported us for so long?

Pomp and ceremony suited Hassan, and I couldn't begrudge him
his pride in the moment. He had worked hard and had actually

accomplished something. To round off the celebration, Ahmad got tickets for the theater in Washington on Sunday. When we came out of the theater, rain was pouring down in blustery buckets. Ahmad balked at driving. By the time the decision was made to postpone our return until Monday morning and I got to a phone to call Manoucher, the rain was a blinding downpour.

"Please, please, just take Nima to school in the morning. I'll be back by three to pick her up."

His answer came screaming down the line. "No! I have to go to my job. I can't take her to school—I don't know how to dress her! You have to come back!"

There was no point arguing. I simply had no choice. "This is how it is," I said. "We can't drive. I don't have the money to take the train. I'll be back tomorrow."

When I got back, he gave me hell. Screaming alternated with begging forgiveness, beating on locked doors, and screaming again over phone lines: a pitiful, angry, groveling cycle. Then one day I simply didn't open the door, didn't pick up the phone. That was all. I had reached the end as far as Manoucher was concerned. I had a life to get on with.

CHAPTER SIXTEEN

Free at last. Ninety-five dollars and twenty-seven cents in the bank. The overlarge apartment echoed like a seaside hotel in the winter, its mood turning from calm solitude to barren bleakness and back again with a shift of the sun's angle or a passing cloud. I checked the mailbox twice a day, hoping beyond hope for some money from home. I prayed Nima stayed healthy. Every day I walked her to school with my portfolio under my arm, then chased magazine editors and agents until it was time to pick her up. Each freelance assignment—a dress design or a textile pattern that I finished in the evening—was a discrete blessing: a load of groceries, a few days' rent. *It's okay,* I told myself. *I'm not starving, I'm not miserable, and I'm not depending on anyone.*

My student tenants were a transient crew, revolving with the semesters. One Indian student seemed the ideal renter, eager as a puppy to help with chores, always ready to babysit Nima. I should have seen it coming: his earnest declaration of love led me to weeks of awkward avoidance, ducking down the hallway, hiding in my room. When two hundred dollars finally arrived from my parents, my patience could afford to run out. It was time for my students to find new lodgings, every last one of them. My admirer delayed his departure till the last possible moment, moping pathetically. The next morning I found him waiting on the sidewalk. He followed as I walked Nima to school; he was still waiting when I came out.

"Enough!" I shouted, then cursed at him in Persian, as if that carried more weight, and let him know that, having already disposed of one unnecessary husband, I did not intend to tolerate his nonsense.

I didn't have the courage to tell my family what had happened with Manoucher. There was no easy telephone connection to Tehran at the time, and letters spent a couple of weeks in transit, giving bad news far too much time to fester before questions could be answered. I don't know whether I was more ashamed to admit the failure of my marriage, or the raw foolishness of having fallen into it in the first place, or the sustained idiocy of having suffered in silence for so long. In any case, the words were too embarrassed to be coaxed out, no matter how many times I sat down to write.

Meanwhile the news coming from Iran was much more worrisome than my small drama. Almost daily there were headlines: "Mossadegh dismissed as prime minister"; "Riots and Looting in Tehran"; "The Shah Flees in Haste"; and finally, "The Shah Returns" in dubious glory. Since I had come to New York, the politics of home had shrunk to a distant island on the horizon of my consciousness. True, when Mossadegh had grabbed the limelight on the world stage two years before with his scheme to reclaim our oil from British control, I was fired up with optimism and patriotic pride. The American press had made much of Mossadegh's eccentric charisma, his hypochondria, and his histrionics, but to me it was only common sense that Iran's oil should belong to Iran. I happily cheered the old trickster for running circles around world powers and for standing up for democratic ideals.

But having been spoon-fed from birth my father's own recipe for our pie-in-the-sky constitutional democracy, I had little understanding of how delicate the concoction was that Mossadegh had whipped up. Now, in August 1953, I was straining to bring distant details into focus through the cloudy lens of the American press, which was fixated myopically on Communist bogeymen. Much happened in those few weeks that would have shocked the innocent daylights out of me if I had known what was hidden behind the headlines. My friend Donald Wilber was very busy indeed pulling strings, distributing stacks of hundred-dollar bills supplied by his employers in Langley, Virginia, feeding lies to the press, and betraying the democratic hopes of the culture that had nourished him, body and soul, for decades. Even my own brother Hassan, who had returned to Iran after his graduation, was sucked into a role—albeit minor—in the unsavory mess.

Of all this I was blissfully ignorant. My father's letters made no mention of the shock waves rocking the Majles and the nation; in his silence I read a stunned paralysis, torn loyalties, bitter disappointment, and unearned shame. I mirrored his politely chatty letters with inconsequential chatter of my own, and neither of us spoke of the real events of our lives.

As relieved as I was to be free of Manoucher, I worried about the effects of the breakup on Nima. She was wetting her pants every day at school. Her teacher sent me to the school psychologist. I explained our circumstances and also talked a bit about how Manoucher had kept Nima at arm's length and under the rule of No. Most particularly, he had forbidden her to touch his paints, a constant temptation to the child. The psychologist took this point and ran with it: "You must give her the opportunity to paint freely, without concern for any mess she might make."

Every afternoon I spread newsprint over the entire kitchen floor, set out paints and paper on an easel, and left Nima to her own devices. I would work in the next room on my textile designs, listening through the quiet of my own concentration to the sploshing and crinkling and occasional burbling comments coming through the open door. The sight that met me when I got up to check on her was always a surprise, no matter how many times the scene repeated—rainbows daubed all over her face, arms, legs, and shoes, splashed across the newsprint, and streaked wildly up the refrigerator and cupboard doors. I scooped up my little Jackson Pollock and put her into the bath, where the colors swirled together into a soapy gray soup, while I cleaned up the mess in the kitchen. The cure worked. Not only did Nima keep her pants dry at school; she started doing beautiful artwork that was even chosen for a competition and shown at the Museum of Modern Art. Of course I proudly fancied that she would follow in her parents' footsteps. I didn't realize yet that Nima was not a follower by nature.

When I started a real full-time job, my fears over money were put to rest. A friend of Alf Evers, Margaret Somerfield, whose own fashion illustrations commanded sums that I could barely imagine, gave me an introduction to Boody, the art director at Bonwit Teller. Boody was a treat—a tiny woman whose ultrapetite frame was dressed with the requisitely obsessive attention to fashion, and who had the sweetest personality one could hope for in a boss.

"You can start tomorrow," she said as she leafed through my portfolio. "You'll be doing layouts. We can offer you eighty-five dollars a week."

Hallelujah. I didn't know what a layout was, but I was confident that if I kept my mouth shut and my eyes open, I would find out soon enough. I had never even heard the term at Parsons, so it couldn't be anything terribly complicated.

Bonwit Teller held its nose even higher in the air than Stern Brothers when it came to their dress code. I had to wear a hat, white gloves, and high heels to work every day, and whatever else might cover my body had to meet the standard implied by these accessories. Honest-to-God fashion police conducted random inspections to ensure that employees dressed with a suitable style and polish. I had to laugh the first time I paraded for inspection. The whole business reminded me of Banu Khanom's daily gauntlet in high school, but now the world was turned upside down: plainness was as punishable as flair had once been. If my fate was to work in fashion, it was a fickle mistress indeed.

The window display department was on the same floor, and just as at Stern Brothers, the entire department was gay. Every one of the staff mothered me. They patted and fussed and made squint-eyed appraisals, and if I gained so much as a pound—

"Monir, take it off!" Loud, with a smack on the bottom. Still, kindness and caring lay behind their treating me like a mannequin, and all in all, coming to work was a pleasure.

When I finished each batch of layouts, another young artist who also worked on shoe illustrations collected them. Conversation was not his strong suit, but we made a connection in spite of his ghostly shyness. He recruited me to help him on a few of his efforts, adding domes and minarets in the distance for a dress slipper that rode a flying carpet. I loved the whimsy of his drawings and intercepted many that were headed for the wastebasket—in particular, a series of shoes set against spectacular flowers, and another of pigs wearing smart accessories with attitude. We lost touch after I left Bonwit Teller, but a few years later I was delighted to learn of Andy Warhol's success. Much later our paths would cross again under a very different sky.

Between my salary from Bonwit Teller and the income from some freelance illustration work I did on the side, I was suddenly very well off. I moved to a smaller but much nicer apartment on Central Park West that was just a few steps away from Nima's school and a lovely walk through the park to work. I could afford to hire a babysitter to pick up Nima from school in the afternoon and stay with her till I got home from work. With a staff discount I could even afford

MY COLLEAGUES AT
BONWIT TELLER KEPT
A CLOSE EYE ON
MY FIGURE.

the wardrobe that the job demanded. Measured against the past few years, I saw myself as safe, successful, secure, and completely content.

About the time when I moved, Ahmad's marriage to Pamela began to fall apart. My brother came over to my place almost nightly to talk over his troubles. His cigarette smoke thickened to a dense fog as I brewed him pot after pot of coffee while he tortured himself with indecision. Me he tortured with sleep deprivation as he measured every possible outcome of the custody battle he was determined to fight, assuming that he did in fact decide to leave Pamela. "To jump or not to jump?" was his melodramatic summary of the predicament, repeated like a nervous tic.

I knew better than to offer an opinion. As far as I was concerned, he and Pamela could both go jump in the lake—Mahopac would serve nicely, I thought. And why couldn't people make their own decisions without having to pass their misery around like a plate of stale cookies? I had never breathed a word to Ahmad—or to anyone, family or friend—of my own misery with Manoucher. (Ahmad was so absorbed in his own dilemma that he did not even notice Manoucher's absence.) I've always found it easy to chat with strangers, and I can make friends in the least likely places; but true *dard-e del,* the talk that lifts the weight of a burdened heart, has never come easily to my tongue. My ears, however, get more than their fair share.

The conversations in my head meandered like this while Ahmad's monologue droned on nightly. Ultimately I always steered back to the same conclusion: marriage had nothing to offer that could possibly outweigh its hazards.

So I certainly was not in search of a new husband when I started dating. Truthfully I couldn't have said what I was searching for, if anything, in exposing myself to countless ordeals by candlelight, dancing duty, and dinner games. Judging by the eagerness of friends to set me up, I could only assume that this was the American way:

A WOMAN IN FULL.

popularity was proof of success, and it was measured by the crowd-ing of one's calendar; hence the term *date*.

Now that Manoucher was neither a deterrent nor an excuse, long-lost acquaintances and forgettable flirtations suddenly revived with new energy. Likewise, a few old friends urgently wanted to be seen in a new light. Some of the more original approaches came from artists I had met at the Cedar Tavern and the Tenth Street Club:

"Will you come to my studio and rub my sculpture? I want to see how the oil of Persian hands affects the wood."

"You're joking! My hands are just the same as anyone else's hands."

"No, seriously. I have a Chinese woman and a Japanese woman whom I pay to come and rub my sculpture with their hands. It gives a different color to the wood. Now I want to see what your hands will do." I passed on that one; I had already swallowed enough nonsense in the service of someone else's art.

There were good souls too, and passably good souls who dangled the temptation of a life of unmitigated luxury. In fact, every single one of them was an interesting human being, and yet I found it a labor and an act of will to stay interested. A very few of these connections escalated briefly into something that threatened to become a relationship, and a couple of cases went beyond goodnight kisses into the domain of actual sex. Dora could do it, and half of Woodstock, my rational mind argued. Other voices in my head, heart, and body argued louder, if not quite so coherently. I learned that guilt can climb over logic's walls, and it doesn't even need a boost up from religion.

All of these dates naturally made babysitters a matter of some importance to me. And consistently throughout that time, the most reliable babysitter I could find was a law student at Columbia University named Abolbashar Farmanfarmaian.

I had come to know Abol through his sister Leila. As the star of her high school basketball team in Tehran, the tall, long-legged Leila Farmanfarmaian was my nemesis. Her team so routinely thrashed us that when I spotted her in New York by chance on the steps of the Art Students League, my split-second involuntary reaction was that sinking feeling of throwing in the towel. Surprise then took over immediately.

"Leila!"

"Monir!" She had moved to New York, was taking classes in sculpture at the league, and was happy to find a familiar face. Soon enough we became close friends.

The Farmanfarmaian name is as well known in Iran as Rockefeller or Rothschild is in the West. Beyond a vague impression that it was a big family with power, history, and money, I didn't know much about them. Some of them called themselves *shahzadeh*—princes or princesses—which I thought a very hollow pretension indeed, given that the fallen Qajar dynasty had not been much to boast about even when they were in power. In any case, Leila had many brothers, though just how many I didn't have a clue. I dated a couple very briefly, but Abolbashar was not one of them. As my friendship with

A CENTRAL PARK OUTING WITH ABOL, NIMA, AND A FRIEND IN 1953,
WHILE ABOL (ON THE LEFT) WAS STUDYING AT COLUMBIA.

Leila developed, Abol was studying in Chicago, doing his doctorate
in political science; he would come to New York once in a while to
visit Leila on holidays.

When Nima was three years old and my need for a babysitter was
most pressing, Abol moved to New York to study international law
at Columbia. Somehow—I barely noticed its beginning—a routine
developed. Abol would show up at my apartment with a stack of law
books and a steak to cook for his dinner. Nima slept, Abol studied,
and I went off to be wined, dined, danced, or whatever. When I got
home, we would chat briefly, and he would say goodnight and disappear until the next time I called:

"Abol, are you home tonight? If you have nothing planned, can you
come stay with Nima? I'll be home by eleven."

This went on for about a year. Once in a while he would come
when I didn't have a date, appearing unannounced at my door,
skinny and tall with his big hands and his big glasses and his little
salt-and-pepper mustache above a broad smile and a dimpled chin.
He would cook steaks for both of us, then settle down to his books
while I worked on my textile designs in the next room. I was comfortable with him around, I counted him as a friend, but I didn't think

about it much. If I did stop to think about why he kept coming—his kindness coupled with his gentle reserve—it mystified me.

On a few occasions I saw him when he wasn't babysitting for me. At a New Year's party at a friend's home, I drank too much for the first time in my life. Normally I didn't drink at all. It was Abol, not my date, who brewed the coffee and checked on me again and again. He invited me to his graduation party, which was flatly uneventful, and one night he asked me out to a movie. If the film we saw was something out of the ordinary, I didn't remember it as such. What stuck in my mind was that we took the bus and saw a movie that cost seventy-five cents. At that time, the better movie theaters charged a dollar. It wasn't at all that I judged a date by the size of the tab, but I was by now no stranger to the inside of a limousine and dinner at the Plaza. Given what I knew of his family, I came to the hasty conclusion that whatever else he was, Mr. Farmanfarmaian was stingy.

When the Shah visited New York in 1954, I got a closer look at the Farmanfarmaian clan. One of Abol's sisters was traveling with the royal entourage as Queen Soraya's lady-in-waiting, and a handful of their siblings who lived in the United States congregated in New York for the occasion. Between Abol and Leila I had several invitations to join the group, and I myself arranged an evening at the theater for the group to see Rex Harrison in *My Fair Lady,* which had just opened. All in all, I was struck by the extraordinary air of self-assurance that seemed to be a family trait. The gene I had admired in Leila at sports expressed itself in subtly muted form in Abol; but seeing it represented en masse, I felt a certain kinship with Eliza Doolittle.

The Shah's visit coincided with the opening of an important exhibition of Iranian antiquities at the Metropolitan Museum, and the royal party was to attend the opening. I had my own invitation, thanks to the curator Maurice Dimand. He had asked me to model some of the two-thousand-year-old jewelry for photographs for the exhibition brochure. We went down to the basement of the museum, and Maurice, with white gloves and infinite care, draped a Sassanian necklace around my shoulders as the photographer adjusted his lights.

"Relax," the photographer ordered. Easier said than done. The two armed guards staring at me were not conducive to relaxation. I thought of my father counting the crown jewels in the basement of the Central Bank. These two characters did not look like they would ever serve tea to anyone. Maurice dealt with them graciously.

"Why don't you two just face the other way? The instant she starts to make off with the jewelry, I'll let you know."

Maurice also dragooned me into doing an interview about the exhibition on Voice of America. It was a painful experience; I was all too aware that I didn't have a clue what I was talking about. It's one thing to mug for a camera and quite another to answer questions about Iranian art history on the radio. I prayed that no one was listening.

The opening was packed, of course, and I was just one in the crowd. Afterward I was invited with the Farmanfarmaian siblings and a handful of friends for dinner and dancing at the Waldorf-Astoria, where the royal entourage was staying. Abol asked me to dance, and then a peculiar thing happened. As we glided around the dance floor in this very public place, I suddenly realized that his hand on my back had somehow unhooked my bra. I stopped dead, and he narrowly avoided tripping over me.

"What on earth are you doing?"

"*Eshteba shod*, Khanom. It was a mistake. Don't worry about it." He looked like a schoolboy trying to suppress a giggle, then lost the struggle and laughed out loud.

I was shocked. Even more than the categorically bold rudeness of his move, I was shocked that it had come from Abol, the paragon of propriety who night after night in my own home had never shown the slightest hint of physical interest.

Soon enough his sisters cornered me for a chat. I recognized the tone of voice immediately—that affectionately *foozool* mode that signals Iranian women on a matchmaking mission.

"Monir *joon*, you're so perfect for Abol. And I think he really likes you."

"No, I don't think it would work."

"Why ever not?" I didn't want to say, but when they pressed me, I had to confess that I thought their brother was stingy.

"Abol? Stingy? Never! Of all the brothers and sisters, he's by far the most generous, the most openhanded, openhearted." I took the advertisement with a fistful of salt: What else could they say? I knew what I knew.

WE CELEBRATED ABOL'S GRADUATION FROM COLUMBIA
AT THE PLAZA HOTEL IN 1956. ABOL AND I STAND ON THE LEFT.

"Besides, he's been like a brother to me for so long. Don't you think I would have felt it if he was interested at all?" They insisted that, being his sisters, they had access to better intelligence. I brushed it off. I really didn't believe it, notwithstanding the incident on the dance floor. I knew what I knew.

The following summer Abol finished his studies at Columbia and decided to return to Iran. He came over to my apartment to say good-bye and in the process presented me with his watch. It was a beautiful man's watch and no doubt very expensive.

"I won't need this now that I'm going, and I want you to have it. But on one condition: you mustn't give it to my brother Karim." *Why on earth would I give the watch to Karim?* I wondered. True, he had shown some interest in me once in the dim past, but that was long forgotten. Abol kissed me on the cheek, said a last goodbye, and left. *He's definitely an odd one,* I thought, but somehow also oddly endearing.

Shortly after Abol left, I had a call from Fred Shoren. "That friend of yours? He's very serious about you. He came to see me about the legal implications of your getting a divorce from Manoucher. He had already done a fair amount of homework. He'll make a very good lawyer, you know. Anyway, I told him it's not possible here. You'll have to go abroad, Mexico maybe."

"Slow down! Have any of you lawyers considered that I might have some say in the matter?" Again, I was shocked. The whole thing was so unexpected, so outrageously unlikely, and if true—though I had no reason to doubt Fred's word—such a bizarre way to proceed.

Things that far off the map have a way of dropping off the edge. I didn't hear from Abol, and I put the whole business out of my mind. Life continued quite happily. I was having fun at Bonwit Teller and making good money. The dating game continued, but a winner started coming up consistently. Geof Sidney was an executive at MGM and the father of one of Nima's classmates. The kids' play dates had led to ours. Geof was determined that one day soon I would marry him. I didn't rule out the possibility, but I was in no rush. And I had that small matter of a divorce to deal with. That summer I used my vacation time from Bonwit Teller to fly to Mexico and finalize the divorce. I left Nima with Pamela, the first time I had ever spent more than a day away from her, and took the opportunity to celebrate my freedom with a few days of sightseeing.

The world is a small place, especially if one has many siblings scattered in far outposts. No doubt Abol learned of my relationship with Geof through a sister or brother, just as I learned that he was engaged to a very beautiful girl that his family had recommended. And then in the same way I learned that he had broken off the engagement—in the most honorable and polite manner possible—because the girl, who was only eighteen, had no interests in life beyond partying and nothing intelligent to say.

After that the campaign began in earnest. Letters from Abol's sisters came regularly, asking if I had got my divorce yet. Khodadad, another brother whom I had not met before, came from Colorado and lobbied on Abol's behalf. I listened to endless accounts of his admirable qualities, the depth of his love for me, and his all-round excellence as husband material. None of it could shake the impression I had formed myself that he was stingy and emotionally cold—if not cold, then why else had he not expressed some of this directly to me? I

SAYING GOODBYE AT BONWIT
TELLER IN MY WORKADAY
HAT AND GLOVES.

wasn't shy about stating my opinion to the many intermediaries.

Finally a letter arrived from Abol himself. Yes, he wanted to marry me. Would I consider coming back to Iran? Or perhaps he should come back to New York . . . Before I had gathered my thoughts to compose a suitably warm but negative reply, a second letter arrived. *Come, please, and see what a beautiful life we'll have. I'll take you on a white horse to the mountains of Hamadan . . .*

White horse indeed! I sat by the tenth-floor window of my Central Park West apartment with the letter in my hand and looked out at New York. Half a block away I could see the rooftop playground of the Ethical Culture School and Nima's familiar form scuttling over the jungle gym. I couldn't make out her face, but I imagined the smile and her own voice in the chorus of happy squeals that blended distantly with the traffic noise. I'd be off to Bonwit Teller in a few minutes, and the German nanny would pick Nima up at three. I was dressed and ready to go. I had a stack of free-lance designs to deliver on my way, a check to collect, and a nicely growing stash in my savings account. Dinner with Geof tonight, plans for the weekend. Where in this life was I going to hitch a white horse?

I had not seen Iran for twelve years. Just once in all that time I had heard my parents' voices over a phone line, a treat that Geof had arranged through MGM. I was a very different person from the girl who had left so long ago, and Iran almost certainly was a very different country. Was it even possible to go back? Would I go crazy if I tried to fit in? I thought of Uncle Dervish. Were the mountains of Hamadan anything like those of Qazvin?

Late that night I wrote to Abol. I told him of my fears, of my reluctance to give up the life I had built, of my contentment. I told him that I would come on one condition: a trial period of three months. If I could adjust to life in Iran and if I could get to know him better, then marriage was a possibility.

Those last few weeks I lived on a seesaw of contingency—planning as if I were coming back, packing as if I were leaving for good. Goodbyes were spoken lightly but were deeply felt. I arranged for a temporary leave of absence from Bonwit Teller, and the fashion gang threw a party at the office. As always they were overflowing with encouragement and innuendo. Ahmad was more than happy to sublet my apartment while he continued to ponder his big jump. The Ethical Culture School would hold Nima's place. Finally I went to say goodbye to Milton and Sally Avery at their home in Greenwich Village. Milton asked me to pose for him one last time. One last time I sat and listened to his brush against the canvas. I watched the dust motes swimming slowly

IN CHRISTIAN DIOR ON THE *LIBERTY*, BOUND FOR IRAN VIA FRANCE.

upstream through sunbeams, tumbling in play but rising still, like little prayers of thanks for the warm glow of friendship. He painted a large portrait, then copied a second version in miniature that he gave me to remember him by. As if I could forget.

I left New York on the *Liberty* for Le Havre. The world had indeed changed much in twelve years. With its art deco furnishings, French cooking, and dancing to jazz, this was no warship. True, we had stormy nights with furniture flying, but I also enjoyed the wonder of things as vast as the ocean, as small as a porthole, seen freshly through Nima's big eyes. Then by train to Paris—finally, Paris!—and the irony of having reached my original destination only as a footnote, a tourist's stopover on my way home.

CHAPTER SEVENTEEN

The flight from Paris landed in Tehran in the small hours of the night in early February 1957. Happily, no sheep was sacrificed on account of my arrival, though I was welcomed at the airport by a huge host of relatives. Familiar faces had a few more wrinkles, and toddlers had turned into teenagers. My mother was a little heavier, my father a little more stooped than I remembered. Many tears flowed amid the hundreds of kisses, and everyone was talking at high speed as if to account in one fell swoop for every missed moment of twelve years.

As we drove home through the silent streets in the clear chill of the predawn, with the stars popping out of the high desert sky, I was overwhelmed by the sheer presence of place, the countless details that fade into familiarity after a few days but that at this moment were shouting at me in unison, *This is not New York!* Later, when the day was warming to the promise of spring and the welcomers had drifted off to their routines, I sat in a jet-lagged stupor and drank in the smells of home: the sooty perfume of kerosene heaters with overtones of dill, parsley, fenugreek, and aromatic rice that hinted at lunch, and the sourceless, ever-present mystery of rosewater. No, this was not New York. I was home.

As I got my bearings over the next few days, I was struck by the changes in the city. Tehran's wide avenues looked far more modern, clean, and Western than I had remembered them. Scores of new buildings, parks, and new-paved roads confounded my outdated mental map. At night every shop front, gateway, and street stall was lit bright as an operating room, strings of bulbs and neon tubes celebrating the god of electricity.

The human landscape had proved more resistant to change. Tehran's garb was now modern and Western, but its heart was still ineluctably Iranian. The city's social energy buzzed not around a new restaurant, a fashion craze, a recent film, an anticipated concert—though these things certainly existed—but around the extended ritual of *did o baz did,* visits paid and repaid in a loosely measured dance of reciprocity, as meandering and symmetrical as the patterned tendrils of a Persian carpet. Multigenerational combinations of cousins, aunts, uncles, in-laws, grandparents, and children partied together as comfortably as American teenagers (and a lot more often), feasting on food enough to stuff us all and still feed the poor of the neighborhood on leftovers for a week. Am I exaggerating? Just a little. But the truth is that human connection—much more than commerce or culture—was the city's engine. My old high school friends, for instance, held a reunion not every few years but monthly. Where the urban Western soul had grown isolated in anonymity, Tehran's growth in that time seemed to multiply the number of characters and interconnections in its village.

I was only too happy to fall into the city's effusive, cheek-kissing embrace. As the prodigal daughter returned, I had far more than the usual social obligations, twelve years' worth. And now, in addition to the web of my own family and friends, I had to negotiate the even more intricate and sticky web of Abol's family. A few times a week Abol would pick me up after he finished work, and we would attend a family gathering in one camp or another.

I knew that the Farmanfarmaians were not an ordinary Iranian family, but I hardly understood what I would be up against. I had written to my father from New York with the news that a certain Abolbashar Farmanfarmaian had asked me to marry him, and that the purpose of my trip home was to explore this possibility. Since his earliest involvement in politics, my father had viewed the remnants of the Qajar dynasty—Farmanfarmaians included—with profound contempt. He called them *moftkhor*, freeloaders, imbibers of alcohol and smokers of opium who had let the country go to the dogs to satisfy their voracious appetites. It did not bode well for happy in-law relationships. But my father, being an open-minded pragmatist as well as a Qajar-hating patriot, had the grace to approach an uncle of Abol's who, like himself, was a member of parliament.

"What an honor for you, Mr. Shahroudy! Of all the many sons of Farmanfarmaian, this one is the best." Faint praise, perhaps, in my father's eyes, but better than none at all. Having ascertained that his prospective son-in-law was an honest and honorable man, and Abol's wealth hardly being a deterrent, my father could not object to the match, even if he could muster scant enthusiasm.

Little by little I came to see how very different Abol's family was

NIMA IS FINALLY IN HER
GRANDFATHER'S ARMS.

from others. Obviously their wealth set them apart. One of Abol's sisters lived on a family compound in a facsimile of a French château that presided over a runway-long garden flanked by tennis courts and a swimming pool. The compound itself, which accommodated several other family homes as well, just happened to be located on prime real estate in the middle of downtown Tehran and seemed almost as big as the grounds of the nearby British embassy.

Less immediately obvious than their wealth was the vast extent of the clan. I knew it was a large family even by Iranian standards. I had met five or six of Abol's siblings in New York and assumed there were perhaps as many again whom I had yet to meet. But every time I thought I had met them all, another one would pop up. One day finally I asked Abol, "Just how many of you are there?"

"There are many of us. Don't worry about it." He brushed the question off. It was years before I learned the actual count: thirty-six brothers and sisters. Forget about cousins!

Beyond wealth and numbers, which are hardly faults, there was the small matter of family pride. Although Abol's siblings were lobbying hard in support of his marriage proposal, a few family members had decided that I fell short of their standards. Occasionally a startlingly condescending remark was lobbed at me from the blue sky, falling like a bird dropping on my face.

If I could find no elegant response to these random barbs, I could count on my own stubborn pride to suffer hard feelings a little longer than necessary. Certain predictable sources of friction emerged. I often brought Nima for family lunches. This was definitely "not done" in certain camps of the Farmanfarmaian family, although Iranian children as a rule are considered completely portable and even at late-night parties will be found sleeping wherever they can find a spot

A FRACTION OF THE FARMANFARMAIANS AT ABOL'S BROTHER'S WEDDING
IN TEHRAN. I AM TO THE LEFT OF THE MAN JUST ABOVE THE BRIDE.

on the carpet in the midst of festivities. Nima in any case was very
well behaved, and it didn't seem right to leave her day after day in
the care of people she barely knew when her whole world had so suddenly changed. But it was also "not done" to decline an invitation for
lack of an ideal babysitter. The Farmanfarmaian children were all
equipped with nannies, most of whom were imported from Europe;
some had brought with them child-rearing practices that seemed bar-
baric to me. I wondered what the psychologist at the Ethical Culture
School would have to say about rich kids tied to their cribs.

Meanwhile an obscure problem had come up in registering my
divorce. It was a time-consuming technicality, nothing of real substance, but it required Abol to send a paper-pushing lackey on several
expeditions to Qazvin and beyond, into the bowels of a surreal
bureaucracy.

"Don't worry, we'll fix it," Abol kept saying. I wasn't worried at
all, or at least not about that. As far as I was concerned, my papers
could continue to drift sluggishly down the hallways of obscure sub-

departments of leviathan ministries. I was in no hurry to find myself nose to nose with a real decision about this marriage. For now, circumstances beyond my control offered a welcome protection. In the meantime the social merry-go-round continued.

One day, on the way to a family gathering, I was riding with Abol and Nima through Elahieh, a quiet suburb in the foothills of the mountains. As we drove down poplar-shaded lanes where mud walls discreetly shielded the vast gardens of old family estates and a few newer embassy mansions, Abol asked the driver to stop.

"I want to show you your future home." I didn't answer, not because I wasn't curious but because I didn't want to say a single word that could be construed as agreeing with his definition of what we were about to see. We entered a gate and drove up the driveway to a clean-lined building: fresh construction, obviously just completed. It was a blank page, I thought to myself with a glimmer of optimism.

No doubt Abol could tell by my poker face that I was determined to maintain a silent neutrality, so he took Nima by the hand and addressed his tour of the house to her. Upstairs he asked her to choose which bedroom she would like if she came to live there. Nima, with an eye for such things even at seven, chose the largest room overlooking the garden. Abol promised it to her. "And you know, Nima," he said, "I never break a promise."

Nima came running down the stairs to me, clung to my hand, and begged, "Mommy, please marry Abol, please. The bedroom is so beautiful!" *Point for Abol,* I thought. It was no surprise that Nima should like him, but few men would show such respect to a child.

A few days later he posed a question that threw me off balance: "How many cesareans can a person have?"

"I don't know," I mumbled. "The doctor said three is the limit normally, but he also said I might not be able to have another child." Was he hoping for a baby factory? I wondered if realism was too much to expect from an Iranian male hell-bent on marriage. Cesarean or no, I was over thirty years old.

Abol paused, then said gently, "Never mind. We have one Nima." A few more numbers flipped over on the scoreboard.

And then . . . one evening I met him at his office. We were planning to go on together to a party at my sister's. His secretary had gone for the day, and the building was empty except for the two of us. Without more preamble than closing the door, he put his arms around me, kissed me for the very first time, and proceeded rapidly to go the next step. And the next, and the next. Stupidly, I was shocked. Not that I couldn't have foreseen the event—I was no longer *that* naïve—but the force of his embrace, and the force-of-nature-not-to-be-denied look in his eyes, presented such a different face from the Abol I thought I knew. Was this the same man who had sat in my living room so passively and patiently surrounded by his books, night after night after night? Or even the one who had laughed like a goofy kid over his bold move on the dance floor?

When I recovered from my shock, it occurred to me that I didn't exactly dislike this new development. And Abol announced, as we lay tangled on his office couch, that he had liked it very much indeed.

The next morning I was barely awake when the phone rang. It was Leila. "Good news, Monir! Your papers are finally fixed. We'll be over before noon for the wedding." I was speechless. So much for my big decision. I ran downstairs and broke the news to my parents.

"Today? It can't be. We have no time to prepare! We have to invite people!" My mother ran for the phone.

"Did you make a decision?" my father asked. No comment. Any reservations I had about the marriage were silenced by primitive guilt. The sophisticated New Yorker, the bohemian artist, the cynical divorcée all vanished, leaving the good girl standing alone on the carpet. Once again I had made my bed and would have to lie in it. I could only pray that this time it would be more comfortable.

I had no time to ponder my stubborn determination not to learn from experience. The whole house was spinning with chaos and reckless motions at cleaning, and my own mind was spinning no less chaotically, when a car pulled up to the house. A procession of strangers filed out of the car bearing mirror and candelabra, sugar cones, boxes of sweets . . . They marched right past me into the house. Leila arrived next and took charge of the dizzy bride. "Do you want to get married looking like that? Get some clothes on!"

"What do you mean? I'm not naked!"

"Come on, let's get you dressed."

I led her upstairs to the bedroom as the strangers took over the living room, spreading a *sofreh* on the table and laying out the wedding paraphernalia. By the time I got back downstairs dressed in my Bonwit Teller best, Abol and his mother had arrived. My mother had

A QUIET MOMENT WITH NIMA
ON THE DAY I MARRIED ABOL,
BEFORE THE HOUSE WAS
TURNED UPSIDE DOWN.

managed to muster Sediqeh and Hassan but could not reach Ahmad and Ali in time, let alone the scores of other relatives who she felt properly should have been present. The turbaned *akhoond* launched into the recitation of the ceremony. My mother-in-law embraced me formally and gave me a pearl bracelet. Abol gave me an emerald ring and a big smile. The sweets were eaten. The deed was done.

First thing the next morning we flew to Abadan for what might be called our honeymoon. It was actually a business trip that Abol had previously scheduled to check on a Coca-Cola factory that he was investing in. Abadan is not the most romantic of cities in any case, and it had changed little since my wartime visit. The British no longer ran the oil company, but their influence persisted in the stratified social life of the place, and the stench of sulfur from the refineries still hung over the neat rows of bungalows.

We stayed for a week at the modest home of a friend of Abol's. After breakfast with our host, Abol would go off to the factory and his friend to his own business. I remained in the house in the company of a servant who was too shy to talk to me. The men would return for lunch and a brief nap, then go back to work until eight at night. Then we would have dinner every night at a club for the upper-level staff of the oil company.

I had plenty of time and solitude to ponder what had just happened. I didn't know a soul in town or how to get around, and I had no business to bring me out. I sat in the garden and listened to sounds from the street drifting over the walls. A man walked by shouting in a long-drawn-out cry, "*Farda! Farda! Farda!*" Tomorrow, tomorrow, tomorrow . . . What did it mean? Today was strange enough, I thought; God knows what tomorrow would bring. Later our host explained that the man was selling lottery tickets for the next day's draw. But all that day his cries echoed in my head like some dread oracle.

I passed the days tossing crumbs and making small talk with the motley menagerie that inhabited the garden—a monkey, a goat, a deer, and a few birds. I also wrote letters. I wrote to my boss at Bonwit Teller and explained that I was on my honeymoon, that I had married a gentleman who was said to be a prince, and that sadly I would not be coming back to work. I learned later that my letter had caused quite a flurry of excitement when it was passed around to all the fashion gang. The novelty no doubt faded over the next few days when another letter, and another, and another, each several pages long in my still-ragged English, arrived for each of my former coworkers in turn. I wondered if it was too obvious to them that I had nothing better to do on my honeymoon than write letters, but indeed, I had nothing better to do.

The trip ended on a more promising note with a few days' visit to Isfahan so that Abol could inspect the proposed site of another Coca-Cola factory. His brother Ali, also involved in the business, met us there. I was prepared for dust-swept, industrial-strength boredom, but the reality of Isfahan swept me off my feet. It was my first taste of the glorious old capital city's architecture, and indeed of the depth of Iran's artistic heritage, a taste that would develop into a voracious appetite and lead me eventually on endless treks crisscrossing the country. In Isfahan's great mosques I marveled at the sculptural balance of space and volume and light: sun-dazzled courtyards framed by deep-shadowed arches, the cool gloom of vaulted halls pierced by golden shafts, blue-tiled domes dissolving into the vast arc of a cloudless, enamel-blue sky. It was architecture that reached for heaven, not with the vertical ascent of a European cathedral but by revealing the weight and gravitas of earth as illusion, dissolving fortress-thick masses of brick into an ephemeral shimmer of glassy skin, where endless skeins of detail wound like the convoluted affairs of men through branch and twig and curling leaf. But take just one step back, and all this meandering would crystallize into larger patterns of mathematical purity, then fade from substance into light and melt into the sky.

Abol and Ali together played tour guide and fed me delicious tidbits of historical background on the mosques and palaces we visited. My own education had omitted so much of this—had I been too busy clowning with my classmates to notice, or had we really skipped so lightly over the history of Iran? Anyway, my guides' grasp of history, colored as it was by family lore and kinship with so many characters in the story, was much livelier than anything I could have found in a textbook.

One page in the story popped into vivid three-dimensional reality when we paid a visit to Saram-ed Doleh, one of the more elderly remnants of the Qajar dynasty. Abol introduced him with the title *shahzadeh,* prince, and addressed him humbly with high-flown honorifics. He certainly cut an imposing figure, over six feet tall, white-haired, extremely elegant and erudite. Indeed, I had heard of him, as the finance minister who in 1919 had been instrumental in handing Iran's oil over to British control. But if a palace was all it took to be a prince, then he certainly was one. He received us in a vast fantasia that was the epitome of Qajar style, the nineteenth-century Iranian equivalent of high Victorian ostentation. The architectural decoration fascinated me, and my eyes kept drifting away from the conversation and the food to the intricate patterns of brick, mosaics of mirror and tile, faience, stained glass . . .

The palace had been built by Saram-ed Doleh's father, the eldest son of Nasser al-Din Shah. Known as Zill-e Soltan or "the King's Shadow," this dark character, governor of Isfahan in his day, was infamous for his ruthless ambition and cruelty to his enemies. I conceived a very personal dislike for the man, long dead though he was. Aside from the graphic tales of torture that stuck to his name, it was he who had obliterated the frescos that decorated the Safavid palaces of Isfahan's golden age. Painted in muted colors with the delicate, calligraphic line of miniatures, their sophistication made Qajar art look crude in comparison. But the mullahs had found the images lascivious, with too many women pouring wine and all of them too explicitly beautiful. The mullahs no doubt found Zill-e Soltan himself lascivious, with too much of a penchant for wine and opium, never mind beautiful women, but the paintings were an easier target. They were also an easy concession for Zill-e Soltan. With a brand-new mansion of his own, why should he care about a few dusty old masterpieces? And so he ordered the frescoes plastered over. Many of them have now been restored, though some were damaged past hope, but when I first saw Ali Qapu and Chehel Sotoon, the blank expanses of chalk-white plaster were testimony to the tragedy of art used as a political pawn.

———

With the shock of the wedding past, and the decision about whether to marry no longer hanging like a sword over my head, I found myself settling into a comfortable ease with Abol. Over the many years of our marriage he treated me always with gentleness and respect, supporting the choices I made without question and indulging my adventures. If he didn't talk much, he was always ready to listen, and much was understood between us with no need for words. In the face of tensions that arose every so often between me and his family—not real conflicts but those casual insults and snobbish slights that caused real enough pain—he dealt big doses of patience. Never taking sides, never pushing, he just quietly went a little bit out of his way to minimize contact between me and them, always with some gracious excuse, until time had a chance to heal the wounds. And always, when he spoke of me, of my work or my interests, to his family or to anyone else, he spoke with pride and respect. These were not things I would ever take for granted.

All this respect might have been a burden if it weren't also tempered with lightness and humor. Though he always politely called me Khanom, often it was "Khaneum" with a Qazvini accent in imitation of my father. He never, ever called me Monir, except in bed.

Throughout our life together I remained oblivious to the details of the Farmanfarmaian mythology: the vast family tree had branches that groaned under the weight of privileged progeny; the family politics had been grafted indistinguishably onto the roots of Iran's existence as a nation; a cult of personality surrounded the patriarch (Abol's own father); and there were elaborate hierarchies of sons and daughters of first wife, second wife, third wife . . . and so on and so forth. I wasn't particularly curious, and Abol wasn't particularly forthcoming. I saw my own position in the family as that of a bird that had chanced to alight on the tip of one branch and found it a suitable spot for a nest. Was the tree any reason to puff up my feathers in pride? I was glad of the comforts of wealth and even more of the freedom it offered. But since when are comfort and freedom—gifts unearned—a cause for pride? I judged people by their actions, not by their name, and I really could not have cared less that Abol was a prince.

Abol himself was modest to a fault, so much so that many of his accomplishments remained hidden from me until after his death. Unlike most of his brothers, who had been sent to Europe for school-

JUST MARRIED.

ing at a very early age, Abol had been raised in Iran until he came to America to study law. When his father died, he was seventeen, and he interrupted his education for several years—he was an engineering student then in Tehran—to move to the country and oversee the family's agricultural lands in some thirty remote villages between Hamadan and Kermanshah. If he enjoyed the legacy of feudal privilege that came with the job, he also took the responsibilities very seriously. Perhaps any good man with money would have paid for the clinics and schools to be built, but the village elders who remember Abolbashar picture him on the back of a truck, hauling vaccines in sacks of fresh snow or fetching a doctor in the night. Although he himself never spoke of this time, I imagine it was an education better than what any boarding school in Europe could offer, and I would see for myself the warmth and dignity in his dealings with people of any rank.

Over time I grew to love the man very deeply.

CHAPTER EIGHTEEN

Miss Shahroudy, come give it a try," said the Shah. "Let's see how well you know the game." I went for it. Who was I to argue with the Shah's command, however casually dropped? Within a few short minutes I was sprawled akimbo on the plastic mat with my ass in the air. If the purpose of this pose was to get a royal look at my legs, I thought, the poor guy was probably disappointed. My legs weren't much to look at. As I stretched one foot for my final move, I caught a glimpse from my upside-down vantage of the Shah's patent-leather shoe moving out to give my own foot a nudge.

"*Afarin!* Bravo! You did it!" a cluster of courtiers clapped with polite enthusiasm as I collapsed on the mat and another victim stepped forward. I had heard that the Shah was fond of parlor games, but I hardly expected Twister.

Except for that little cheat of a kick, the Shah did not join in the fun. He stood very stiffly, watching the general efforts to entertain him with one foot forward, hands behind his back, smiling artificially as if posing for a photo. Gossip had it that he was very relaxed at his nightly poker games with a few close friends, laughing and telling dirty jokes, but that evening he was hardly the life of the party. He barely made an effort to speak to anyone, though he did compliment my father when I was introduced to him, and he asked a few questions about what I had studied. He persisted in calling me Miss Shahroudy.

The party was a very big affair hosted by Abol's sister, who was then still lady-in-waiting to the queen. The queen, Soraya, sat demurely in a corner most of the night, but she did not seem unapproachable. She had a natural beauty with peachlike skin, lustrous hair, and lovely light green eyes. She was dressed very simply with a bare minimum of makeup and jewelry. I thought she looked sweet and unaffected. But she would soon be gone, divorced for not producing an heir. Abol's sister was very upset by the whole affair. The new queen, Farah, naturally favored her own friends and cut all ties with those at court who had been close to Soraya.

Meanwhile we were still partying, and our hostess spared no effort to entertain the royal couple. An orchestra played, and the Shah watched us dance. After dinner there was a performance by the young Googoosh. She was just seven or eight years old, a very ordinary-looking child dressed up in a tutu, but already you could see the unaffected, luminous stage presence and transparent pathos that would make her an international pop diva. "*In kun kaj-eh?*" she sang, swinging her hips in demonstration. "*Ki migeh kaj-eh?*" Her father accompanied his little puppet on the *daf,* the round moon of the drum bouncing high above his shoulders with the beat. He wore a big mustache like a Turkish bandit.

CHAPTER NINETEEN

We moved into the house that Abol had built in Elahieh a few days after we arrived back in Tehran from the honeymoon trip. The house was designed by Abol's brother Aziz, who had studied architecture in Paris, and was supposedly based on a home by Frank Lloyd Wright that Abol had seen in a magazine. Abol's taste didn't normally lean to the modern, but he was eager to please me and knew that I admired Wright. I didn't actually recognize anything of Wright's style in the design, but it was clean-lined and modern, untainted by the aspirations to French baroque that plagued our social circle. Just as I had hoped, it was a blank slate. In fact, it was more than a blank slate; it was absolutely raw construction, barely finished and completely empty.

Abol kept his promise to Nima, and she got the large bedroom overlooking the garden, which at that point was a moonscape of rocks and broken bricks surrounding the crater of an empty swimming pool. My mother-in-law sent over a mattress and a little boy who was supposed to cook for us. My own mother provided some sheets and blankets, a few pots and pans. Anything else would require an expedition to the bazaar or a search through many small shops. Tehran had nothing resembling a department store in those days, let alone a phone book. In fact, it took six months to get a telephone at all, using every bit of family influence at Abol's disposal.

I was determined to keep the house modern regardless of how many eyebrows my choices raised. I put venetian blinds on the windows instead of heavy tasseled drapes. I covered the concrete block floor with gray linoleum as a foil for the Persian carpets. This was seen as particularly perverse and cold. Until imported marble flooring became available later, it was normal to show off one's wealth by spreading carpets like a patchwork over every inch of the floor.

The Farmanfarmaian homes were decorated in European style and filled with antiques, many of them family heirlooms from the Qajar period or fine objects that recalled the court life of earlier dynasties. Abol's sisters took me in hand and introduced me to a few high-end antique shops in Tehran, where I asked a lot of questions. I began, in a small way, to learn something about fine carpets and miniature paintings, crystal and enamel and silver—the ornate and highly refined decorative arts that Iranians have always treasured. But it was not until later, when I found my way home to Qazvin, that I began to make real discoveries of my own.

Just two months after Abol and I were married, I got pregnant. I celebrated by eating chocolate, putting on a huge amount of weight, and staying ferociously active. I may have looked like a meatball, but I danced defiantly at parties, and I learned how to water-ski, much to the dismay of my mother-in-law and the family surgeon, Dr. Yahya Adl. He was no obstetrician, but any cutting that the family needed fell to him, and he seemed genuinely fearful that I would demand his services in the middle of one of those grand parties. I worked too, painting ads on the side of Abol's Coca-Cola trucks. I went up and down ladders like a bulbous yo-yo, creating a six-meter-long reclining woman holding a bottle of Coke.

When the waters finally broke, Dr. Adl performed the cesarean. All three of us survived, mother, baby, and doctor. It was a girl, so entrancingly pretty that I wanted nothing more than to lie there and look at her huge eyes and black curls.

A couple of days later Abol informed me that he had taken care of the birth certificate. "I named her Zahra Iran," he said. He didn't need to explain. On his own he had chosen the names of my mother and my beloved sister Iran. His words stirred in me a wave of sentiment so pure that it seemed refined. *This is love,* I thought, *of an unfamiliar kind.*

"It's perfect," I said. "She is Zahra Iran."

Home from the hospital and still weak with pain, I bowed to family pressure and accepted the Swiss nanny they recommended. It drove me nuts that she slept in Zahra's room and gave her a bottle in the night instead of waking me to nurse. If I mentioned it to Abol's mother or sisters, who were prominent in the stream of visitors who came daily to pay their respects, they were adamant: "You've had an operation—you can't possibly manage alone!" Meanwhile they sat there drinking tea and chatting endlessly. I was propped up painfully on pillows to receive them, and from the corner of my eye I watched the nanny hovering in the hallway, bouncing my hungry baby and waiting for the visitors to leave so that I could nurse without offending anyone.

Two weeks of that, and enough was enough. "Khanom, it's your decision," Abol said, "not theirs." I let the nanny go.

SHE IS ZAHRA IRAN.

Once Zahra was a couple of months old and Nima was well settled in school, I took a job working mornings at the Ministry of Agriculture in the Point Four program, which was headed by Abol's nephew Shahrokh. It was a program set up under the Marshall Plan at the end of the war, part of America's effort to win friends and influence people by undoing at least part of the damage that the Allies had inflicted on the Iranian economy. The main thrust was technical assistance, teaching modern methods of agriculture, banking, and mining and laying the groundwork for industrial development. Much of the work floundered at the hands of foreign experts who had little understanding of how to dish up their superior knowledge in a form that was digestible to the people they were trying to help.

Knowing that I had studied at Parsons, Shahrokh recruited me for a project adapting traditional handicrafts to appeal to foreign markets, with the intention of promoting exports and tourism. I was supposed to research local crafts and come up with new designs that satisfied Western tastes. At the same time I was to act as a guide and translator for Bill and Hugo, the foreign experts who would teach modern production methods to the craftsmen.

Bill was American, a specialist in textiles, and gay. I felt right at home with him, and he was an instant friend. Hugo's field was ceramics. He was Italian, handsome as a film star, and determined to get me into bed. Much of our time together was spent in a comical dance as I tried to keep Bill safely between me and Hugo, and Hugo tried to maneuver closer to me.

The variety of local textile traditions was so rich that it was hard to know where to begin. Ceramics, however, were a serious technical challenge. It was not difficult to redesign shapes that had been made the same way for thousands of years. The potters had skill enough to turn a baking pot or a water jug into a flower vase. But the fragile, porous earthenware didn't stand up well to shipping, and there was a tremendous amount of breakage in the kilns, which were fueled with thick black oil and heated very unevenly. While Hugo struggled with the temperamental kilns, I begged the potters to teach me to use the wheel. The workshop where I learned, in the southernmost reaches of Tehran's slums, specialized in blue-glazed yogurt bowls like those that had inspired Donald Wilber's dinner set. No electricity was used beyond a couple of bare lightbulbs; we powered the wheels with our feet as potters had done for countless generations. In a whole week I succeeded in throwing, glazing, and firing two not-quite-perfect bowls, while the small boy at the wheel next to mine made forty or fifty, all of them flawless. I played like a child in the mud on a rainy day, loving the slippery feel of the clay alive in my hands, the mess dripping down my arms. I wondered if the child so hard at work beside me still enjoyed this same muddy pleasure, or if it had dried up with the tedium of daily labor and the load he carried as a wage-earner. I wondered too if he would ever see the inside of a school-room.

I decided that we needed to look farther afield than Tehran in our search for traditional handicrafts. Qazvin came to mind immediately. I arranged for a car and driver and, waiting to see where Hugo and Bill sat, chose my own seat accordingly. We took off down the high-way, and I watched as the mountains on the horizon resolved into the familiar shapes of my childhood. It was my first trip back to Qazvin since the war, though I had seen my relatives when they came to visit my parents at Noruz. It felt very strange to be going home as a tourist.

As soon as we stepped out of the car, a crowd of children gathered. They trailed us through the bazaar like a cloud of mosquitoes, crowd-ing close as we stopped at each shop.

"Are they French?"

"No, German, I'm sure. Look at his camera."

"I'll bet the woman is Russian."

I decided to keep my mouth shut if I wasn't speaking English. Our driver tried again and again to shoo the kids away, but they stuck to us. "Are they beggars?" Bill asked, ready to turn annoyance into com-passion.

"Not at all," I said. "They're just curious. Very few foreigners come this way."

Finally it was impossible to concentrate on the work. I turned to face the sticky cluster of boys and said loudly, in the deepest Qazvini accent I could pull from buried layers of memory, "If you don't leave us alone, I'll kick your ass so hard you'll fly to the sky and catch a baby crow before you come down again!" They froze. Their mouths hung open, and their eyes popped out of their heads.

"*Khak bar saram!*" said one, slapping his hand to his head. "She's speaking Qazvini!" And they all turned together and ran. I laughed so hard I could barely stand. Even the driver was shocked.

"Khanom, how do you know Qazvini?"

"I was born here," I said. "This was my home."

Qazvin proved to be a treasure trove, and we came back many times. I found some beautiful *jajeem*, big squares of very rough, hand-woven wool in checkered patterns of deep pinks, oranges, and greens, all natural dyes. They were used to wrap up bedding during the day. The soft, colorful bundles served a double purpose in traditional homes with minimal furniture, becoming comfortable cushions to lean against a wall when sitting on a carpet. We spoke to the weavers about making the same fabric in a tighter weave, more practical for cutting a coat or a winter suit. It worked, and for years I wore the prototype that I sewed myself, a beautiful suit that looked like something from Chanel. Another success was an adaptation of traditional silk-screened scarves worn by the Turkoman tribal women. We provided quality linens and taught the craftsmen to print tablecloths and bordered sheets.

One day as I was wandering in the far corners of the Qazvin bazaar, I came across a huge wooden door that opened on an abandoned caravansary. It was four meters wide, studded with huge iron nails, and decorated with shieldlike bosses and a big lion's-head knocker. Behind the door was a courtyard with a round platform in the middle, ringed with iron hooks to tie up horses and donkeys. Small rooms for travelers lined the perimeter of the courtyard, each with a little porch framed by an archway to sit outside in summertime. Such a caravansary, perhaps the very same one, would have seen the comings and goings, the wheeling and dealing of my grandfather's import-export business. The sight of that door was a revelation to me. It was the first time I realized that there was history captured in ordinary objects, embedded in the alleys and byways of my own hometown.

In Qazvin I discovered an antique dealer who would open many old doors for me. When I first met Javad Agha, his little shop was more of a recycling center than anything else. He used to buy broken glass by the kilo, brought to him in big burlap bags by people who picked through the trash. He would empty the bags in a glittering heap in the basement of his shop and sell the glass in turn to a factory that made new bottles. He also had a few kilims and several piles of small, square, wooden panels. I picked one up and wiped off a thick layer of dust. A nightingale appeared in the midst of roses. I remembered the ceiling of my childhood, bower of bedtime stories. Javad Agha told me how they were tearing down the old houses to make room for new concrete boxes, and he had found the ceiling panels abandoned in the wreckage. He sold them to me for about five cents each, which to him was a premium for garbage, and to me a very good price for art.

It was the beginning of a long friendship. I visited Javad Agha each time I went to Qazvin. Often I would have lunch at his home, and always I brought gifts for his wife and children. When he came to Tehran, my home was open to him.

As soon as he realized that someone else cared for the old ceilings, the painted door panels, and the *orsi*—intricately decorated sash window frames—he rescued many more. He began taking me to old homes before they were scheduled for demolition, and the wreckers

SALVAGED SAFAVID DOORS BECOME A CABINET IN MY DINING ROOM,
AND I INSTALLED A MIRRORED CEILING.

learned to proceed more carefully once a value was set on the old woodwork. Every so often my phone would ring:

"Khanom, I have found some window frames" . . . "Khanom, can you come quickly? There are some paneled doors from the Safavid period, with gold leaf and black lines on a dark blue background. They are incredibly beautiful." In exchange I taught him to recognize many other treasures that were sold off from the old homes: Qajar paintings and Russian glassware and Baccarat crystal.

The notion of using architectural salvage to decorate a new home was unheard of then, but to me it seemed perfectly obvious. I used those beautiful Safavid doors to build a cabinet that covered one wall of our dining room and lined it with antique fabrics. I used pieces of *orsi* window frames as curtain rods. I framed and hung the ceiling panels on a wall and gave many away as gifts.

And so I caught the collecting bug. I didn't buy fur coats or jewelry; I never gambled. In fact, I never lost the frugal ways that had served me so well in hard times. But when it came to antiques, the arts of Iran's past, or the timeless traditions of folk art, money was no object. When I began, there was so little regard for these objects. And when others did begin to value them, I argued to myself: *If I don't buy it, someone else will. If it's sold abroad, a piece of our culture will be lost, and that would be a shame.*

I developed relationships with many other dealers, though none as sweet as Javad Agha. I bought far more than I had any notion of using myself. I bought as if I were rescuing strays, feeding and nursing them back to health. I bought four hundred pieces of wooden *orsi*, hired a worker to come to my home, and taught him how to clean and repair them. In Isfahan I bought a whole room that was decorated with Qajar paintings on plaster, scheduled for demolition for a new avenue that cut through an old neighborhood. I had it disassembled and the pieces carefully packed and stored. I bought stone columns from Shiraz that would have been crushed for hard core, and stone lions that marked the graves of young warriors from Lurestan, headed for dealers abroad.

Although the job at Point Four had unlocked amazing treasures for me, I stuck with it for only a few months. Fending off the constant sexual harassment from Hugo and others at the office was exhausting. I

REDISCOVERING QAZVIN: COLORFUL STAINED GLASS WINDOWS
FRAMED WITH WOOD IN AN OLD HOME.

also resented the fact that the foreign experts were paid many times more than what I was making, even if I didn't need the money. I spoke to my boss, Shahrokh, and he conceded that I had a point. He proposed that he would not renew Bill and Hugo's contracts when they expired, and I could then work full-time instead of just half a day. The salary he offered—all that the budget allowed, he said—was still just a third of what foreigners made, and I would replace two of them.

In the end I quit before the contracts expired. I arrived home from work one day and reached eagerly to take Zahra from the nanny's arms. She turned her face away and refused to come to me. That was the last straw. No job was worth my daughter's treating me like a stranger. I quit the next day.

Being at home all day, I turned my attention to the garden. Zahra played on a swing and seesaw I bought from an American family while I planted flowers or paced the grounds, trying to figure out what to do with the rocky wilderness. I knew less than nothing about gardening. In New York cut flowers were the closest I got to nature, and all I could remember from childhood in Qazvin was agricultural in scale. Harriet Holmes, the American ambassador's wife, gave me a stack of old *House and Garden* magazines, and another friend gave me a beautiful book on the gardens of Kyoto. I studied them cover to cover. The most basic knowledge, even the fact that grass can be planted, was news to me.

Aside from the rocks and the huge empty pool, the garden had only two rows of plane trees planted at rigid intervals like soldiers lined up at attention. I knew from the start, when I knew very little else, that I wanted the soldier trees gone. It seemed a radical step to remove them when so little grew there at all, and I worried that Abol would object. But no: "Khanom, I trust you completely in this as in everything else."

The gardener, known simply as Hajji, had rather less confidence. Every step I took in the garden, magazines under my arm, was a trespass to him. Any instructions I gave were met with a fierce frown and stony silence. The first day I took a trowel in hand, he grumbled ferociously under his breath and walked away. I tried to reason with him. "It's true, Hajji, I don't know this work. I certainly don't know it better than you. But there are other people who know more than you and me both, and they wrote a book about it. Here, look."

"I'm sorry, Khanom, I can't read."

"Never mind, it's written in English anyway, but I can read it."

After a while we came to a working compromise: "Hajji, that part of the garden is yours, and this part is mine. You do it your way, and I'll do it my way; all right?" In the competition that developed between us, I had luck as well as science on my side. Perhaps if he had known the traditional lore of his own trade better, it would have gone the other way. My roses bloomed while his grew long and straggly stems without a bud. When we grafted trees, mine took and his died.

It took several seasons, more than a year, to win him over. But slowly he softened, and the boundary between my territory and his was no longer fiercely defended. Little by little he listened to me, and little by little we became friends. It was then that the garden really blossomed.

The work consumed me with a passion. I dug endlessly, and every rock that I dug up found a use. I came back from trips to Europe with suitcases full of bulbs and hand luggage loaded with water lilies and evergreen saplings. I tracked down what looked like volcanic rocks and discovered they were remnants from the brick kilns south of Tehran, where I bought them by the truckload. I designed a driveway in brick laid in lattice patterns like the brick floors of mosques, with the spaces planted with grass. Then I argued for days with the mason to convince him it could be built.

The rows of soldier trees went, leaving only a few strategically placed sentinels. A huge old walnut stayed, too venerable to disturb, and I planted a stand of pines for a far vista at the bottom of the land. In the middle of the lawn a tall umbrella of wisteria dripped blossoms in the spring.

At the bottom of the garden, shielded by a hill and drop from the house and pool, I indulged my fantasies of Kyoto with a rock garden. I sculpted a stream with large stones so the water burbled down little falls into a large pond, filled with water lilies and frogs and framed by a backdrop of bamboo. Three boulders sat in meditation amid goldfish. Here and there splashes of color appeared in a perennial sequence of surprises: first snowdrops, then crocus, then tulips and short-stemmed irises, then narcissus.

Many of the treasures I discovered in Qazvin and on trips around the country found homes in the garden. Stone faces of monkeys, lions, and dogs—fountainheads from old homes that were being demol-ished—bordered the flower beds. The lions from Lurestan guarded the pool. Scattered in the grass were the round, hollow bases and crowns of old stone columns, overflowing with flowers. On some I rested large containers of hand-blown green glass, made originally for transporting sour grape juice in a bedding of mud and straw. Goldfish swam in them above a bed of white pebbles, and the delicate green glass made a striking contrast with the heavy white stone of the columns. For parties I spread kilims on the grass and raised a colorful Egyptian patchwork tent.

When Zahra was still a baby, and Nima on school vacation, we often accompanied Abol to Abadan when he went to check on the Coca-Cola factory. We usually stayed for a couple of weeks at a time in a house we rented from the oil company. There was a certain irony in the fact that we were bottling Coca-Cola when the tap water was still unsafe to drink, so Abol decided to set up another factory to produce chlorine for water purification. He was much concerned with the country's prospects for economic development and sought out such projects eagerly. There were great opportunities to make money, of course, but more than that he felt a personal duty to contribute to Iran's development as a modern nation. He pressed his enthusiasm also on his younger brothers and encouraged them to go into industry.

Abol's brother Cyrus visited us on one of our trips to Abadan, having recently returned to Iran with a degree in astronomy and physics. Abol was eager for him to turn his learning to more practical matters and join in the chlorine project. Abol took us to look at a piece of land he was considering for the site of the chlorine factory.

It was a neglected date plantation, several hundred acres of land beside the Karoun River, where it begins to widen into delta. The date palms were in blossom then, with umbrellas of gold and yellow budding shoots spreading under the green canopy of palm fronds. Small olive trees scattered among the palms shimmered with silvery leaves, and beneath it all spread a carpet of wildflowers.

A small adobe house stood on the land where a farmer had once lived, just two rooms on either side of a courtyard with a small fountain, and a stable at one end. It was primitive but beautiful. Thick wooden beams supported the flat roof, the fountain was finished with tile and stone, and French doors opened wide onto a view of the river. Nearby was an old dock in disrepair that had been used to load the dates onto small barges.

When the decision was made to buy the land, I begged Abol not to demolish the adobe house: we would build onto it as needed. We kept the original building for our own bedrooms, adding wings with a kitchen, dining room, living room, and seven bedrooms for the engineers who came from Italy to supervise the building of the factory and train the local workers. I had noticed that the intensely humid weather of the Gulf was hard on the old British furnishings of the oil company houses, so I decorated the adobe entirely with wrought iron that I designed myself and with the tough striped fabrics that were locally made for awnings. It was a lively, comfortable look that fit the energy of the household. Dinner was a big communal affair each night, what with engineers and houseguests and children. Food was important to the Italian engineers, who brought their own cook and taught the Iranians to make pasta.

In the evenings after dinner Abol and I would walk the half-kilometer to the factory, watching the sunset gild the date palms. He would proudly show me the work that was just completed, the new pumps, and the huge pool of water with a layer of mercury floating on the top like a giant mirror. We stood on the rim looking down at our reflections, and Abol poked at them with a stick, launching slow ripples across the silver. As we walked through the plant, he would lay a hand gently on each of the pumps. "Does it have a fever?" I teased him.

Once the factory was up and running, Abol invited the Shah for a formal inauguration. He was coming to the Gulf anyway to inspect a battleship for the navy. When Abol heard that the Shah had agreed to the visit, he was suddenly nervous. "Khanom, he's coming! What shall we do?" I offered to make the arrangements for an appropriately royal welcome.

I got carried away. It wasn't that I cared so much what the Shah thought, but I wanted to make Abol proud. I set up a sewing machine in the courtyard and hired two workers to sew yards and yards of red, white, and green fabric into little flags to decorate the dock, now repaired, and the road to the factory. I whipped the garden into shape, planting hundreds of flowers around the house where I planned to serve tea before the factory inspection. I set up my Egyptian tent and rented an antique Qajar tent as well, to accommodate the retinue of bodyguards and attendants. On the road that led from the factory to the highway, I built an archway of date palm branches decorated with small flags.

The evening before the Shah's arrival, everything was complete and I was exhausted. That night a sudden storm blew in from the Gulf. I lay awake all night listening to the flags flapping furiously. In the morning I toured the wreckage. The tents were down, the arches broken in pieces, and the landscape littered for miles with my stupid flags. There was no time to fret; on to plan B.

We decided to move the whole reception into the salt storage room at the factory. I grabbed what I could of the least-mangled decorations and improvised. I had just screened off the hill of salt with the Egyptian tent and was laying out teacups and cookies when the advance security team arrived to inspect the site. That meant the Shah would be there within the hour. A SAVAK agent poking around in search of bombs stopped to admire the patchwork tent and asked where it was from.

"Egypt," I told him, in all innocence. All hell broke lose. The SAVAK agent started yelling at me to take the tent down at once. Iran was not on good terms with Egypt at that particular moment, it turned out. I argued that it was decoration only and had nothing to do with politics. Abol and Dr. Adl, who was our liaison with the court, heard the fuss and came running. They agreed that the tent had to go.

By the time the Shah arrived at the little dock, red-nosed from a cold and inspecting the battleship in the rain, I was shaking. Dr. Adl advised me to add some cognac to the Shah's teacup; I needed a good swig myself. When I served the tea, the Shah inquired after my father, then asked me questions about the house and the engineers we were hosting. I started to explain the accommodations we had built, but I was so addled with nervousness that I got it all wrong: "There are five bedrooms and twelve engineers, and each engineer has their own bedroom . . ." It was bad enough to hear the words coming out of my mouth, but worse when the Shah pointed out the faulty arithmetic. I bowed out quickly and went back to the kitchen for my own cup of tea and cognac.

CHAPTER TWENTY

The car was inching around Tajrish Square through a traffic jam of proportions that would prove prophetic. In 1958 the behemoth that Tehran would become had not yet swallowed this suburb in the foothills of the Alborz mountains. The weekend picnics spread on carpets beside the roads leading out of the square, complete with samovars and kebabs over smoking charcoal, had not yet become stubborn islands in a rising sea of exhaust fumes, and the melted snow still ran fast under Tajrish Bridge, with only a few melon rinds bobbing in the froth. But that day, the traffic in the square was as slow as glue, and I had time to take in every detail, from the white-capped mountains looming above, to the brightly colored hills of fruit in the greengrocers' that fronted the small bazaar. On the upper balcony of a building that jutted into one corner of the square, something caught my eye: a warrior astride a white horse looking down from a large painting to the bustle below. I asked the driver, Mostafa, to pull over.

"Impossible, Khanom, we can't stop here," said Mostafa. A chorus of horns blasted confirmation.

"Then go around the square and stop at that building," I pointed. Our detour allowed time for his suspicions to gel, and he asked what I wanted there. "I want to go upstairs."

"Impossible, Khanom. You can't go up there. That's a coffee-house." I might as well have asked to drop in at a brothel. Mostafa took it for granted that his job description included taking personal responsibility for the family honor. He was only the first of several drivers who, being the man in the car, were tested by my disregard for boundaries when curiosity stirred. But where the others would squirm, torn between manly concern for my virtue and respect for my authority as employer, Mostafa bossed me around like a junior wife. It didn't take me long, though, to figure out that the same cockiness made him a ready accomplice once he realized there was no stopping me.

"So what if it is a coffeehouse?" I said.

As I climbed the stairs, the smell of tobacco smoke, lamb fat, and stale sweat met me halfway. A young man carrying a greasy tray of empty *abgusht* pots shoved past me on his way down, mumbling a curse. I approached the manager at his post near the top of the stairs, greeted him politely, and asked if I could look at the painting on the balcony. He seemed surprised. He grunted something to the boy behind him who was filling a row of hubble-bubble pipes with charcoal, heaved himself out from behind his desk, and led me across the room. As I walked through the maze of tables, the din of voices subsided suddenly. Tea glasses hung in midair as all eyes followed me.

On the balcony I examined the painting. It was primitive but powerful. The broad-shouldered hero with flaring mustache and forked beard was no doubt Rostam, the epic warrior whose strength upheld the throne of king after king, and whose tragedy was to kill his son unwittingly in single combat. He sat in perfect proportion on a white steed defined by curves that coiled with energy. In the background, devoid of any perspective except that of imagined history, were a few loyal riders and foot soldiers. Their wide eyes—and Rostam's own sad, distant stare—seemed to gather up all the glowering of those male eyes that had followed me across the room and discharge their energy on the plains of legend.

"Will you sell this?" I asked the manager.

"No, Khanom, this is a painting for the people." I had recognized as much, but he explained it from his point of view: "The people see it, and they come to the coffeehouse."

"I'm a person too, just like those people." I meant it sincerely. Hadn't the painting drawn me here? "If you're willing to sell it, I'll buy it and you can use the money to get another one."

He wouldn't sell, and the painting hung above the square for many more years. But he did give me directions to another coffeehouse where more such paintings could be found. One coffeehouse led to another, and over endless glasses of tea—tea was the only drink ever served; the name "coffeehouse" must have stuck from an earlier time—I began to learn about these "paintings for the people."

The oldest were said to date from the beginning of the nineteenth century, but the layers of grime that gathered on them in the smoke-filled rooms made even the new ones quickly look old. The paintings illustrated scenes from Ferdowsi's epic *Shahnameh,* ancient stories that stirred the pride of every Iranian. Professional storytellers had made the paintings come alive, reciting the epic in a sonorous chant to an audience gathered for an evening at the coffeehouse. Religious stories were also painted—the martyrdom of Hossein and his family at Kerbala, or the torments awaiting sinners at the final judgment. These too were recounted with much emotion poured out by both storyteller and listeners. Timeless events were cast as fresh news: you could often recognize the features of Reza Shah in the grimace of hell's gatekeeper, stirring a boiling pot of sinners—or else those same familiar features appeared on a sinner's face in the pot, depending on the artist's political persuasion.

Sometimes the storytellers performed outside the coffeehouses, moving to a public square or the entrance to the bazaar for a broader audience that included women and children. For these street performances the paintings were rendered on loose canvas, called a *pardeh,* or screen, and hung from two sticks held up by assistants. A curtain would veil the image until the storyteller dramatically flipped it over the back to announce the beginning of his tale.

With the advent of radio, professional storytellers fell out of favor, and coffeehouse paintings were seen as old-fashioned. Eventually television would deal the final blow, and the old canvases were

THIS COFFEEHOUSE PAINTING DEPICTING ROSTAM DEFEATING ESFANDIAR WAS SHOWN AT THE IRAN-AMERICA SOCIETY'S 1967 EXHIBITION IN TEHRAN.

junked or picked up for a pittance by antique dealers. In their stead a framed photograph might take pride of place in a coffeehouse, perhaps of the Shah or often of Takhti, the wrestling champion who had caught the country's imagination, the new Rostam.

But at the time I first became aware of the paintings in 1958, the earliest television broadcasts had just begun from a single private station, and artists were still painting the stories in the old way. The paintings were commissioned by the coffeehouse owners, who would also choose the subjects. The artist, and perhaps an assistant, would sleep in a corner of the coffeehouse for the duration of the job. In addition to offering a roof, the coffeehouse owner paid for the paint and canvas, provided food, and ensured a supply of cigarettes and opium. The artist would not negotiate a fee but could generally expect a donation.

As I scoured the city in search of these paintings, I soon realized that no one would sell to a woman in the unwaveringly male environment of the coffeehouses. So I would make an initial visit to scout the scene, under cover in a chador and escorted by Mostafa, who took some pride in his new role as art critic; then I would send Mostafa back alone to negotiate.

Once we got word that there were six or seven especially beautiful paintings in a coffeehouse near the Sepahsalar mosque. Soon we were sipping tea, whispering across the table with a wink here, a nod there. I fumbled awkwardly with the tea glass as I tried to keep the chador in place with one hand.

"Mostafa, what about the one behind me? How does it look?"

"It's interesting, Khanom, but you have to judge it yourself."

I stole a glance over my shoulder. Rostam had a stranglehold on the throat of a *div*. The monster's plaster-white skin was pocked with pustules, his eyes popping from their sockets, his tongue protruding fearsomely. I turned back to face a man looming over our table, leering at me. His clothes were smeared with white plaster. He slammed his huge mason's hand down on the table and said to Mostafa, "Get up, man, it's my turn with her." Mostafa rose without an instant's hesitation, as if his moment had finally arrived.

"Who are you talking to?" As he squared his shoulders, I fled, pulling the chador tight across my face and mumbling through it that I would head for my mother's house. I ran across the street and hailed a taxi.

Half an hour later Mostafa showed up at my mother's door with a proud grin under the blood that was streaming from his nose: "Khanom, you got me into a good fight!" I fussed over his wounds as my mother groaned over my ill-conceived disguise. I had forgotten to remove my makeup. A chador worn with lipstick and eye shadow was anything but a signal of modesty; it was the normal advertisement for a prostitute.

Eventually the collection grew to nearly sixty paintings, though both my own family and Abol's criticized me mercilessly for wasting money on this "garbage that smells of opium." Two artists figured especially prominently in the collection, Hossein Ghollar Aghassi and Mohammad Modaber. Both had earned a considerable reputation as coffeehouse painters in Tehran, but to my eyes Modaber was the better. (It was he who had done the paintings at the coffeehouse near Sepahsalar mosque.) When I heard about an exceptionally large *pardeh* that he had painted, I immediately sent Mostafa to the owner to make an offer, sight unseen. He refused to sell it. I went myself and begged him. In all my searching, I had never seen such a masterly work. It was more than five meters wide, divided into small panels that portrayed, in sequence, the complete story of the martyrdom at Kerbala. The story unfolded in passionate detail, with a surrealistic vision of the universe emanating from this core of the Shi'ite faith.

The owner was a deeply religious man and feared to see the painting fall into the hands of an unbeliever. I myself feared that if it ever got into the hands of a dealer, believer or not, it would soon be sold out of the country. For a year I tried sincerely, over and over, to win his trust with every angle I could think of. It was no use. Finally I realized that I would have to lie, even if I boiled in hell in the same pot as Reza Shah. My sister Sediqeh, who was bound to a wheelchair by then, agreed to back up my story. I told him that I had vowed to donate the painting to a shrine in hopes that my prayers for Sediqeh's recovery would be answered. At this he finally agreed to sell. The painting was mine, the particular shrine became vague, and poor Sediqeh stayed in her wheelchair. What will happen in hell remains to be seen.

In spite of their renown, both Modaber and Ghollar Aghassi remained very poor all their lives. Modaber had passed away before I could track him down, but after a long search I found Ghollar Aghassi in a hospital bed near the end of his life. He would not accept any offer of help and said very little, uncomfortable to be receiving a female stranger at his bedside. When I told him that I had many of his paintings, and they had brought much pleasure, he said only, "Very good, Khanom. God willing, you'll take care of them."

I did. I was concerned about the condition of the paintings, darkened by years in the smoke-filled coffeehouses. The ones that were beginning to appear in antique shops were kept rolled and often were damaged. The artists used a cheap, locally woven canvas that they prepared themselves, and sometimes when oil paint was too expensive, they made do with a gouache of egg yolk and powdered pigment that chipped badly when rolled. As an art student, I had not learned the technical skills of restoration, but I knew that it was possible. I found a dealer who did some repairs and brought a few pieces to him. He was less than agreeable to deal with, and secretive—whenever I walked into the shop, everything on his worktable would suddenly disappear. But I recognized the chemical smell that filled the room and began to read and experiment. Finally I hired a man who came to my home to work on the paintings. I taught him what I had learned by trial and error, rubbing the surface gently with a soft cloth moistened with denatured alcohol, cleaning the back of the canvas and oiling it, repairing the broken stretchers. The retouching I did myself.

I took care of the coffeehouse paintings in other ways too. Barbara Spring, director of the cultural center at the Iran-America Society, had become a very close friend. Together, in 1967, we arranged to exhibit the collection at the Iran-America Society. The show was mounted beautifully: we transformed the galleries into a coffeehouse with tea served from a huge samovar. A traditional storyteller explained the paintings to visitors, and a fine catalog was printed with a scholarly preface by Karim Emami. The opening was attended by the American ambassador and his wife, and by more ministers and ministers' wives than I could be bothered to count.

When the coffeehouse paintings had first appeared on the walls of my home, my in-laws had laughed. "What is this garbage you've found? Why don't you save your money and buy a real Qajar painting?" Yes, I was buying the paintings at a typical price of twenty or thirty dollars—less than a tenth of what Qajar court paintings sold

I AM AT THE IRAN-AMERICA SOCIETY'S EXHIBITION OF COFFEEHOUSE
PAINTINGS, WITH THE WIFE OF THE MINISTER OF COURT,
A GUEST, THE MINISTER OF COURT, AND NICHOLAS THACHER,
THE AMERICAN CHARGÉ D'AFFAIRS.

for. But that wasn't the point. I loved the primitive paintings, their sincerity and their surrealism, their view into the people's soul. To see them honored finally was a victory worthy of the old heroes of the epic.

That first exhibition shattered the elite prejudice against folk art, and the coffeehouse paintings suddenly became fashionable. I continued collecting, regardless. One day the phone rang, and I was shocked to hear the queen introducing herself to me at the other end of the line. She had heard about my coffeehouse paintings and wanted to know more. I put my hand over the receiver and asked Abol in a panic how I was supposed to address her.

"Tell her, 'I bow to you,' " he said.

"That doesn't make sense! How can I bow on the phone?"

"Just say it, Khanom." *How silly,* I thought. I decided to forgo the protocol and speak from the heart. I told her that I believed these paintings were an important national treasure. Eventually Queen Farah arranged for the collection to be shown in Paris at the Maison de l'Iran. The opening was packed, so much so that people were leaning on the paintings in the crush. When the queen's progress through the crowd brought her to where I was standing, she found me with both arms outstretched in front of a canvas. "Why are you standing like that?" she asked. I explained: I was trying to protect the paintings.

CHAPTER TWENTY-ONE

The year after I began working on the garden in Elahieh, the flowers bloomed in a feast of color. I picked huge bouquets to decorate the house and immersed myself in the ritual of arrangement, but I wanted to drink still more deeply of those purples and yellows and reds. I cleared a corner of the bedroom and unpacked my paints and brushes, untouched since New York. Zahra had started preschool by then, and Nima was settled in comfortably at the international Community School. They left with Abol each morning, leaving me to my own devices for most of the day. I painted flowers endlessly, not still life in the traditional sense but fireworks of color, direct emotional responses to the life that was exploding before my eyes.

I took a trip abroad for a couple of weeks to visit Leila and her husband, who had moved to Egypt. When I arrived home, Abol announced, "Khanom, I have a surprise for you." He took me upstairs, then up more stairs that had not existed when I left. They led to a large, well-lit room on the roof. "I think you have a space now where you can do your artwork," he said.

It felt so good to be making art again. I had hardly been idle, but without realizing it I had missed the absorption of playing with color and composition for its own sake, free of the constraints of practical design. I felt a certain nostalgia too for my student days and the exercise of making art just to see what you could learn from it. The spacious new studio was an invitation to experiment with new techniques, to spread out without worrying about making a mess. I recalled the monotypes that Milton Avery had taught me to do, painting on smooth linoleum and then pressing canvas onto the painting to make a print of it. And I wanted to try some nudes again, to reconnect with fundamentals. I asked Abol if he would pose for me. We shut ourselves up in the rooftop studio on a weekend when most of the servants were gone. I laid a sheet of linoleum on the floor and painted an almost life-size portrait of Abol in the nude, then printed it as a monotype. It wasn't my best work by far—the proportions were distorted by working so large on the floor—but we were having too much fun for that to matter.

The flower paintings lent themselves quite naturally to monotypes, the transfer process muting my explosions of color. The linoleum was heavy and hard to handle, so instead I tried painting on a piece of glass and printing from that. Then I realized that I could pull prints even from paintings on canvas if the paint was wet enough with linseed oil and turpentine. One day, frustrated with trying to print from a painting on glass that was not quite wet enough, I grabbed a metal spray pump of insecticide that was lying around and sprayed a few flits at the canvas. The tints bled softly together, reminding me of Renoir's translucent layers of color on color. By spraying the same painting again and again, I found I could make several prints, each one unique. I pressed the paper onto the glass or canvas with my hands, the uneven pressure bringing out subtle effects.

"Khanom, just use kerosene," Abol advised me. "That's the base of it anyway. Please don't soak your hands in DDT!"

By 1963 I had finished around a hundred of the monotypes of flowers. It seemed like a good time to do something with them beyond letting them pile up. I approached the fine arts department at Tehran University, which held exhibitions that rotated every month, and asked if they would give me a show. The teachers I knew there had all left years before, but I hoped that someone might look kindly on an old student. They did, and it was my first solo exhibition.

(I had never shown my work in New York, except to close friends. I had, however, shown a couple of pieces in Venice a few years before in 1958. I had stumbled on a small gallery of modern art in Tehran and got to know the owner, Marco Gregorian, who was also an artist. One day he called me: he had been asked to recommend an Iranian artist for the Venice Biennale and wanted to see my work. I had not yet started on the flower paintings then, so I showed him a few small abstract monotypes that I brought from New York, rather like miniature Jackson Pollocks. He was impressed and submitted them. I flew to Venice for the opening, very excited. I wasn't prepared for the strange shock of seeing my work amid hundreds of other images, all of them far better, I thought, than those miserable little prints hanging in a corner labeled "Iranian Artist." I was even more shocked when I learned that I had won a gold medal. Perhaps that experience

MONIR SHAHROUDY FARMANFARMAIAN AT
HER FIRST SOLO EXHIBITION.

was a necessary initiation in self-exposure. In any case, I was far
more comfortable with the show at Tehran University.)

I found a frame-maker and worked side by side with him to make
frames that suited the delicacy of the images and avoided the heavy,
ornate style that was then fashionable in Tehran. I set the prices very
low, the most expensive at about a hundred dollars and small ones for
less than twenty dollars.

I even steeled myself to do a brief television interview to publicize
the show. I mentioned my childhood in Qazvin and how the flowers
and nightingales on the old wooden ceilings had given me a taste for
painting flowers. Later Parviz Tanavoli, a friend and artist whose
family also came from Qazvin, told me that his mother had scolded
him: "You see—she is not ashamed to say she is from Qazvin!"

My parents were even more excited about the show than I was.
When my father saw the crowd at the opening, he said to me, "Don't
forget to tell them your name is Monir *Shahroudy* Farmanfarmaian."
It was probably the most explicit compliment I ever received from

him. There was a very nice write-up in one of the Tehran papers, but not all of the feedback was favorable.

"You went all the way to America to study art, and now you paint flowers?"

"Have you sold enough to cover the cost of the frames?"

One of Abol's sisters bought a painting after long deliberation, then returned it a few days later. I took these slights far more seriously than I should have, but all in all I was very happy with the exhibition.

After all the fuss I went back to my rooftop studio, now suddenly quiet as if with anticipation. What could I do next? I made a few more monotypes on glass, working from sheer habit. Once, after I lifted a print and picked up the glass to move it to another table, I realized that the image seen from behind the glass itself was quite lovely, with the brush texture of the flowers showing semitranslucent. I started to play with painting behind glass. I propped up a sheet of glass and built the image in reverse, twisting one arm around the back of the image or on larger pieces moving back and forth to see the effects of my brushstrokes. I tried a few on very thick sheets of glass that added a new depth and brilliance to the colors. Sometimes I added backgrounds of gold and silver leaf behind the flowers. I experimented with monotypes printed from one piece of glass to another: when I pressed with the palm of my hand, the paint sandwiched between the two sheets of glass spread in abstract, organic tendrils blending in jewel colors like an undersea dream.

The materials themselves were leading me, but at the same time I was being pulled by the memory of paintings behind glass from the Qajar period that I had seen in antique shops or in the old homes that Javad Agha showed me in Qazvin. I started to collect these antique paintings on glass, making expeditions as a break from experimenting in the studio. Many of them were familiar stylized flowers and nightingales, or fish that promised good luck in a dry land. There were landscapes too, and paintings of famous buildings from earlier centuries with primitive attempts at perspective. Many were portraits of the Qajar court: I recognized their features from other paintings on canvas. I found an especially fine portrait on glass of the infamously beautiful princess Taj-ol Soltaneh.

Many of the Qajar glass paintings, especially those used as architectural decoration, were done on oval or square panels of mirror. The painted images of flowers, nightingales, and fish spilled into the surrounding border of mirror. I thought to copy the effect and took one of my paintings to a mirror factory in Tehran. I asked them to pour the mercury backing around the edge of the painting. I was surprised that the mercury formed a heavy black line where it met the oil paint. It was not a bad effect in itself, but it seemed to flatten the image and was very different from the delicate Qajar paintings that floated on a mirrored background behind the thickness of the glass. When I looked more closely at the old panels, I realized that the mirror coating had been laid on first and then scratched off in precisely the areas that were to be painted. It was an incredible investment of labor, and I could find no other way to reproduce the effect. I put the mirrors aside for the time being.

In 1966 I had a second exhibition at the Italian Institute in Tehran. The show caught the attention of Heydar Ghiai, who, as the Shah's official architect, was designing a new building for the Senate. He asked if I would paint some panels of *gol o bolbol*—flowers and nightingales—for the reception room. It was my first commission, and I was excited for a variety of reasons. I could relate to Ghiai's work, which was determinedly modernist in style and yet incorporated traditional themes. I felt a curious pleasure in returning to the architectural roots of the imagery that I had chosen, and even a sense of poetic justice in this modern incarnation of court art. Not to mention a certain delight in being able to make my father proud on his own turf, right there in the lofty halls of the very imposing new Senate building.

A hundred wooden panels in various sizes were cut and prepared by the master carpenter, covered completely with fine gold leaf, and then carried up to my rooftop studio. I painted the bird and flower motifs in blue-green acrylic, which, unknown in Iran, was brought specially from Germany. After some practice I found I could use a single, continuous brushstroke for each section of the design. The line that emerged was as fluid as calligraphy. It was definitely my own, and yet it echoed the practiced ease of the craftsmen who had made thousands of panels in the old homes of Qazvin. I was very pleased.

I was not so pleased when I saw the panels installed. In fact, I was appalled. They had been coated with a brownish shellac, then scratched roughly with a wire brush. In the heat of a righteous fit of anger, I chased down the architect and demanded to know why my work had been destroyed. Mohandes Ghiai, who was a very large man to begin with, grew several feet before my eyes and informed me that he was the conductor of this symphony, and I was one small violin. He wanted the panels to look old, and so he had had them "distressed." I acknowledged that the panels were very distressed indeed, and so was I. I took my revenge in a small way. Ghiai had stipulated a particular condition when he first gave me the commission: that I not sign the work. I took a pen and a bottle of ink into the reception hall and signed each one of those poor, distressed panels, threading my name, sometimes in English and sometimes in Persian, through the leafy tendrils.

After that small drama I was surprised that Ghiai came back to me a few months later with another request. There was a problem with the windows on one wall of the building where the Shah himself would stand exposed to outside view when he addressed the Majles. Security demanded a curtain. Aesthetics crumpled at the thought. Would I consider designing a treatment for the windows, an artwork on glass that would screen the Shah from view? After some discussion the conductor and I settled on a plan to repeat the same bird-and-flower motif that I had used on the panels, painted in enamel on colored glass. A kiln was needed to bake the enamel into the glass, and so I located a factory that specialized in reproductions of the ornate painted glassware and chandeliers of the Qajar period, which in turn were modeled on glass imported from Bohemia and Russia. The factory was located in an old neighborhood in south Tehran and was essentially a large workshop using traditional methods. The workers would not welcome a woman in their midst, so I arranged to use the facilities after hours.

For three weeks I went down to the factory every evening at six o'clock, descending for more than an hour through narrowing streets as the winter darkness fell and the city lit up and the sidewalk crowds grew dense with people leaving work and shopping for the evening meal. My friend Nicole came along, officially as my assistant, but more than anything to keep me company during the long nights. The proprietor unlocked the deserted factory and then left for the night. One of his workers, Mr. Azizkhan, stayed to keep an eye on things and run the kiln. Mr. Azizkhan was a wrestler in his spare time, his huge arms covered with religious tattoos, and he was giving up his evening practice at the *zoorkhaneh* for this business of protecting the Shah with glass. The driver would drop us off, fetch a dinner of *chelo kebab* for the group—one portion each for me, Nicole, and himself, and three for Mr. Azizkhan—and then doze off in the car.

The night factory was magical. I experimented first with colors, playing with the many types of glass and enamel, including much gold, that were used for the chandeliers and ornamental glassware. I settled on a salmon-pink glass imported from France, with white enamel, painting the *gol o bolbol* again as much as possible with a single continuous brushstroke. It was coming up to Christmas, so I took the opportunity also to paint several glass bowls and bottles for gifts, signing them with a parody of the gold inscriptions on the antique Qajar copies of Bohemian glass that named the courtier who had commissioned the work. Nicole kept the brushes washed and Mr. Azizkhan mixed the enamel glazes. At times I chattered while I worked, teasing Mr. Azizkhan at every opportunity. At around two or three in the morning I would run out of steam and wake the driver. Mr. Azizkhan would load the kiln and light it—by the time the factory came to life in the morning, that batch would be done—and we would head home through the deserted streets, dark except for the dusting of snow in the headlights.

After the job was finished and Mohandes Ghiai had expressed his complete satisfaction with the work, it occurred to me that perhaps I should be paid. I had no contract, not even a word and a handshake. The architect had never discussed a fee, as if he didn't want to offend the dignity of the wife of a Farmanfarmaian with such venal concerns. Money was not the real question; it was professional pride that was screaming inside me like an ignored two-year-old. I wrestled with the knowledge that I would never have found myself in this situation if I were not a woman.

In a sudden bout of certainty I called the speaker of the Senate, Mr. Sharif Emami, and made an appointment. I dressed for the occasion as if for a meeting with my boss at Bonwit Teller, Chanel shoes and all. He very graciously promised to look into the matter, without revealing the slightest hint of condescension or the certain knowledge that nothing whatsoever would come of my request.

After the meeting I hailed a cab for the long ride home. Perhaps it was the democratic inspiration of the Senate building or the feminist bee in my bonnet that day, but for some reason I sat in the front seat next to the driver. He took the recently opened Jordan expressway, the first thing resembling a freeway to be built in Iran, and was clearly enjoying a radically new experience of speed—when he hit the center divider, barely missing a cluster of workmen who were planting bushes on the center strip. The car flipped into the air and landed on its side, with the driver in a heap on top of me. He was shouting in confusion and panic directly into my ear, and I tried to reassure him from my compromised position that really everything was all right. Through the window I could see boots, then a face bending close.

"Khanom, are you all right?"

"I'm fine, but he's on top of me."

Ten or twelve men with hard hats and shovels surrounded the car. With much heaving and many cries of *Ya Ali!* they pushed it over onto its wheels. They managed to pry the door open and pulled us out. My legs were shaking, so I sat down on the edge of the gutter. Traffic had stopped, and the crowd was growing. A woman approached me.

"Can I help you? Are you pregnant?" She seemed seriously worried. I assured her that my brief entanglement with the driver had not resulted in any roadside impregnation, but she insisted on driving me home anyway. I hesitated to leave the scene of the accident, which was rapidly escalating into chaos. The taxi driver was sitting on the ground weeping loudly, surrounded by a crowd pouring curses and threats of civic action on his head. A couple of the hard hats were waving their shovels ominously. I pushed through the crowd to give the driver his promised fare, which only increased the volume of the threats and redirected some of them toward me: "Why are you paying this *pedar-sokhteh*? He almost killed you!"

As it happened, my rescuer was an obstetrician on her way to the hospital and was simply eager to offer help in the way she knew best. I had to reassure her several times more that I was not pregnant. The only damage at all was one torn Chanel shoe. In the end I never got paid for my work on the Senate building, or for most of the commissions I did in Iran. And whenever I had a hankering to stand on principle, I couldn't help but ask myself if it was worth the trouble, whatever bizarre form that trouble might take.

With the excitement of the Senate commission behind me, I continued painting behind glass. A couple of years later the mirrors entered my life again, this time in dazzling force. Marcia Hafif and Robert Morris, the minimalist artists, had come to Iran for a visit, and I offered to take them sightseeing.

We went to Shiraz, the city of poets in the ancient heartland of Pars. At the Shah Cheraq shrine Marcia and I donned chadors, and the three of us sat for hours in a high-domed hall that was covered entirely—every inch of every surface—in a mosaic of tiny mirrors cut into hexagons, squares, and triangles, each piece set at a slightly different angle. The very space seemed on fire, the lamps blazing in hundreds of thousands of reflections. I imagined myself standing inside a many-faceted diamond and looking out at the sun. Women came and went, ethereal in white chadors, trailing children awed into silence. The motions of their prayers, bowing, rising, prostrating, echoed in angled fragments. Splashes of color rippled like jagged lightning across the walls and domed ceiling. It was a universe unto itself, architecture transformed into performance, all movement and fluid light, all solids fractured and dissolved in brilliance, in space, in prayer. I was overwhelmed.

I had seen mirror mosaics of Shah Cheraq before, as well as those in the shrine at Mashhad and the Golestan Palace in Tehran, and they were often used in a smaller way on trim and molding in the old Qajar homes. But I had never experienced them with such intensity as I did that day in Shiraz. The art had originated a couple of centuries ago, when the aristocracy began to import mirrors from Venice. Too often the mirrors arrived in pieces, so craftsmen salvaged the fragments and used them in much the same way as they worked with tile mosaics. I came home from Shiraz fired up with ideas, determined to bring the mirror mosaics into my own work. I poured my enthusiasm out to Abol. "Of course. It will be easy," he said.

Not so, I thought; but Abol was intrigued by the technical challenge. When he learned that a friend was building a new home using mirror mosaic in a traditional way for the decoration, he arranged for us to visit the building in progress. We found a man sitting on the floor, cutting mirrors into tiny pieces with the speed and assurance of a lifetime of practice. His two assistants were setting the glittering pieces into wet plaster directly on the wall. The man cutting mirrors stood up to greet us, and the owner of the home introduced him as Hajji Ostad Mohammad Navid—Hajji because he had made the pilgrimage to Mecca, and Ostad, which means "teacher," because he

THE MIRROR MASTER, HAJJI OSTAD MOHAMMAD NAVID.

was recognized as a master craftsman. Few meetings have been so important in my life; Hajji Ostad immediately became my teacher.

I asked about the medium he used as a base. He explained how they "killed" the plaster by kneading it for hours so that it would stay pliable instead of setting hard immediately. He showed me the *sereesh,* a liquid brown glue made from the pounded root of a tree that they added to the plaster to further slow its setting. It was also used in bookbinding, he told me. It smelled foul. I asked if he would come to my studio when his work on the house was finished and teach me more about his craft. He put his hand on his chest and politely made modest excuses.

In the end he agreed to come, but it wasn't easy. He was a very religious man and wasn't comfortable working for a woman. His usual clients—the sort of people who could afford to decorate a room with mirror mosaics—were men of exceptional wealth and old-fashioned tastes. Hajji Ostad was puzzled, to say the least, by what I wanted him to do.

I quickly gave up on the idea of asking him to teach me to cut the mirrors myself. This was master's work that he had done since the age of seven, and even his assistants were no match for him. The mirror he used was unusually fine, specially made in Belgium for the

Iranian market and half the gauge of the thinnest mirror found in America. Hajji Ostad could cut it like butter, producing strips so narrow and long that they bent under their own weight like stalks of grass when I placed a handful in a vase. I gave him patterns on paper—stars, triangles, strips, and crescents—and asked him to cut twenty of these, a hundred of those . . . I gave him also some of the abstract paintings behind glass I had done and asked him to cut those in pieces. He was mystified but curious enough to continue.

For a long time I pondered the problem of how to create a frame or a base that would hold the plaster and mirrors independent of a wall. Abol was eager to help and came up with the idea of using steel frames around a steel mesh to hold the plaster in place. I made the first few pieces on those frames, but they were too heavy to be practical. It took three or four men to lift the finished artwork when the steel was covered with plaster and glass. Then I happened to visit a factory owned by a friend who was starting production of plastic chairs molded from an epoxy mixture. He had asked me to look at the process and see if I might contribute some designs. The epoxy was noxious stuff, but I thought somehow it might be useful, so I begged a couple of cans to experiment with. I mixed the chemicals and spread the mess on a piece of plywood, hoping it would serve as a base to hold the plaster. Hajji Ostad shook his head. "It will never work; the surface is too smooth." So I tried again, this time strewing coarse sand on the epoxy before it set. "This might do," said Hajji Ostad, still looking doubtful. I also bought a big jar of Elmer's glue and suggested that we might mix it into the plaster instead of *sereesh*. Hajji Ostad was pleased. The glue worked well, it didn't smell, and it was much easier to handle.

With all the pieces finally at hand, I began to compose, building images spontaneously from fragments of mirror and painted glass. I incorporated small fragments also from some of the Qajar paintings on glass that had broken: a glimpse of a nightingale, a few petals of a flower, a fish swimming through waves of glass. Something new, something old, all swirling together in a dazzle of light and color and unpredictable angles.

Hajji Ostad couldn't quite believe it was working. Every so often he would pick up a piece we had finished a few weeks before and shake it to see if anything fell off, then shake his head in disbelief. His reluctance to work for me faded gradually. It didn't hurt that I paid him whatever he asked, and his price crept up every few weeks.

IRISES, MIRROR, OLD AND NEW REVERSE-GLASS PAINTING,
PLASTER ON WOOD, 1973.

"Khanom, Dr. Fallah has asked me to work on his house. He's offering me ten *toman* more than you are paying."

"Don't go, Hajji Ostad. I'll pay you as much as he will."

"Thank you, Khanom."

"Never mind, you're worth it. No one else can do such beautiful work as you do."

"Yes, Khanom. Thank you."

Hajji Ostad's coming and going through the bedroom to the rooftop studio was awkward, so Abol had another stairway built outside. Finally we outgrew that room and built a much larger studio in the garden, where Hajji Ostad set up quite a camp. With his assistants there were sometimes as many as seven or eight of us working together, especially later when we did some large installations. I saw to it that tea was served throughout the day, with cakes at ten o'clock

and a big lunch for everyone. Two of his workers smoked opium and
would droop a little at intervals, but Hajji Ostad would wake them
with a shout: "Ahmad Agha, get up! It's time for work! No snoozing!"

When I was confident of Hajji Ostad's support and comfortable
with the technique, I decided to work on a larger scale and return to
the architectural roots of the art. I did the ceilings of the girls' bedrooms and the wall of our fireplace. The work was admired by family
and friends, which led to many commissions: another fireplace for
Abol's brother, a ceiling for a friend, two walls and columns for the
Intercontinental Hotel, two more for the Farhangsara cultural center.

I call them commissions, but I was rarely paid. The business skills
I had learned in order to survive as a designer in New York seemed to
vanish when they were no longer needed. With Abol's support I
needed nothing, and it seemed inappropriate to ask for money from
friends. On the contrary, I felt a responsibility to support other artists,
and I bought far more than I could possibly hang in my home, bought
like a collector, simply to show my appreciation. But it bothered me
in a quiet way that my own work did not seem to deserve the same
respect. It was as if my marriage had automatically conferred on me
the status of a dilettante, and I feared my art would never be taken
seriously.

My silent dilemma came to a head on a visit to Paris. Teresa Bat-
testi, a journalist who had written a very generous review of one
of my shows in Tehran, gave me an introduction to the Galerie de
France. It was perhaps the most important gallery of modern art in
Paris, showing Picasso, Matisse, too many great names to count.
What the hell, I thought, *I have nothing to lose.* I brought them a few
small abstract paintings behind glass.

"Very unusual. I like this. Can you do this work on a larger scale?"

I was flying. I would have built the pyramids if he asked. "Of
course. This is only what I could fit in my suitcase."

"Can you stay in Paris?"

"For how long?"

"For good."

My heart sank. "But I have a family, a husband, a home . . ."

He made a gesture with his hand as if to brush all that away. "Your
work is very fresh to Western eyes, and I like it. But we can't give a
show to everyone who walks in the door. We have to believe in the
artist's commitment to the continuity of the work. This is our policy.

It takes time to develop relationships with collectors and critics. But I like the work well enough to tell you that in two years I could give you a show here. That's not a promise, but a half promise."

"I'm sorry, I'm married, I have children—but I could come often to Paris."

"There's no way I can give you a show if you live in Iran. Forget it."

Forget it? Easier said than done. I came home to Tehran very upset. When I was barely over my jet lag, I went with Abol to a big dinner party. The guest of honor was Sir Eric Drake, head of the British oil consortium who was visiting Tehran. We had met before, and at one point during the evening we found ourselves talking alone in a corner of the garden.

"What have you been up to, Monir?"

I told him what had just happened in Paris. By the end of the story, I couldn't control my tears and they came flooding out. He took my hand, and I expected empty noises of sympathy, but instead he gave me hell.

"Monir, what are you doing at this party? Why did you come?"

"Well, my husband—"

"Your husband can take care of himself. Quit this stupid social life! You're wasting your time! Go home! Go home right now and work on your art. If the Galerie de France thinks you're an artist, then you're an artist. Yes, you look beautiful, but in two or three years, who will remember what you wore tonight? Go home and make art that will not be forgotten."

I thank him still for that knock on the head. I didn't entirely become a hermit, but I let a great many social obligations go unfulfilled. People talked, said I thought myself too good for their company, but I didn't care. I wanted only to work.

Shortly after that the mirrors led me into the mysteries of geometry. I asked Hajji Ostad to show me the traditional patterns, the ones he used in his own work. He gave me a few samples. When I looked at them closely, I realized that they were variations on a mathematical theme. Under all the intricate angles a simpler rhythm repeated itself on a larger scale, honeycombs of implied hexagons, or octagons. I asked Hajji Ostad how he laid out the patterns on a wall, and he

IN MY STUDIO AT HOME, 1975.

showed me using a piece of string, anchored with his thumb to make a compass. Rubbed with a little charcoal dust, pulled taut, and snapped, it drew a straight line. With nothing more than this string, he could make an infinite variety of patterns grow like crystals over an entire wall and fit the tiles with perfect symmetry, the last one slipping neatly into place without the tiniest margin of error.

This was a marvel indeed. I wanted to get to the root of it. I needed to learn geometry. I bought books. I went to the math teacher at Nima's school and asked him to tutor me. I read up on Sufi cosmology and the arcane symbolism of shapes, how the universe is expressed through points and lines and angles, how form is born of numbers and the elements lock in the hexagon. I traced the logic of the great Iranian astronomers, even made a pilgrimage to the ancient observatory at Maragheh. Much of what I learned I have forgotten. Was Hajji Ostad aware of the volumes of knowledge that twisted through his patterns? When I tried to use too many words, we always came back to his string.

The geometric patterns began to infiltrate my own art. I used them not quite faithfully but with a minimalist twist, relishing the clean, modern lines that appeared when the mathematical logic was distilled from the traditional designs. I mixed the mirrors and painted glass with stainless steel, each tiny piece angled just so in small patterns repeating precisely over huge fields. I grew the hexagons large and pure in isolation, drew them with long, sheer lines of mirror on voids of clean white plaster incised and beveled to echo the lines of light. Revealing the plaster opened a whole new vista of possibilities. The snowy matte surfaces made a beautiful contrast with the glistening mirror, like earth and water distilled into two different faces of purity, and the colors of painted-glass accents gleamed with a startling clarity against the intense white.

Carving the plaster gave the pieces a sense of sculptural relief, and it was a short step from that to freestanding sculpture. Freed from the limits of two dimensions, the geometric shapes seemed to extract their mathematical essence from space itself. I designed steel forms—returning to Abol's original idea, he was more than happy to see to the fabrication—but they were lighter now, the shapes embracing large open voids. And I leaned again on Hajji Ostad, who was no less skilled at *gach-bori*, the traditional art of carving plaster for architectural decoration, than he was with mirrors.

The amazement I felt at watching his skill in action never faded, no matter how familiar it became. It was magic to me every time to watch the strips of mirror peel off under the steady motion of his hand. It was pure wizardry to see the universe of patterns that tumbled out of the twang of his piece of string. I came to an even deeper appreciation of that wizardry when I later did an installation of mirror work in New York without his help. It took a firm of architects many expensive hours of computer time to calculate how to extend my design in the space. Hajji Ostad could have laid it out in a few minutes with his piece of string.

CHAPTER TWENTY-TWO

The few brief tastes I had sampled of the country beyond Tehran—my forays into old Qazvin, or to Abadan with Abol, or vacationing with friends on the Caspian coast—made me hungry to explore the vast and wildly varied landscape of Iran. I jumped at any excuse for a trip: a chance meeting with an archaeologist who had come into town from a distant dig, an invitation from the khan of a tribe to visit his tents, a tip from an antique dealer that led to a remote village. Because every mile between here and there was ripe with serendipitous possibilities, I traveled by road whenever I could.

That required a driver. By 1965 we had hired and fired a succession of them who were nothing but trouble. Then Sasha came into our lives and never left. At the time he came to work for us, he was in his midforties but already his hair was white. He was an Armenian whose family had escaped to Iran from the revolution in Russia when he was a child. He spoke Armenian, Russian, and Persian very well and picked up a little English too. When Sasha became part of our family, his family was part of the package. Sasha's mother sewed beautiful patchwork quilts for me. His wife, Emma Khanom, was a seamstress too, and they had one son, Varoush, who was an exceptionally polite and intelligent child. When he was older, we helped to send Varoush to Europe for college.

Sasha was indeed a character, but the sweetest of souls. He was very much a gentleman, mild-mannered, soft-spoken, always punctual, and impeccably honest. It's usual for a driver to compete with the cook for top position in the hierarchy of servants. While the cook controls a substantial budget for groceries and influences a vital portion of the family's day-to-day sensorium as well as their hospitality, the driver is entrusted with an outrageously expensive piece of equipment, access to the world at large, and the opportunity to eavesdrop on private conversations. Before Sasha, all of our drivers had fought with the cook and lorded their power over the other servants. Mostafa, the rogue who accompanied me into the world of the coffeehouses, had once even

ABOL AND HIS DOPPELGÄNGER, SASHA.

pulled a knife on the cook. But Sasha had too much dignity to stoop to such nonsense, and he kept a polite distance from the other servants.

He was very distinguished looking. Once after a long absence we stopped at the boatyard where Abol kept his sailboat. Some of the workers mistook Sasha for Abol and addressed him with effusive respect. He was painfully embarrassed and tried to move a distance away from me. "Never mind, Sasha," I said. "Nobody knows the difference. If they think you're my husband, then that's who you are for the moment."

Sasha was deeply devoted to Abol and even more so to Zahra, who had a special empathy with him. Once on a long drive she asked to sit in the front seat, then suddenly broke into song—in perfect Russian! Sasha blushed and covered his face with his hand. "Zahra Khanom!" he pleaded, laughing with embarrassment that the songs he sang for her on their drives to school were being exposed to other ears.

My own relationship with Sasha developed slowly. He was reluctant at first to take me out of town, fearing the burden of responsibility as the man of the car. If anything untoward should happen to me, how would he answer to Abol? Whenever curiosity beckoned and I told him, "Sasha, let's turn here and see where that road leads," he turned pale.

"I'm sorry, Khanom Doctor, the Volvo can't go there." He always called me "doctor" as a gesture of respect, however baseless. The Volvo was always his first excuse.

"Well, let's try it and see. If worse comes to worst, we'll turn around." The first time we hit bad luck and got stuck in the mud, Sasha was in such a frightful panic that I made him sit down— "Sasha, calm down, it really doesn't matter"—and went for help myself. Within minutes I found two farmers who put their shoulders to the task, and we drove on, Sasha's hands shaking on the wheel.

Gradually he warmed to me and took the adventures in stride. He was especially impressed by our visits to ancient ruins and archaeological sites. He developed his own eye for any little bump in the landscape that might be a midden. Speeding down a highway in the middle of nowhere, we would suddenly slow to a crawl.

"Khanom Doctor, I see some ruins! Shall we go there?"

"Of course, Sasha *joon,* why not?" We would stop and tromp around some small embankment that a shepherd had shoveled up to create a little shade, and I would announce knowledgeably, "I'm absolutely certain there's something under here that hasn't been excavated yet." Then, having stretched our legs agreeably, we would pile back in the car and continue on our way.

There were companions I invited regularly on these trips, friends whose curiosity matched mine and who were not too fussy about creature comforts. My old friend Azizeh, who had returned to Iran before me, came along on a few especially memorable journeys.

ON A BELGIAN ARCHAEOLOGICAL DIG.

BEENIE AND I SPENT THE NIGHT IN A COFFEEHOUSE MORE
THAN ONCE. THE LITTLE POTS ON THE TABLE ARE
FOR A PEASANT FOOD CALLED *ABGUSHT.*

Nicole, a Belgian writer who became a very close friend, often came with me, as did Beenie, the wife of an American diplomat, who was eager to explore Iran and always up for adventure. When school was out, Zahra or Nima might come, or a couple of my nieces, who added a younger energy to the general enthusiasm. We were often all women, which added to Sasha's headaches.

Certain rituals developed around our travels. The deep seats of the Volvo gave me a backache on long rides, so Sasha covered a kitchen chopping board with a piece of velvet to make a firmer seat for me. I always brought knitting to keep my hands busy while my eyes traveled. And the car was always overstocked with fruit, biscuits, bread and cheese, and a bottle of vermouth for times of special need. Sometimes we ate a picnic lunch by the side of the road when the nearest settlement was hours away. More often we ate at the roadside coffeehouses that served tea and a simple meal of bread and soup or fried eggs to the local farmers and truck drivers.

In provincial towns we stayed at the inns run by the Ministry of Tourism, which were functional, if a little fusty, or sometimes with family or friends. There were odder accommodations too. The Hotel Miami in Gorgan featured a huge mural of the Florida Everglades with shocking pink flamingos, apparently copied from a postcard. The rooms were infested with bedbugs, and their service, at least for women, was rude to the point of meanness; but their *shishlik* with pickled garlic after a long day on the road made the rest almost tolerable.

Farther off the beaten track, we would aim to find a coffeehouse before it closed at sundown. I would negotiate with the coffeehouse owner to use the space for the night, and we would spread our sleeping bags out on the tables. One night I went into the kitchen with the coffeehouse owner to improvise a dinner. When we emerged, laden with hot bread and omelets in tin pans, Sasha had gathered a huge bouquet of wild almond blossoms. The blossoms in lantern light transformed the bare concrete room. We lingered over dinner, chatting with the coffeehouse owner about local affairs and sharing the bottle of vermouth. In the morning I awoke to the smell of almonds, the sounds of a nearby stream, and the wind in the trees.

Our destination might be an ancient ruin, remnant of civilizations that thrived here before Islam came to this land: the Achaemenians,

SASHA WATCHES ZAHRA AND MY NIECE JUNI RIDE A STONE LION NEAR HAMADAN.

THE ROAD OFFERED MANY OPPORTUNITIES FOR FEASTING.

who balanced vast imperial power with enlightened notions of justice and tolerance, or the Sassanians, who were the last to go, with a brilliant flowering of the arts before they faded in the twilight time of the coming of Arab armies. The landmarks that remain are the tumbled stones of palaces and fortresses swept by winds for millennia, and giant figures carved in relief on the sheared-off rock faces of mountainsides or deep-river gorges.

The names that archaeologists have deciphered for these kings are forgotten by the shepherds and farmers who live in the shadow of their tombs and are blended in memory with heroes of poetry and legend. The sun rises for them on the same plain where Rostam raised his bow. Their flocks graze where Jamshid taught men language and Solomon passed judgment. Their horizon is ringed by the same peaks where the Simorgh soared like a phoenix.

The stone of the ruins is echoed by the stone of the land, harsh crags and sudden mesa cliffs, heaps of boulders and mile-long runways of scree, young mountains split by some geological cataclysm to reveal layers of swirling rock formations like the fingerprints of giants. Standing on a windswept height, you can feel in your bones that your feet are anchored at the center of a continent, at the mid-

MY NIECE JUNI, ZAHRA, AND I ON A ROOF NEAR SOLTANIYEH.

point of endless time. The stones bake under a blazing sun in a vast cloudless sky and cool each night under galaxies just an arm's reach away. Between those diurnal extremes lie a thousand colors that shift from hour to hour. Purples slowly deepen; oranges flare to reds, then bleach to yellow and shades of white. The infinitely subtle carpet of color is stained here and there by the miracle of desert flowers: blood-red poppies and shocks of pink that draw you in from the vastness to a tiny world of petal and stamen, framed by the crazed pattern of cracks in the brick-hard earth. Over it all the wind continues, an eternal moaning from the innards of silence, a thrumming of the essence of solitude.

It is not hospitable country. The people who live there must be very strong-willed. Near the ruins at Persepolis and Pasargadae you can see the homes of the Qashqa'i tribes in the distance, black tents dotting the plains. A shepherd passes, knee deep in a dusty foam of sheep, or a lone woman strides across the landscape with skirts swinging, keeping a few goats moving fast in line with swats from her stick. The clang of their bells travels far in the clear air.

In the winter the Qashqa'i camp on the plains that stretch south of Shiraz to the Persian Gulf; their summer pastures lie on the far slopes of the Zagros mountains. Twice a year they gather their herds and load tents and toddlers and chests of belongings on camels and pack-horses for the long trek through the mountain passes. They number close to a million, a confederation of tribes of different origins that have lived in the area for centuries, and they are a force to be reckoned with. Reza Shah's army corralled many of them into sad villages, outlawing their traditional dress and relieving them of their rifles. When he abdicated in 1941, they abandoned their concrete prisons and returned to the open pastures, but the new Shah's land reforms in the 1960s and 1970s again forced them into settlements and stole their lands. They resist the central government sporadically in an ongoing war of "incidents" and assassinations that are reported, if at all, as common banditry.

The city of Shiraz lies at the hub of the Qashqa'i migration routes, and I had caught glimpses of the tribeswomen in the bazaar there. They had an air of freedom that was startling in the narrow passageways of the bazaar: tall, unveiled, trailing gauzy scarves in a riot of colors, they walked with long strides that seemed to end with a kick of their many-layered skirts in a rhythmic flounce. So when I was introduced to a Mr. Bahmanbegui on a visit to Shiraz and he invited me to see one of his tent schools at a nearby Qashqa'i encampment, I jumped at the opportunity and insisted that Nima come too.

Mohammed Bahmanbegui was an extraordinary man, charismatic and clearly adored by the people he served. He was on a mission to bring modern education to his fellow tribesmen of the Qashqa'i. He himself had learned to read and write from a scribe in the service of the Ilkhani, the ruler of the confederation of tribes, and he had studied law in America as well as Tehran. Beginning in 1952, he had started a program of schools that met in tents—white tents that stood out like beacons among the black tents scattered on the meadows—and taught the basic curriculum both in Persian and the Turkish dialects spoken by the tribes. The program gradually spread to the many clans and subgroups that make up the Qashqa'i confederation. Bahmanbegui founded a teachers' training school too and later a high school and technical schools for the graduates of the white tents.

The scene in the tent school was impressive—as impressive in its own way as anything I ever witnessed at the Ethical Culture School in New York. The children, boys and girls together, sat with notebooks and pencils on their laps on a floor of tamped-down earth in the soft light that filtered through the canopy of white canvas. The classroom was open to the landscape on all sides with only the black-board as a barrier. I marveled how the children could keep their attention focused when eagles swooped across the panorama that surrounded them. They ranged from first to sixth graders, and the teacher directed each of his questions to a specific group. But they all paid attention—so much so that it was not unusual for a whole group to complete six grades together in two years.

I was saddened to learn that even the tent schools were a source of conflict between the tribes and the government, ruffling feathers at the Ministry of Education. Never mind that it was in those breeze-blown classrooms that the Qashqa'i first learned that they too were Iranians. On a later trip when I flew to Shiraz with Zahra, I happened to recognize the minister of education sitting in the row in front of us on the plane. As we flew low on the approach for the landing, Zahra and I had our noses glued to the windows. When we spotted the white dot we were looking for, we cheered, "A tent school! Bravo Bahmanbegui!" and the minister scrunched low in his seat.

We toured the encampment that day for a couple of hours. When

THE WOMAN OF THE QASHQA'I CAMP PERFORM
FOLK DANCES FOR BAHMANBEGUI'S GUESTS.

Bahmanbegui saw our enthusiasm and unbridled curiosity, he invited us to stay for the night. The tent where we slept that night was as big as some of my New York apartments. One side was completely open to the landscape; you couldn't have found a better penthouse view. Chests were stacked to form walls, and the black wool of the tent itself was hung with beautiful kilims, strings of tassels, and woolen bags for utensils. It was colorful, spacious, and cozy at the same time. Meals were cooked and served there, toddlers played, and babies rocked in leather hammock cradles. At night the heavy cotton quilts that in the daytime served as pillows to lean on were unrolled and spread on the carpet. There were even clean sheets for the guests.

Before the daylight faded, Bahmanbegui arranged for a performance of folk dances. Women circled with scarves waving in their hands and skirts swirling with layers of colors. The men answered with white handkerchiefs and stamping feet, and the music of reeds and drums carried far on the wind. I knew that whatever he said in politeness about dancing to honor his guests, it was Bahmanbegui himself they were dancing to honor.

When I traveled in those days, I often carried a camera. There were too many images begging to be captured and no time to sketch them all. We were driving one day in the Turkoman country east of the Caspian Sea. We had set as our destination the ruins of an ancient fortification, but took a detour to see Gonbad-e Qabus, a Mongol tomb tower of spectacular brickwork that stands like a giant monolith on the plain near Gorgan. I stopped to take a picture: a long adobe wall at the edge of the town was punctuated by a beggar huddled in a black chador with outstretched hand, the tomb tower looming in the background. I was composing the image carefully when I heard a car pull up behind me. The door slammed, and footsteps crunched in the gravel. A uniformed officer stepped into the frame. He adjusted his hat, straightened his shoulders, and waited for me to shoot. Annoyed, I stood there with the camera at my eye and waited for him to move. Minutes passed. Finally he gave up and left, and I snapped the picture.

Unfortunately that was not the end of it. I should have known better than to toy with an officer's vanity. When we got on the road again, a police car came after us with sirens blaring. My first thought was a prayer of thanks that Sasha was not with us: he would have had a heart attack then and there. It happened that my friend Nicole was driving on that trip. We pulled over, and the policeman asked us to come with him to the station.

"Why?" I asked.

"It's nothing. It will just take a minute. Were you going somewhere?"

"Yes, we're looking for a wall that was built against the Mongol invasion. Do you know it?"

"Just come to the station. Someone there will give you directions." There was no use arguing. We followed him to the gendarmerie.

I recognized the officer in charge, though I had seen him only through the viewfinder. He was none too photogenic up close either, I decided. He subjected us to a list of questions, writing the answers down at length—What is your name? Where are you coming from? Where are you going? What are you doing here? Nicole was obviously an object of special curiosity. I translated for her, dictating what amounted to a full curriculum vitae. When the officer reached the end of his paperwork, his tone suddenly changed. "It's an honor to meet you! We are very happy to welcome such distinguished guests. Please allow me to offer you tea. Then I will send an officer to escort you and show you the way to the ruins." A nuisance, I thought, but at least we'd be on our way.

Before we even got back to the main road, our escort told us to stop at another building, "to look at the map inside." It was a small, windowless brick cube with only one door. There was no map inside— just two SAVAK officers who asked us the same set of questions all over again. Finally it seemed we were finished. The two men excused themselves, walked out, and shut the door behind them. It locked with a heavy click, and my heart sank in stupid recognition of the sound. I was as angry at myself for falling for the trick as I was fearful of what would happen next. I banged on the door long, loud, and hard. It didn't accomplish a thing, but it felt good. Nicole and I took turns sketching out various doomsday scenarios and trying to pick holes in each other's logic. "They would never . . . !" It was an exercise in optimistic realism. For all the good times we had shared, we were never so glad of each other's company as in that one hour that seemed to stretch forever.

Finally the door opened, and a SAVAK officer bowed and scraped his way in, dribbling apologies, elaborate honorifics, and offers of tea. The explanation leaked out with all the other froth. They had become suspicious when they saw foreigners photographing things that could not possibly interest tourists. We might be spies. At the very least we seemed to be photographers with poor taste who would show their town in a bad light and cause all Iranians to lose face if such pictures were seen abroad. While we were locked up, they had spent the hour trying to phone Tehran for instructions. Having finally got a connection, they were informed of the terrible mistake they had made. Hopefully we would take their good intentions into account and find it in our hearts to forgive them. I fumed all the way home, knowing full well that if I had only flattered that vain little officer with a snapshot, none of this would have happened.

WE CROSSED PATHS WITH KURDISH TRIBES
MIGRATING THROUGH KERHMANSHAH.

The memories of many random scenes on the road stay with me like perfect snapshots, unfading. On the road from Shahroud to Gorgan, two trucks stop on the snow-covered road just ahead of us, between drift-piled verges where partridges run. I wonder if we will have to wait while they put on chains. No. A gang of men jump off the trucks waving gunny sacks, chasing the partridges that thrash in the powdery snow, unable to get purchase for their feeble little leaps of flight.

"Let them go, please!" I scream at the frantic scrum.

"No, Khanom! We're going to have a good soup tonight!"

In a barren mountain wilderness on the approach to Takht-e Suleiman, we stumble on a hot spring. A half-dozen men and women soak and splash together in the shallow water under a blanket of drifting steam. They are all fully dressed. The men are identifiable as Luri tribesmen by the baggy black trousers that now cling sodden to their legs. They look like cats suddenly shrunken by a soaking, but infinitely happier. The women's broad skirts float and swirl slowly around them in pools of color.

Approaching Kerman, there is an emerald island in the desert, an orchard of citrus trees—oranges, lemons, limes, and bergamot—bordered by tall cypresses. The gardeners are drying limes for cooking, and the air is dense with their tangy perfume. Miles of white muslin stripe the sun-drenched ground between the trees, covered with lime polka dots: emerald green limes just lifted from the big pot on a fire dug into the ground where they boil to extract the aromatic oil; yesterday's batch, now fading to yellow; and shriveled little brown ones that are gathered one by one into heaping baskets.

On the road from Gorgan to the Caspian coast, there are wild tulip fields. You can smell them on the wind before you see them, and then you can see nothing else: mile after mile of undulating purple, yellow, red. Young girls are bent over in the fields, and others stand by the roadside at intervals, surrounded by buckets of color and waving handfuls of the heavy-headed blossoms. We haven't passed another car for miles; I wonder how they can possibly hope to sell what they have cut. We stop and buy their entire stock for a handful of coins. Then again at the next cluster of girls, and again and again, until the floor and seats of the Volvo are piled deep with tulips of every color, the green stalks dripping puddles around my feet and the smell of springtime racing along with us.

In a deep-river gorge between Firuzabad and Sarvestan, where ancient reliefs are carved into the cliffside, we sight an old dervish, no longer wandering but sitting in front of his small hut. He tends a pot of tea perched atop a kettle on a charcoal fire. He wears a white robe with long flowing sleeves, just like Uncle Dervish's, and a domed hat of embroidered felt. He talks to us about the civilization that left its mark on the rock cliffs, older than the Achaemenians, with connections to Babylonia, and about the scholars and hippies who visit this spot. It is a hard climb up to the carvings, but no one ever gets hurt, he says proudly, as if the gorge is under his special protection. I give him a package of biscuits and tuck some money under a corner of the quilt where he sits. A big toothless smile carves wrinkles on his wizened face.

Not every encounter was so happy. There is an area in Mazandaran, not far from the tulips, where wheat fields stretch for miles and miles. I had heard that the farms were owned by the Shah's brother. As we drove, I spotted an odd structure beside the road and stopped out of curiosity. It was a little shack built entirely, roof and walls, of small tree branches stripped of their leaves. A woman and three chil-

THE SHAH'S BROTHER'S IMPOVERISHED TENANT AND HER TWO GEESE.

dren sat on the rough dirt floor. In a corner a sad white goose flailed and screeched in a dry metal tub, desperate for water. There was none that I could see; no jug, no bucket.

"Do you live here?" I asked.

"Yes. My husband goes in the daytime to work in the fields. When they bring him back, we sleep here." They had come from Baluchistan, she told me, far away on the Pakistani border, with the promise of work in the prince's fields. As we were talking, a truck pulled up, piled with stacks of flatbread. A man sat on top of the bread. He called out a name from a list and then tossed a few folds of bread down to the woman. I asked about water. She said that her husband brought a jug when he came home from work at night. They had no donkey, no horse, and no way at all to come and go except for the prince's trucks that delivered the workers and the bread.

I was truly shocked and too embarrassed to offer the children a packet of biscuits. *To hell with biscuits!* I thought. *What am I, Marie Antoinette?* I gave them most of the cash I was carrying. When I got back to Tehran, I made an angry phone call to a friend who was a cousin of the prince—the closest link I could find. "Tell him this is no way for a man to treat his workers!" I doubt that it did any good, and I can't even say that it made me feel better.

CHAPTER TWENTY-THREE

Many of the roads I traveled around Iran began as a path traced by a finger through dust on some obscure object in an antique dealer's shop. Tehran's antique shops in those days had none of the polite polish that the term might suggest, but tended rather to shadowy cubbyholes of eccentric hodgepodge. Among moth-eaten needlework and rusty dervishes' axes and padlocks forged in fanciful shapes and hand-copied Qorans and Afghan pistols and Russian bric-a-brac might be found articles of mysterious function and provenance, any one of them the starting point for a shaggy-dog story served up by the proprietor with glasses of tea. I cultivated relationships with a handful of dealers who came to know my taste and alerted me to any promising new find. One of them, Valiollah, became a good friend.

It was his rag that wiped the grime from a sheet of glass to reveal a primitive but beautiful painting. And another, and another: he had come back from a trip to the Persian Gulf coast with a whole stack of paintings behind glass. Brilliant folk art in Matisse-like colors, these were poor country cousins of the Qajar paintings behind glass. Instead of portraying decorative flowers and nightingales, most of the paintings were large-eyed portraits. A few were scenes from religious stories that reminded me of the coffeehouse paintings. There were peacocks too and prophets on horseback. They were flat and coarse, drawn in heavy black lines that were completely formulaic, even traced from the same template; but somehow each face was alive with expression, and the colors were unique to each and boldly eccentric.

I traveled with Valiollah to the southern coast by the Strait of Hormuz, where he had found the paintings. It was a world apart from the rest of Iran: tropically humid, with marshes and mangrove forests lining the shore. In ancient fishing villages, women with their faces hidden behind stiff black masks looked out to sea, where their men tossed nets from high-prowed sailboats against a backdrop of oil tankers and battleships queuing through the strait.

VERNACULAR PAINTINGS BEHIND GLASS.

In tent encampments—the most makeshift of slums—on the outskirts of the ports of Minab, Bandar Abbas, and Khorramshahr, the
glass paintings served as humble decoration. They hung by a strip of
fabric from a nail in a tent post, frames skewed and splitting, the glass
fly-specked, greasy with cooking smoke, and coated with the dust
that blew through the tents. The paintings were forty or fifty years
old at the most, a very brief fashion in the time span of traditional
arts, and one that was disappearing fast as the paintings were sold off
for a pittance and replaced with poster prints of religious images or
photographs of the Shah.

We found a painter who still made a small living from his art. His
brother who had also painted had recently died, and he himself was
half blind, one eye glued shut. He worked on the dirt floor at the back
of a shop where his wife sold cigarettes and odds and ends. Bending
over the glass with brush in hand, he traced the lines from a drawing
placed beneath the glass and then blocked in the colors—shocking
pinks, purples, blazing orange, and brilliant green. An apprentice, a
boy of about fourteen, sat to one side, mixing powdered pigments into
a paste and wiping clean the panes of glass. The artist identified the
woman in the portrait: "It is Tooba Khanom. I have painted her a

COUSIN MARYAM POSES BEFORE THE PAINTINGS
BEHIND GLASS THAT DECORATED ZAHRA'S ROOM.

hundred times." That was all he would say about Tooba Khanom, and I was left to imagine their story.

Over a few years I collected about sixteen hundred glass paintings from the Gulf, buying almost anything that was offered for sale. My patronage no doubt prolonged the life of the tradition artificially for a few years, but I saw no harm in that.

I was poking around in another antique shop in Tehran, one that specialized in silver, hoping to find a good tea set, when a man entered with a sack slung over his shoulder like Santa Claus. He wore a furry black lambskin hat, and his pants were tucked into tall boots as if he had just galloped in from the Russian steppe, but his features looked almost Chinese. He dumped out the contents of his sack in a jumbled heap on the table. It was blackened silver, badly tarnished. I recognized some of the shapes as bracelets and necklaces, some studded with carnelian and colored glass, some chased with gold; but many of the objects were mysterious. The shopkeeper sifted through the heap, piling objects on his scale. They haggled furiously, the stranger speaking with an odd Turkish accent, but finally they agreed on a price for seven or eight pounds of silver. As soon as the man left, I started asking questions.

He was a Turkoman, the shopkeeper said. I had heard of the Turkoman tribes that inhabit the plains just east of the southern tip of the Caspian Sea. They were famous as bandits and horse thieves, skilled riders descended from the Mongol armies who invaded Iran centuries ago, now part of the patchwork of different ethnic groups that make up the country. Like the Qashqa'i tribes in the south, the Turkoman had been forced to give up their arms and their nomadic ways and settle in villages as Reza Shah consolidated power in the central government. They had adapted with less resistance than the Qashqa'i, becoming successful cotton farmers and horse breeders. But I would learn, as I delved more deeply, that their unique culture was still very much alive.

I was not aware that the Turkoman were highly skilled at crafting silver, and no one else seemed to know much about it either. I was appalled to hear the shopkeeper say that his purchase would be melted down and recycled. The silver was good, he said, but the stuff had no value as jewelry.

I disagreed; there seemed to be beautiful work hidden under all that tarnish, quite unlike anything I had seen before. "Maybe so, Khanom, but there is no market for it." Still, he was more than happy to sell me a few pieces for the price of the weight of silver. I took home a bracelet and a pair of anklets with tiny bells, thinking Zahra might wear them and I could keep track of her whereabouts. When I polished them they were indeed beautiful. But every time I heard my toddler tinkling down the hallway or up and down the stairs, my mind went back to the shop, the Turkoman with his sack, and the heap of silver condemned to the melting pot. I went back several times, bought more pieces, and asked more questions.

As it happened, the first trip I made into Turkoman country was by chance. I was visiting Azizeh at her family's home in Shahroud, a few hours' drive from Gorgan. Azizeh suggested an excursion, and the two of us drove alone, ending up at the infamous Hotel Miami. We decided that the shocking flamingos and sneering waiters could be tolerated only if we ordered vodka with our *shishlik*. It was 1961; such behavior from women was unheard of in a small provincial town. Every eye in the whole room of men was on us, and every eyebrow raised. But we were back in college days, on a lark, and cared no more for their opinion than we had for all those boys who hoped for dates.

In the morning we made our way to Qombad-e Kavous, one of several towns in the area where the Turkoman hold a weekly open-air market. We found the market by following the crowd to a large open square. It was a loud and raucous party. There were camels in one corner, horses in another, and sheep and goats everywhere. Goods for sale were spread on blankets on the ground, potatoes next to saddles next to onions next to stacks of sheepskin. The women wore long caftans of spectacular colors, their heads or shoulders draped in brilliant shawls with silk-screened floral patterns. They were extraordinarily beautiful, with oriental eyes and high cheekbones but very fair coloring, many of them almost blond. They milled around or crouched

I WEAR AN UZBEK SCARF,
TO THE AMUSEMENT OF MY TURKOMAN FRIEND.

at the blankets, sorting vegetables, gossiping, laughing, haggling. A horse and cart piled high with carpets came hurtling through the crowd; the driver stood high on the pile with legs planted wide and reins stretched tight, whooping his head off.

I looked for jewelry but was disappointed to see that the women wore very little if any. What they did wear—a necklace of coins, a few gold bangles—was nothing like what I had seen in the shop in Tehran. There was obviously more to this story than met the eye.

Determined to track down the silver, I came back again to Gorgan every few months. The several jewelry shops in Gorgan sold only modern pieces, mostly gold—the same styles that could be found in bazaars everywhere in Iran. They did, however, buy old silver jewelry, or accept it in barter for gold, and then melt it down. They told me that the Turkoman women no longer wanted to wear the heavy silver; the same value of gold was much lighter and more comfortable. Where could I find the old silver for sale? They couldn't say except perhaps to check the open-air market that moved in a circuit among three towns on different days of the week.

So it seemed a stroke of luck when, traveling with Nicole almost a year after my first visit to Gorgan, we found a few old silver bracelets spread on a piece of red silk in the dust between baskets of eggs and cucumbers. I asked the old man who was the proprietor of the red scarf for the prices.

"English?" he asked, eyeing Nicole.

"No, I'm Iranian, just like you," I answered.

"Very well, Khanom. Then a different price for you." I wondered how many Englishmen had passed this way recently in search of old silver. Even if they paid double what I paid, they would have got a bargain. I bought the lot. As we were finishing, another stroke of luck struck with a variation on the same theme.

"I speak English," announced a young man who had been observing the transaction. He was a Turkoman named Mahmad, about seventeen years old. His English was not actually as good as his confident advertisement would have had us believe, but he was very eager to practice. From that time on Mahmad became my guide into the world of the Turkoman. He had energy and curiosity enough to match his confidence, and he became fiercely loyal to me. In the process he learned as much as I did about the old silver.

I went back to Gorgan every two or three months, and each time I would find Mahmad. He lived in a village nearby and came into town every day to attend classes. I would look over his notebook, coach him on a few English sentences, and have him practice some simple conversation. Then we were off in search of silver. He introduced me to a few dealers and made them understand my strange request: if any old silver came their way, they should offer it first to me before melting it down. I developed relationships with a few of them, and eventually they came regularly to Tehran to offer me the first choice of whatever they found. But Mahmad preferred to bypass the middlemen and go straight to the source. He took me to several homes where he had somehow found out that a woman had something to sell: jewelry, clothing, a saddle . . . I felt guilty at first, removing heirlooms from their rightful place, but I reasoned that if I hadn't been there, they would have been sold to the dealers instead for a much lower price and the silver would be melted down, an ancient heritage rendered into faceless commodity.

In their homes the women unwrapped silk-tied bundles of treasure. There was an incredible abundance of different pieces, mostly worn around the neck and shoulders because of their weight: collars, breast plaques and pendants, necklaces that weighed up to four pounds each, buttons as big as six inches across, earrings so heavy they were supported by headbands, and wide bracelets that came halfway up to the elbow. There were silver-covered purses of leather and cylindrical cases, worn hanging from a chain, that carried a rolled-up slip of paper inscribed with a prayer or a quotation from the Qoran. There were magnificent crowns: they showed me how they bound them on their heads with scarves over hair worn in many narrow braids. Different styles of braids signaled who was married and who was still available. They showed me clothing as well, embroidered coats and others of *ikat*-dyed silk, many of which were decorated with hundreds of coins.

I learned why I had never seen the old silver worn. It wasn't just a question of changing fashion or the weight of the stuff. Even in the past the jewelry had been worn only on special occasions. A woman might dress for a wedding in thirty pounds of silver, a serious display of wealth. I learned too why so many of the bracelets I had seen were dented or had cracked stones. A ritual battle took place at every wedding as the bride's mother, sisters, and cousins resisted her removal to the groom's home. They fought their new in-laws using their heavy

WEARING A TURKOMAN COAT YEARS LATER IN NEW YORK AND
POSING FOR A PHOTOGRAPH BY LENOR CARABALLO.

silver bracelets as armor, clanging wrist to wrist. The religious holiday *'eid-e ghorban* was another day to dress up; it is celebrated all
over Iran but is especially important for the Turkoman, who are
mostly Sunni. The biggest occasion of the year was the horse races
that gathered the tribes of the whole region for days of celebration. It
was not only the women who showed off their silver then. Even the
horses were decked out in silver ornaments and beautifully decorated
saddles and bridles. I was lucky enough to find a complete set of trappings for a horse that was made from twenty pounds of silver, set
with agates, and decorated with patterns in black enamel and gold. It
seems that the men were content to let their women and horses carry

TURKOMAN JEWELRY ON A TABLE BENEATH MY COLLECTION
OF SEVENTEENTH-CENTURY PORTABLE HOOKAH BASES,
DESIGNED FOR SMOKING WHILE TRAVELING.

the burden of wealth. I found silver belts that were worn by men but
very little else.

There were two distinct styles of craftsmanship, belonging to two
different tribal groups, the Yamut and the Tekke. The Yamut silver
was decorated with lozenge- and crescent-shaped patterns of very
thin embossed gold and set with cornelian agate or colored glass.
Designs were often repeated, pressed from the same embossing mold.
The Tekke jewelry was more refined. The silver was plated with
gold, then chased with floral arabesques that echoed designs I had

seen in ancient metalwork from Sassanian times, before Islam reached Iran. The Tekke used agate too but never colored glass, and every piece was unique.

I was told that no one made the old jewelry anymore, at least not in Iran. Things might be different in Afghanistan, where many Turkoman still lived. But one day a dealer sold me several Yamut pieces that I could have sworn were new in spite of his claims for their antiquity. "Someone must still be making this stuff," I told Mahmad. He did some scouting, and on my next trip he brought me to a small house where a very fat Turkoman woman sat on a pile of cushions in front of a stone table. She had a charcoal brazier burning, with a small boy working the bellows. She held a piece of silver in the fire with small tongs and then beat it with a hammer.

I showed her one of the bracelets I had bought. She claimed it proudly: "Yes, I made it. Isn't it good?" I admired the work but mentioned also that the antique dealer in Tehran had not been entirely honest with me: he had sworn the piece was old. "It's your own fault," she laughed. "They told me about you. I hadn't worked the silver for many years, but now you've made it fashionable. You come and buy, and now the dealers want me to make more. Thank you!"

One day Mahmad brought me and Zahra home to his village near Gorgan. His family lived in a substantial adobe house, though it had no electricity. (It was rare to find anyone that still lived in a yurt, the domed round tent of felt that was the traditional Turkoman home, although many families kept a yurt for storage or extra sleeping space when guests came to stay or when newlyweds wanted a bit of privacy.) The instant we entered—and every time after—a plastic tablecloth was spread on the ground and tea was served in bowls with a separate teapot for each guest, and freshly baked bread and cheese were laid out on the side.

Mahmad's father was out of the picture, but his mother and sisters seemed to be managing well. His grandmother, a woman of great cheerfulness and dignity, lived with them too. There were also two brothers who lived under the same roof. The younger was recently married, and his bride was a shy, smiling presence. She was bound by tribal tradition not to speak in her mother-in-law's company for a year after her wedding, or until her first child was born, whichever came first. Mahmad's elder brother's wife was named Tushan, which means "rabbit." She was tall, with fair hair and deep blue eyes, and

THREE GENERATIONS OF TURKOMAN WOMEN:
MAHMAD'S GRANDMOTHER, SISTER-IN-LAW
TUSHAN, AND NIECES.

she had a great many children, all of them girls who looked very much like her. The little ones had their blond hair cut boyishly short to keep down lice; running around in long caftans of brightly colored satin, they looked like elegant imps. It was a very female household, and happily so.

Dinner was served: rice and fatty lamb on a big tray. Two spoons were procured for the guests, but everyone else dug in with their hands, so we did too. After we ate, two of the older girls wanted to show us the carpet they were weaving. They picked up kerosene lanterns and led us to a large outbuilding. The imps trailed behind. In most of Iran carpets are woven on vertical looms, but the Turkoman looms are horizontal. The carpet was nearing completion, and it stretched the length and width of the room, but a couple of feet above the ground. It was fine work, and we told them so. I told them also about my own experience with weaving and the lure of bees, and they had a good laugh. As the girls led the way out to return to the main house, I looked back for a moment and caught a glimpse of the imps bouncing in silent glee on the taut carpet like a trampoline. Their shadows flew wildly up the walls in the receding lamplight. I wondered how long the game would last in the dark, and whether they ever got caught.

I asked Mahmad's mother about the obstacles to getting electricity. It wasn't just their house but the whole village, she said. A wire had to be run out from the main road, and it wasn't clear if the government would pay or the villagers had to raise the money. When I got back to Tehran, I took care of it. I figured it was the least I could do to thank Mahmad for all his help. On my next trip to Gorgan we celebrated with a big feast served under several glaring bulbs. I missed the subtle lamplight, but they were very happy, not least for the comfort of being able to weave in decent light. Mahmad's sister made a special carpet for me with my name woven into the design.

I continued to collect the silver for almost twenty years. I didn't refine the collection as many collectors do, getting rid of lesser pieces to make room for new finds. As far as I was concerned, it was all worth saving. One day, I hoped, all of it would be given the place it deserved in a museum. If not, then at least it had not been melted down. I even bought a few extraordinary pieces from dealers in New York and Paris and brought them back to Iran. They had probably come from Afghanistan—I doubt that any dealer in Iran would have gone around me—but I figured that was close enough to home.

CHAPTER TWENTY-FOUR

Not all of my journeys in Iran were driven by curiosity, leisure, or the pursuit of art. There were darker trips too.

Late one evening in 1964 we were sitting in the garden under the tent having drinks with a friend who suddenly came to the conclusion he had drunk too much. Then the earth lunged beneath us all, the glasses spilled, and the swimming pool was heaving like the sea. Earthquake! I tore through the house and grabbed Zahra from her bed, then ran back downstairs and out to the garden.

The news in the papers the next morning was bad. Hundreds of villages had been destroyed, and more than ten thousand people were dead. The epicenter was near Buin Zahra, between Qazvin and Hamadan, country that both Abol and I felt close to. I got on the phone and started dialing friends and relatives—"Bring money, clothing, blankets, whatever you can," I told them. "I'll hire some trucks." A dear friend called from London and said she was sending money, then called right back again—"Can you wait for me? I'll be on the next flight." I went to the bazaar and ordered tents, samovars, kerosene stoves, shovels, blankets, and food—enough for thirty families. The gear we collected filled two whole rooms in the house. It was nothing, I knew, a drop in the bucket, but you had to start somewhere.

We left on the morning of the fourth day after the earthquake, the Volvo leading a convoy of three trucks. At Qazvin we stopped to pick up Javad Agha, the antique dealer who had first opened my eyes to the notion of architectural salvage. I figured we needed a guide. He knew the area well and could speak the Turkish dialect that was common in the villages there.

The road was impassable in places where the earth had split open right across the asphalt. Before the trucks could safely pass, we had to fill the deep cracks with whatever large stones we could find near the road. On one side a hill had been sheared in two, and the roots of a huge tree hung fifteen feet up in the air. Seeing the earth itself ripped wide, we could imagine what lay ahead of us in the villages built of adobe and sun-dried mud brick.

It is hard for me even forty years later to describe what we found: the devastation of homes reduced to hills of dust and rubble; the scenes of raw grief. We saw very little of any official relief effort. The spread of the disaster was too vast—hopefully they were busy elsewhere. What little we did see left Javad Agha even more distraught. "Shame on the corruption of this government! They're supposed to send seven meters of white cloth for each shroud, but they've cut the cloth in five-meter lengths. How can you bury a man decently like that?"

As we went from one village to the next unloading the trucks, I was appalled to see men sitting in the shade of the stubs of walls, smoking, waiting. The stench of death was everywhere. The carcasses of cows and sheep were bloating in the stables. There was no water anywhere because the channels of the underground *qanat* had collapsed. There was so much that desperately needed doing. What were they waiting for?

"Khanom, we don't have any equipment."

"I've brought shovels. Come on. Let's clear this mess out of the stable." I started to dig. Javad Agha was furious.

"Khanom, you can't do this work for them. These people are lazy." They weren't lazy, I knew, but shock and grief can do strange things to people. Perhaps the sight of a city woman shoveling broken bricks would jolt them back to their senses.

We left after sunset, the trucks empty. At three in the morning I fell into bed exhausted and allowed myself finally to cry. The shower, the clean sheets, the pillow, the solid ceiling above me all seemed unreal, as much an illusion as any notion of justice on earth or in heaven.

CHAPTER TWENTY-FIVE

The more I came to know my country in all its vast diversity, its many human faces, and its deeply creative heritage, the less credence I gave to the imperial posturing that claimed dominion over it all. When our King of Kings, Light of the Aryans, decided that 1971 was the appropriate moment to celebrate twenty-five hundred years of the Iranian monarchy, it occurred to me—though I didn't dare say it out loud—that he was getting a little too big for his britches.

Of course, the very notion of two and a half millennia of empire was a politically convenient fairy tale. It belied the constant invasions of this land, not to mention the humble origins of the Shah's own father. The icon that held the fragile story together was Persepolis, the spectacular ruins of the Achaemenian palace that had fallen to Alexander the Great. The stone columns and carved stairways that stood on a windswept platform in the desert near Shiraz were indeed twenty-five hundred years old. The rest was open to interpretation.

The hope implied in setting the celebration at the ancient site was that kings, presidents, and glitterati would line up to pay tribute to the Shahanshah, just as the stone-carved emissaries bearing gifts from the far reaches of the Achaemenian empire marched in bas relief up the stairways at Persepolis. In exchange for the propaganda value of their bows and curtsies, we would dazzle them with the most lavish party that Iranian hospitality and oil money could offer.

I politely declined an invitation from the Ministry of Court to act as one of the official hostesses of the celebration. But I didn't say no when I was asked to design a glass wall and a mirror mosaic for two new luxury hotels that had been built for the occasion. I figured I was just one of countless artists whose business it was to adorn the revels. Should the carpet weavers who had been hired to weave piled-silk portraits of each invited head of state be blamed for the politics of their assigned subjects? Court patronage of the arts was a venerable Iranian tradition that had less to do with politics than kings might wish. After all, it was the work of the stonemasons and sculptors that survived at Persepolis, not the institutions of government.

Preparations began a year in advance of the big bash. During that year I made several trips south to Shiraz and Persepolis to work on the hotel installations. To my eyes it looked as if a bomb had dropped. Bulldozers were plowing roads through centuries-old neighborhoods of Shiraz and leveling the plain at Persepolis for the tent city that would house the visiting heads of state. Cables and scaffolding were scribbled all over the ruins. The mountain-ringed landscape that had once taken my breath away with its windswept solitude was now interrupted by miles of plastic fencing and an instant forest that looked like nothing so much as an embryonic Christmas tree farm.

Often I didn't know whether to cry or laugh. A group of young soldiers on a break from construction lounged in the shade of a tree. It was miserably hot. They had taken their shirts off and were munching on watermelon. Each wore shoulder-length hair and a full beard, grown under orders in anticipation of marching in the celebrations. The idea was to dress them up as the Achaemenian army. Each of the poor conscripted actors was scratching his furry face compulsively.

I stumbled on some other actors too: Peter Brook's company rehearsing in the ruins at Persepolis for their performance of *Orghast* at the Shiraz Arts Festival that same summer. It was another blazing-hot afternoon, but I stopped to watch. The cast included two cows that refused to learn their cues. Stagehands pushed and shoved, and actors spoke commands in a language that no one understood, but the cows just stood there chewing their cud. It was obvious that the cows had been hired locally: these ordinary Iranian cows had no training in Western avant-garde theater. It was equally obvious what was needed. I picked a handful of grass and gave it to the actor who was supposed to walk ahead of the cows, which then followed.

On a road outside Shiraz, on yet another oven of a day, I passed a huge mound of construction trash. White stone faces peered out from under piles of broken plaster, lions smiled at me upside down, and carved columns poked at the sky in topsy-turvy angles. I had stumbled on the gravesite of the old houses of Shiraz that were being leveled for new roads leading to the big party. I marked a few pieces that I especially admired with chalk, and when I got back to Tehran, I sent Valiollah on an expedition to salvage the pieces I had chosen.

In spite of all the civic mayhem and the destruction of a beautiful heritage in the name of an ersatz claim to ancient glory, the celebration launched a great many cultural projects that otherwise would not have seen the light of day. The Goethe Institute, which represented the German government for cultural affairs, pitched in by sponsoring an exhibition of the paintings behind glass that I had collected from the Gulf coast. I chose some two hundred of the most interesting paintings and insisted that they be shown in a venue that would be accessible to the man on the street. Given their humble origins, it seemed absurd to hide them away in an exclusive uptown gallery. We finally settled on an exhibition space in Tehran's central City Park, but I had to wrangle over every detail of the arrangements with the project director and his wife. An unpleasantly sticky and ambitious couple, they were far more interested in pushing themselves up the social ladder than in bringing art to the people. The news that the queen herself would attend the opening sent them into orbit, far out of reach of any rational communication.

My patience with these characters wore thin because something much heavier was pressing on my mind. Four years earlier my father had fallen while hiking in the mountains. He broke his hip, but worse, the X-rays revealed an inoperable cancer of the bone. He suffered in much pain, confined to a wheelchair and dosed up with drugs. During the last weeks leading up to the big celebration he was failing rapidly, and I visited him almost daily in the hospital.

On those visits we often talked politics—as if the snippets of news I brought could somehow tether him to the known world; as if the whiff of a good debate could reel him back in from the cloud of morphine. I griped about the chaos I had witnessed in Shiraz and the corruption that was all too visible in the general frenzy, and I mocked the egotistical absurdity of the royal celebration.

"You are right, Monir Khanom," my father agreed sadly. "But listen to me: There is nobody who can step into the Shah's shoes. Who could you point to and say, 'This man has the intelligence, the honesty, the vision that the job requires'? Who would you choose?"

"I don't know," I mumbled. He was the one who always had the answers; where were they now? I was unnerved by his resignation, as if the disease of the body politic was as unstoppable as the cancer in his bones, as final as the skull waiting behind his gaunt cheeks and paper-pale skin.

His death hit me like a fist in the chest, literally. I couldn't breathe, couldn't move for the fierce pain under my heart. There was too much pressure on nerves in my diaphragm, the doctor said, but it felt like a hole had been punched in the middle of my being. I asked the project director at the Goethe Institute to hold off on final plans for the opening of the exhibition of glass paintings, but they had sent out invitations without consulting me. They had managed to squeeze themselves into the queen's schedule, and nothing else mattered. I was deeply upset by their rudeness, which made the pain in my chest even worse. That in turn upset Abol, who was distressed to see me in such a state. He took the very uncharacteristic step of writing an angry note to the German ambassador, who, as it happened, had troubles enough of his own at the time. I sent a message to the queen, apologizing that I was too sick to attend the opening, and she in turn sent a message back saying, in effect: "Whatever you do, please don't cancel, because our relationship with the Germans is strained, and we need to repair it." *Damn it,* I thought, and I imagined the diplomatic dominoes falling toward some unthinkable conflagration. So the opening went ahead as scheduled, with Abol and the queen and the German ambassador in attendance. I stayed home in bed. The project director's wife stayed home too in a fit of pique, missing her grand moment with the queen. It was all my fault, she said, for making such a fuss "over a few lousy pieces of broken glass."

Finally, after all the sideshows, the long anticipation, the propaganda, and the preparations, it was time for the party at Persepolis. Like most of our fellow citizens who were not invited, we watched it on television. The occasion prompted a low-key gathering of family and friends at the home of one of Abol's brothers.

"They're starting!" someone shouted, and we settled around the television. Conversation subsided, leaving only the clink of ice in tall glasses of vodka lime, the voice of the announcer wavering between breathless awe and flowery pomp, and soon enough the sound of my giggling. I couldn't help it. I hadn't laughed at anything since my father's death, but the sight of the long-haired, itchy-bearded soldiers lined up in cheap satin robes was too much for me. They looked like strays from a school Christmas pageant or, at best, extras in a very low-budget biblical epic.

Once I started laughing, I couldn't stop. Each moment seemed to me more ridiculous than the last, and it didn't bother me in the least that I was the only one laughing. The coup de grâce was the Shah's address to his adopted forefather, Cyrus, the Achaemenian king of kings, at his tomb on the plain of Pasargad. *"Asudeh bekhab, ma bidarim,*" he reassured the old ghost: Sleep in peace, for we are awake! At that I was falling out of my chair laughing hysterically. Abol's brother hissed at me to be quiet. Abol went pale and whispered, "Khanom, the walls have ears!" If laughing was treason, then I was one helpless traitor.

CHAPTER TWENTY-SIX

My home in those days was a caravansary: people coming and going endlessly, houseguests staying for weeks at a time, Hajji Ostad and his crew trooping in and out of the studio. Guests having drinks by the pool at sunset might look up—and feign a twinge of good Muslim guilt—to see an old Turkoman bending to his prayers on the balcony, an antique dealer who stayed for a couple of days each time he brought silver to sell. The constant ebb and flow peaked every Friday, the final day of the weekend in Iran, with an open house.

The Friday gatherings had started when Nima was home for vacation from boarding school. I remembered when I was her age: Ahmad and Pamela in the upstairs apartment, the gramophone, dancing and card games . . . It seemed that the least I could do for my daughters and nieces was to welcome them just as warmly into the grown-up world and introduce them to some interesting people.

THE FAMOUS EGYPTIAN TENT.

ZAHRA DIVES FROM THE GLASS PLATFORM.

Lunch was always a barbecue and very informal buffet—hamburgers and hot dogs, kebabs and a traditional rice dish—with people carrying their plates out to sit in the garden, under the impolitic Egyptian tent, or by the pool. A gang showed up regularly, many of them artists and writers, and friends would bring along friends of their own. Kids always splashed in the pool, a cluster of Zahra's classmates, Nima's old friends, a few cousins and nieces and neighbors. There were always fresh faces, often someone just passing through—an archaeologist or a journalist, even the occasional stray hippie waylaid en route to points farther east. It never failed to be a lively mix, very relaxed but varied enough to generate good conversation and interesting connections.

At these gatherings one flower in the garden attracted far more than her fair share of butterflies. My niece Vida, the daughter of my brother Ali, was blessed with extraordinary beauty. She didn't just turn heads; she literally stopped traffic when she walked down the street in London, Paris, or Geneva. She had been an aspiring fashion designer and worked with Christian Dior and Valentino, both of whom begged her to model for them at whatever price she cared to name. So it was hardly surprising when artists started bringing paints and canvas to the Friday gatherings and asking her to sit for them. Once it started, it was unstoppable. Later others sat for portraits too, but Vida just kept multiplying.

Vida's resplendent beauty had a dark shadow, though. As a teenager in high school, she had fallen in love at first sight with a very intelligent young man from a powerful family. They nursed their grand passion through several years of separation, then finally married and moved to Geneva, where he was studying architecture. They were the perfect young couple, very much in love and living the happiest of fairy tales, but the story came to an abrupt end. Finding his name missing from the posted list of those who had passed an important exam, he checked into a hotel and blew his brains out. That he had actually passed the exam and his name was omitted by mistake was but a sorry footnote to the whole sad affair.

OUR BEAUTY, VIDA SHAHROUDY.

Vida never entirely recovered, it seemed to me. She came back to Tehran and stayed with me for a while in her darkest time, and we became very close. She was a wonderful traveling companion and a great confidante. She had a knack for paying attention to people so that the most casual acquaintances would reveal their life stories and their deepest self-doubts to her. At parties I used to joke whenever I could see an introduction approaching, "Vida, get the couch ready!" But as she engaged with the world again after her tragedy, it was with a certain recklessness, as if nothing ultimately mattered anymore. For all her magnificent empathy, she didn't really give a damn for any of the men who were mesmerized by her beauty.

Once a month the Friday gathering escalated into "poetry night." As many as fifty or sixty might show up, and often half of them were new to me. Many poets came and went, but there were a few loyal regulars. I could count on Nader Naderpour to recite, and Esmail Shahroudi would always deliver a memorable performance. I picture him standing on the terrace, declaiming dramatically over Beethoven's Ninth Symphony, "*Baz kon, baz kon . . .* Open! Open! Open these gates!" Sohrab Sepehri came often, but he never recited. He sat

TOWN & COUNTRY PHOTOGRAPHED VIDA IN TURKOMAN ROBES
WITH TANYA FOROUGHI IN OUR GARDEN.

very quietly in a corner, observed the goings-on, and spoke only when spoken to.

On poetry nights I served only a big pot of *abgusht* with all the fixings. *Abgusht* is poor man's soup, the standard fare of the coffeehouses, and it was unheard-of then to serve it to guests in a wealthy home. But it is also comfort food, delicious when well made, and after I started serving it, *abgusht* parties became quite the fashion.

A current of laughter and good fun ran through our lives in those days. If I was reckless enough to laugh at the sight of an emperor with no clothes, I was also sane enough to laugh rather than cry over the more absurd obstacles that littered the path of daily life in Iran. But so often Abol's quiet, off-the-wall humor reminded me also to laugh at myself.

Somewhere between the work I was doing with glass and a memorable ride on a glass-bottomed boat in Greece, I came up with the notion of making a glass island for the swimming pool, resting on four of the stone columns from Shiraz and large enough to sit four people comfortably on chairs. The idea sparked Abol's enthusiasm

MR. FARMANFARMAIAN AT HOME.

and also fired up my nephew Kayhan, a young engineer who had grown very close to Abol. They conferred endlessly over the technical challenge, which was just as well because it turned out to be quite a feat of engineering to stabilize the columns and build a stainless-steel frame for the glass and a bridge to the island, not to mention obtaining thick, shatterproof glass from a manufacturer that supplied the local automotive industry. In the end the effect was delightful. Abol and I sat out on the island for a drink in the evening, admiring the play of light beneath our feet and quite pleased with our work.

"Abol *joon,* supposing we painted a picture on the bottom of the pool?"

"Khanom, you know best."

"It could be lovely if I find the right image."

It was Abol who found the image. The very next day, with a big grin, he handed me a cartoon he had clipped from *The New Yorker:* three nude women cavorting, with a horned devil eyeing them hungrily from behind a leafy tree. *Okay,* I thought, *why not?*

About fifteen years had passed since I painted a reclining Coca-Cola drinker on the side of a truck, and I knew I needed some help with the physical labor of working on such a large scale. I called a cinema and tracked down a team of three Turkish brothers from Tabriz who painted the huge billboards that advertised the latest movies. When I showed them the drained swimming pool and the cartoon, they looked dubious to say the least.

"If you don't know how to start, I can sketch it for you." I climbed down the ladder and made a rough sketch with a lump of charcoal, then climbed back up to check. The proportions were okay; it was in their hands.

A few days later when I came outside for a routine check on the work, I found Vida and a friend sitting on the edge of the pool, legs dangling above the emerging image. I brought out a tray of *sharbat* and sat with them awhile to chat. But our own conversation faded: we couldn't help but listen as the painters on the pool floor debated where exactly to place the nipple on the breast of one giant nude.

"Don't worry, I know exactly where the thing goes," I said. "I happen to have a couple of them myself." I climbed down the ladder and took the brush from the hand of one open-mouthed Turk. I corrected the line at the bottom of the breast, dabbed in the nipple, and smudged the edges a bit with my finger. Vida and friend were choking on fits of giggles above us.

"Khanom, do you know this work?" asked one of the brothers.

"Yes, I know a thing or two about painting."

THE SWIMMING POOL AS WORK OF ART.

It was finished in about a week. When we filled the pool again, I had to admire Abol's inspired madness. The leaves of the tree rippled in the breeze, the women's flesh undulated, and the devil's grimace came alive. We found that young children needed some reassurance before they were willing to jump in the pool, but otherwise it was a great success. Not long afterward we were flying into Tehran from the Caspian in a small plane. The flight path happened to cross Elahieh.

"Look, Abol! Look!" Not just Abol but all the passengers got an eyeful of our swimming pool. I thought it looked especially nice from above, the rectangular pool framed by a red brick border and the surrounding mat of green grass, like a painting hanging on the wall. After that I realized why the Shah's helicopter occasionally circled right over our house on its way to the palace. And when it circled two or three times on one trip, I knew the Shah himself was not on board, and it was probably a new pilot.

CHAPTER TWENTY-SEVEN

Abol's family owned a stretch of some forty acres of land known as Farmansara beside the Caspian Sea. Many of his siblings had built villas there and went up for weekends away from Tehran. A plot was available to us, and Abol suggested building there, but I wasn't thrilled. It felt too crowded, the landscape was uninteresting, and the beach was muddy. Never mind the social obligations that came with the territory. "Let's look a bit further," I said.

One day when Abol, Sasha, and I were driving up the coast from Chalus toward Babolsar, I spotted a smooth, wide beach with white sand, a rare sight on the Caspian. It was a magically beautiful location with sand dunes leading to the mouth of a broad river flanked by flowered wetlands alive with frogs and turtles. The ground rose rapidly into thick forest, clearing in spots where huddles of thatched roofs marked small villages. Above the forested slopes hovered snow-capped mountains facing the sea. There was a glowing gentleness to the place, a soft light, and a fresh breeze danced through the wild-flowers.

Looking for some clue as to who owned the land, we found a narrow road heading up into the mountains. A fog settled in as we drove through the forest, the road narrowing through the undergrowth. Sasha complained that the Volvo wouldn't make it, which I translated to mean that we were now officially on an adventure. Finally we came to a village and asked for the *kadkhoda*. Abol did the talking, inquiring whether the beach land might be for sale. The *kadkhoda* claimed he was embarrassed to sell such poor land to such a great man. Nothing would grow there, he said. Wouldn't it be much wiser to buy land in the village where we could plant oranges? Abol struck a deal: we would buy the village plot he was so eager to sell, provided that we could also buy the land from the beach to the river. The price was settled before we learned that both river and village were named Dozdak, which means "little thief."

By Iranian law, property is not fully owned until it is built on, so we quickly had a small cottage built there for a gardener to look after the land. Whenever we visited the Caspian we still stayed at the hotel in Chalus, a grand if rather fusty remnant of Reza Shah's plans for our own Riviera. I tired of ferrying the kids back and forth to the beach and then making us all presentable three times a day to eat in the hotel dining room. I wanted to camp on the beach. Abol was nervous at the idea of our staying in a place that he considered dangerous wilderness, but I figured that we would be safe enough with the gardener and Sasha nearby. I started to round up camping equipment, some borrowed, some bought. Before I could gather all the gear, the phone rang.

"Khanom Doctor, what color do you want the bathtub to be?"

"What bathtub?" I asked.

"The bathtub for your house."

"We have a bathtub. There's nothing wrong with it."

"The bathtub for the house at Dozdak." Determined that we wouldn't have to pee in the woods, Abol had sent a team of builders up to add a bathroom and a little kitchen to the gardener's cottage. I was determined to sleep in the tent nonetheless. Abol joined me reluctantly. That very first night Dozdak lived up to its name and we were robbed. The thief took only one kilim, but he also grabbed Abol's eyeglasses. Although he had the last word, vindicated in his judgment of the dangers of the place, Abol was very upset to spend the rest of his vacation out of focus.

That was the end of camping on the shores of the Caspian Sea. The cottage grew, room by room, until it was large enough to squeeze in many weekend guests, comfortable in a rough-and-ready way. As often as not there was a houseful, and between Zahra, Nima, my nieces, and their friends, it was usually a young crowd. If we happened to find a few hippies camping on the beach nearby—not a rare event in those days—we would invite them over for a drink. I figured it was good for them to get a taste of Iranian hospitality, and the kids in my care enjoyed the scent of freedom and adventure that these young travelers brought with them.

One afternoon I was going for a walk on the beach when I came across a battered van and makeshift campsite. I chatted briefly with the campers—two young Englishmen and a Canadian couple—and invited them for the evening to Dozdak. (The name by now had become attached to our cottage.) When their van pulled up to the cottage a few hours later, I was working in the garden. I welcomed them

OUR COTTAGE ON THE CASPIAN.

and introduced them in English to the weekend gang, "These people have come on a very long trip; take good care of them!" I added in Persian to Vida, "Get the couch ready!" I went back to finish up in the garden, and by the time I had showered and dressed, they were settled in front of the fireplace with drinks and a spread of hors d'oeuvres, including a generous heap of the best local caviar.

Vida gave me a short report: one was a medical student, another studying botany, the Canadian was a policeman, and his female compatriot was extremely nervous. I asked them if they would stay for dinner.

"No, we have to go soon. We have food in the van." Her eyes never settled, flitting from one corner of the room to another as if she feared an attack at any moment. The others were more relaxed, and they overruled her, happy enough to accept a hot meal in a congenial setting.

Ghasem, one of the gang, brought out a pipe after dinner and offered it around. It shouldn't have come as much of a surprise: Ghasem looked as if he had just stumbled off the bus from Kathmandu himself, with his shoulder-length curls, his beard, and his granny glasses. I abstained, preferring the familiarity of my vodka lime. The Canadian girl refused too, for whatever reasons of her own, but the rest puffed eagerly. The policeman puffed most eagerly of all. After a while I noticed tears running down his cheeks.

"Are you okay?"

"I'm in heaven," he began. "I'm having such a good time. This is the first time I've been under the roof of a home in three months, and the fire in the fireplace, and the magnificent dinner . . ." He ran out of words and started sobbing out loud.

I said to Ghasem in Persian, "Enough! Don't give the poor guy anything more to smoke. He's crying."

Ghasem leaned back in his own universe, a silly smile crinkling his eyes into vague slits above his glasses, "Monir *joon,* he's just laughing."

"As if you could tell the difference!"

The evening ended uneventfully: we said goodnight at a civilized hour, and they drove back to their camp on the beach. The girl remained tense to the end, as if she were still not convinced that we wouldn't drug them senseless, steal their van, and demand ransom money from their parents. The next morning when we had packed up and were ready to head back to Tehran, we swung by their campsite to say goodbye. There were hugs and kisses all round, and warmest of all from that cold-fish girl who had obviously suffered a sea change.

"Thank you," she said over and over again. "You gave me the most beautiful memories of a lifetime." I asked her why she had been so

ZAHRA AND I WENT SKINNY-DIPPING IN THE CASPIAN SEA.

tense. She apologized. "I just couldn't believe that people could be so nice to strangers."

"Obviously you haven't been in Iran very long!"

Abol spent most of our weekends at the Caspian on his sailboat, meditating patiently in the middle of a perfectly calm sea. There was wind, it was true, but of a most unpredictable sort, and usually just enough to get him stuck far out at sea for hours. He didn't mind at all;

ABOL AND HIS BELOVED SAILBOAT ON A TYPICALLY CALM SEA.

it was his quiet time. He claimed that he was communing with nature, and it was obvious that he was happy as a clam: a perpetually seasick clam, yellow in the face, who could barely utter more than a syllable in response to my bored chatter. How can someone be seasick when nothing moves? If I was lucky, a fly might keep me busy observing its crooked path across the deck. If I was really lucky, a seal might poke its head through the water and stay for a chat.

And so most of the time Abol found somebody else to accompany him sailing, and I experienced his pleasure vicariously, reported at the end of the day. The boat was his baby, and it was indeed beautiful, forty-five feet of mahogany, built for racing and brought all the way from Norway. Just figuring out how to move it from the Persian Gulf port to our mountain-ringed inland sea without passing through tunnels was a task that had kept him happily challenged for days. But the unpredictable wind was the real challenge. The sea may have been calm, but there was drama on the shore when Abol went missing for too long, and more than once I drove up and down the coast for hours straining to see any glimpse of a mast on the horizon.

I wasn't the only one worried. Because the boat had too big a keel to get close to the beach, Abol kept it at the deep dock in Noshahr, where the Shah often stayed at his seaside villa. The security arrangements meant that Abol had to get permission each time he took the boat out. One day when the wind dropped and refused to stir again, he was gone long into the night. We learned later that the Shah had asked the guards many times whether Abol had returned yet. The royal order was communicated soon after: henceforth Abol would be allowed to take the boat out only on condition that he was back before sunset. *Tell that to the wind,* I thought.

It was at Dozdak that I entered into a collaboration that has remained a secret, more or less, until now. It was a moody, cold, wet day: a log was burning in the fireplace, and condensation fogged the window beside my bed. My view of the garden was a gray-green blur, but in close focus a bug tiptoed a zigzag path up the misted glass, leaving tiny footprints of clarity on his search for freedom. Finally I opened the window and let the poor little guy go, but he left behind an idea.

When I got back home to the studio, I recruited an unsuspecting wasp. Holding him ever so gently by the wing with a pair of tweezers, I dipped his feet in ink and set him on a sheet of good white paper. Bugs can't fly with wet feet. He scooted off on an errant path, leaving delicate tracks. Each tiny footprint was not just a stamp but a hair-thin brushstroke of the kick and drag of its gait. The tracks faded gradually to white. When the ink ran dry, he could manage liftoff. That first wiggly line was promising. I caught him again, washed his feet gently in a saucer of water, then dipped them in ink once more and set him off on a second line.

I needed more bugs, better bugs. I got help from one of the servants, and the two of us could be seen chasing around the garden waving the large construction sieves that were used for sand and cement. The wasps were difficult to catch; we had much better success with what we called date-bees, *zanbur-khormai*. Brown and gold and as big as plump dates, they were slow in flight, and they left big footprints as they waddled across the page. I became quite adept at catching each one again when its ink dried out or when it walked off the edge of the page. At the end of a session I would wash its feet one last time and place it under a large sieve with a good meal of fruit and meat, ready for the next day.

The drawings that resulted were a true collaboration: I could choose the color of the ink and the starting point for each line, but beyond that it was up to the bug. The compositions were abstract, of course, delicate and spacious. People saw many things in them, reporting sometimes as if I had set them a Rorschach test. But no one ever told me that they saw the path of a small creature on a mist-veiled windowpane, each step a pinprick of clarity, a microscopic fraction of a hint of the green world beyond the glass.

When Zahra and Nima had both grown up and gone off to study abroad, Dozdak became a quieter place. It seemed to me that the cottage had a spent feel, like the morning after a party. The empty beach seemed always to be waiting. But I was not disenchanted with the coast. The landscape still exerted its pull, a deeper current undisturbed by the ebb and flow of teenagers. Part of me longed to cross the arbitrary boundary of weekends, to stay winter and summer in a green, calm place and learn the subtler rhythms of its seasons. Abol had bought another, much larger parcel of land nearby. A spectacular hilltop vantage set between sea and snow-capped mountains made me wish only that Cézanne was there to paint these slopes, planted with broad strokes of tea and orange trees and emerald-green rice paddies. We made up our minds that one day, sooner or later, we would build a home on that hilltop and leave the noisy business of Tehran to younger people.

CHAPTER TWENTY-EIGHT

My close friend Beenie was married to Nicholas Thacher, who was the chargé d'affaires at the American embassy in Tehran before being appointed ambassador to Saudi Arabia. She had been an eager and intelligent companion on several of my trips into the remoter regions of Iran and a frequent visitor to Dozdak. After she moved to Jeddah, I happened to phone her there when I was in London. I caught her in a rare low moment. Life in Saudi Arabia was constrained, even for an ambassador's wife, and she was lonely. She begged me to come visit for a couple of weeks.

That required a visa. Beenie said she would send an invitation through diplomatic channels and instructed me to go to the Saudi embassy in London. When I arrived there, I was interviewed by a very proper young diplomat.

"We received the request for your visa from the American embassy in Jeddah. Are you planning to go to Mecca also?"

BEENIE AND ME, SELLING PAPER DRESSES FOR CHARITY.

"Of course!" I hadn't actually thought about it till that moment. "How can I go all the way to Saudi Arabia and not do the *haj*?"

"How will you go?"

Is this a trick question? I wondered. "By airplane, of course. How else?"

"Will you be accompanied?"

"No, I'm going alone." I should have seen what was coming next.

"You will not be accompanied by someone who is *halal* for you? Your husband or a brother?" Women were not allowed to travel alone in Saudi Arabia; I needed a chaperone with appropriate kinship credentials.

"No, I don't have any *halal* coming with me."

"I'm very sorry," he said, gathering the papers in front of him.

"Will you be my *halal*?"

"No, madam, no! You need a husband or a brother!" He was so shocked by my proposition that he blushed deeply and kept his eyes glued to the table for the remainder of our interview. I imagined him thinking: And this shameless woman is going on *haj*!

"Let's just say that the American ambassador is my *halal*." Somehow that got him off the hook. In any case, my passport was handed back to me with a fresh visa stamped in it.

Beenie and her husband met me at the airport, and I spent a few days enjoying the generous hospitality of the embassy residence and the gracious good fun of Beenie's company. But sadly she could not come with me to Mecca. The holy city was off-limits to infidels. Beenie, for all the goodness of her heart, was technically an infidel just as I was technically a Muslim by birth. It didn't matter that my father despised the mullahs or that I had never been instructed in the most basic practices of the faith: Mecca was my birthright, and I wouldn't have missed the adventure of the *haj* for anything.

Still, there was the small matter of a woman traveling alone, and besides, I didn't have a clue what I was supposed to do when I got to Mecca. Beenie and I called on the Iranian ambassador's wife—the diplomat's world runs in tight little social circles—and asked for help. As it happened, her son was home on vacation from college, and his father had decided that it was time for the boy to make the pilgrimage. She planned to go along for the drive, and I could go with them. She also gave me some guidance on how to prepare for the spiritual experience of a lifetime.

"Take off that nail polish, and wash your face completely. No makeup. Take a shower and do *ghosl.*" The ritual ablutions she described were vaguely familiar to me. As a child, I had watched my mother and other women in the bathhouse go through the motions of washing away the temporary stain that sex with their husbands had left on the soul: face the direction of the *qibla* in Mecca, pick up your right foot from behind with one hand, toss a basin of water over your left shoulder, repeat with the other hand and foot.

Back at the ambassador's residence, I was standing under the shower, drenched and ready to perform my little dance, before I realized that I didn't know which direction Mecca lay in relation to the bathroom. Determined to proceed with complete seriousness, I covered my ass by repeating the ritual four times facing front, back, and both sides. I toweled dry and dressed in the white robe, jacket, and scarf that the Iranian ambassador's wife had lent me, thanking Allah that I could wear my own underwear, which by luck was the required white.

The half-day's drive from Jeddah to Mecca was uneventful, the landscape barren, and by the time we arrived, I was genuinely ready to suspend doubt and cultivate a reverent state of mind. A young clergyman was assigned to guide us through the pilgrimage route and instruct us in the rites. He was a very handsome young man and clearly quite conscious that he cut a dashing figure in his turban and robes.

The pilgrimage threads a prescribed route through the holy places surrounding the Ka'aba—seven times counterclockwise around the black stone; back and forth seven times to the Zamzam well; hop on one foot across a certain segment of the route marked at either end by a red light . . . I figured that if I could maneuver successfully through this obstacle course without choking to death on suppressed laughter or making some dire misstep that would call the wrath of God down upon my head, I might indeed emerge from the process with a more disciplined soul and a deeper faith.

The Iranian ambassador's wife had already done the *haj* herself on a previous occasion, and so she sat out the more energetic portions of the route. That left me in the company of her son and the good-looking mullah, whose prayers were punctuated repeatedly with an eyeful of a gaze that seemed to me a little too soulful for the circumstances. As we walked from one station to the next, his cloak brushed against me as if by chance, then again. This time there was no mistaking the fingers groping under the cloth. I took a step sideways and opened a space between us, which closed again instantly. Then came a pinch so aggressive that I had to twist my bottom free of his pincers. At that point it dawned on me that it really is important to bring along someone who is *halal*—husband, brother, or father—as a chaperone on the pilgrimage. I would have to make do with the ambassador's son. I didn't want to make a fuss or do anything that might shake the teenager's faith, but I did scoot around him and ask him, in Persian, to stay between me and the mullah.

In spite of this distraction, there were indeed moments that inspired a profound sense of awe: to be one of thousands of people in prayer together in the huge courtyard surrounding the center of the world, all bending, bowing, rising in unison; the vast silence and calm of the crowd, each individual in prayer, solitary before God, and yet immersed in this ocean of human solidarity. The black stone, as tall as a three-story building, was covered in black velvet embroidered with gold inscriptions; the stone itself was visible only in one spot on the corner, the size of a man's face. It was perfectly smooth, polished to a gleaming mirror by millions of hands over many hundreds of years. I rubbed a Kleenex on the blackness to bring back to my mother. She herself had done the *haj* but had never touched the stone. She had not been well enough to walk the route, so she had hired two strong men to carry her on a litter, but they couldn't get close enough through the crowds to touch. I also filled a plastic bottle with water at the Zamzam well to bring to her.

At the end of the circuit I joined up with the ambassador's wife again in the women's section of the mosque. She explained that I would have to do one more set of prayers before I could be permitted to have sex with my husband. It didn't make sense to me—I figured I was as pure by that point as I would ever be—but she offered to demonstrate, so I followed along.

I was concentrating hard on repeating the motions and words a breath behind her, when suddenly a burst of wet chemical fog exploded in my face. I had noticed the man in the distance with the tank of disinfectant on his back and the spray pump in his hand working his way up and down the rows of the faithful, but the blast in my face still caught me off guard. I let out a loud, involuntary exclamation of surprise. My mentor halted her prayer midstream, as shocked by my outburst as I was by the mouthful of disinfectant.

"You interrupted the prayer—it's ruined! We can't repeat it again!"

"Never mind, I'll sleep with my husband anyway. Believe me, it won't make any difference."

I don't know if that branded me as an irredeemable *kafir,* but as we made our way back to the car, I was struck by awe one more time. Our route took us through the bazaar, which had emptied completely for the noon prayers. Every single soul had gone to the mosque court-yard, and the shops were left open, unlocked and unguarded. House-hold goods, pilgrims' souvenirs, fabrics, gold bracelets, and diamond rings—the whole economy of the bazaar lay exposed in absolute faith that no thief would dare to steal anything while the city prayed.

On the drive back to Jeddah, the ambassador's son turned on the car stereo in the Mercedes-Benz, and the two of us, still in our white pilgrims' weeds, bounced in our seats to some rousing good rock music. The ambassador's wife did not bounce. She hissed at her son in Persian, "Turn it down! Can't you see the driver is shocked?"

They dropped me off at the American embassy residence, and we said our goodbyes. As I entered the house, the servants beamed at the sight of my white outfit. They bowed and welcomed me with Muslim greetings of exceptional respect. I was now *hajjieh,* the pilgrimage accomplished. Not many of the ambassador's houseguests held such an honor. But once again I blew it. When a uniformed servant approached me, bowed, and asked in polite English what I would like to drink, I answered without thinking, "Whiskey soda, please."

"Monir, shut up! Shame on you!" Beenie scolded me under her breath. "Couldn't you have asked me?" The embarrassment I felt in that moment was genuine, so I guess the experience of the *haj* had indeed had some effect on my wayward soul.

Later, on the flight back to Tehran, I picked up a newspaper and read that an epidemic of chicken pox had broken out. The source had been traced: water from the Zamzam well was to blame. I broke the news to my mother and apologized when I handed her the plastic bot-tle. She emptied it into a flowerpot with a whispered prayer.

CHAPTER TWENTY-NINE

The conference table was polished to a high sheen, a dark pool reflecting eight heavily made-up faces and eight sets of lacquered nails that drummed for a turn to speak or brandished pens emphatically. *Mirror, mirror, on the wall,* the rhyme ran inappropriate circles in my brain, *who's the most virtuous of us all?* Was it the general's wife with the huge girth and husky voice who assigned tasks with such monumental authority? Or would the honor go to Khanom with the towering hairdo who was reporting every last penny of her charitable disbursements in a nasal drone? Or perhaps to the perky weasel with the face-lift and the gift for business-school jargon? I was half asleep, hypnotized by the slow sweep of the minute hand on the big gold clock, when Mrs. General boomed, "Khanom Farmanfarmaian! What would you like to do?"

"Ladies . . ." I groped for a polite way to do this. *To hell with it,* I thought, *it's now or never.* "Ladies, I would be happy to do anything, anything at all, as long as it doesn't involve coming to meetings. Give me a job, and I'll happily do it. I'll clean toilets in the poorest slum. I'll scrub floors. I'll change diapers in an orphanage. Just don't ask me to come to meetings."

Silence. Eighty red fingernails perfectly motionless. The weasel broke the spell. "Khanom is an artist." I feared her smile would crack something.

"Khanom takes photographs," growled the general's wife. That took me by surprise. How did *she* know?

I had begun taking photographs simply to capture some fraction of the kaleidoscope of my travels, but it was impossible to ignore the extreme contrasts that appeared in my viewfinder. It seemed as if the camera itself packed a social conscience. Point it at a human being, and the very frame makes a statement. This is included, that is not. No comb has tugged at this child's matted hair. The sneakers on these little feet are wet with snow; no socks in this picture. Returning home from one trip stunned and laden with distressing images of poverty's scars on children, I had raced Zahra off to an exceptionally ostentatious birthday party, the camera still slung around my neck. As she added her offering to the mountain of ribbon-wrapped, chrome-trimmed, battery-operated loot, I thought of the kids whose very best toy was an empty milk carton recycled as a soccer ball. Somewhere between the cavorting clowns, the regiment of nannies at attention, and the squeals of children who had never suffered any indignity worse than getting their cheeks pinched by overzealous aunts, I hatched the idea for a documentary photo essay.

My photojournalistic ambitions were equally a reaction to the luxury that surrounded me and to the poverty I witnessed. I didn't want to anesthetize myself to the pain I felt at the deep gash that divided rich and poor. I couldn't deny that I was enjoying the good life myself, but I knew better than to presume I had any special entitlement to what luck had brought my way. Money is one thing; the burden of class is quite another. And so for a while I tagged along to every birthday party that Zahra was invited to, working under cover, just one more mother snapping away at the spoiled darlings. In the end, the photo essay remained a private project, shelved for years because I didn't know how to publish it without giving undue offense to friends and relatives. Hence my surprise that the society sisters of mercy had me pegged as a photographer. Was I exposed as a double agent in the class wars, or did they think I had something useful to offer the cause?

My own approach to charity had always been personal, serendipitous, and discreet. I knew I wasn't going to solve the world's problems. Even with all my connections and the weight of the Farmanfarmaian name, my righteous angry phone calls to people in high places rarely accomplished more than beating a shortcut through the bureaucracy. My complaints just fell on deaf ears that much sooner. But I did feel a responsibility to share the luck that had come my way, at least with those less fortunate whose paths crossed my own. If a servant worked in our home for any length of time, he would find in due course that he owned his own home.

The upshot of the charitable society ladies' meeting was that I would teach art twice a week at a public school in Shah Abdolazim. It was the poorest neighborhood on the southern fringe of Tehran, lying under a blanket of soot from the belching chimneys of the kilns where whole families worked at molding mud into bricks. It was a long haul there, a crawling hour and a half through heavy traffic each way. Once a week Zahra came with me—her own school ran on a different schedule—and taught English to kids a little younger than herself.

Considering the neighborhood, the school was remarkably well appointed: a modern building, well lit, equipped with wooden tables and chairs, and a huge sports field. The children, all boys, were orderly, polite, and rather more cheerful than their dingy prison-gray uniforms and shaved heads would have suggested. They seemed, if anything, a little intimidated by their surroundings and the lucky escape they had made from the brick factory into the hallways of learning. Art as I knew it was terra incognita to them. I might as well have told them that we were going on a field trip to Mars.

What was beautiful, in their estimation? I asked. "A flower," one said when I made it clear that I expected answers to this seemingly rhetorical question.

"A garden full of flowers!" said another, clearly bent on one-upmanship. I wondered aloud if he had ever seen such a thing. "Yes, at the cemetery."

"A carpet is beautiful?" one ventured to whisper.

Another, more confidently, "A shiny new motorcycle."

"A shiny new car. That's more beautiful." We were on a roll now.

One named a local movie star. Had he ever been to the movies? No, but his brother had.

Finally one earnest little face said shyly but with utter conviction, "My baby sister." Now I was satisfied that we had moved from the realm of consensus and cliché into direct experience.

Remembering the postcards and slavish copy work that had so rigidly regimented my own perception, I decided that free expression was a far more urgent priority for these kids than any technical skills. Remembering also the advice of the psychologist at the Ethical Culture School, I decided that finger painting was a good place to start. The art supply stores in Tehran did not stock finger paint, so I cooked up a few bucketsful using soap and powdered pigments.

The kids were afraid to even touch the stuff. I was surprised. I knew that many of them had worked in the brick factory trampling the lumps out of wet clay with their bare feet, and others had no doubt done dirtier work. But I had confused them by introducing something so mucky into the pristine sanctuary that school represented to them.

I dipped my fingers in the blue goop. "Look! It's not poison. It washes right off. It's clean. It's made from soap." One of the bravest tested a single fingertip. Tentative dabs at the wet paper. A trailing streak. The finger, examined, proved unharmed. Little by little they ventured into the goop and discovered the possibilities of smushing, swiping, and splatting, fist curls and thumb wiggles and palm pats and sweeping waves. I watched brows furrow and tongues twist in concentration. I was amazed at the uniqueness, the complete individuality of each finished sheet, unclouded by *should* and *must* or any preconceived notion of what a picture ought to be.

When we graduated from finger painting to brushes, they froze once again, as if the little pieces of wood and hair were instruments of an occult technology, heavy with expectation in their hands. I pondered how to break the curse. Jackson Pollock should do it, I thought, and I pulled some art books from the shelves of my studio.

"Look," I told them. "This guy just let the paint drip, and they put his pictures in a book. You see how important this book is? It cost a thousand *toman!*" Their families probably lived on that much for two or three months. I didn't dare tell them what the paintings themselves were selling for. Pollock made a real impression, as did many other pages in the book and, most of all, the unbounded diversity of what was included between the covers. This is art? Yes. And that is art too? Yes. And that, and that, and that? Yes, yes, yes! I watched their huge dark-lashed eyes as they scanned the pictures. I saw no judgment there, no skepticism. I saw innocence, curiosity, discovery, and faith in my word that anything indeed was possible. The results were a testament to that faith. They painted with exuberance and a startling freshness, each one of them embracing his own vision with confidence.

How could they do so much with so little? So little prompting, so little exposure, so little in the way of materials . . . I sat in the car and daydreamed as Sasha wove through the choking traffic; Zahra was sound asleep with her head in my lap, exhausted by the day's work. What kind of an impact would it have if these children could see good art firsthand, not just reproductions in a book? There was no contemporary art on public display in Tehran at the time, except in a few small private galleries in the wealthiest neighborhoods on the far side of town. These children would never set foot there. The one real museum in the city, Iran Bastan, contained only ancient artifacts that were not even properly labeled—but that was another matter. I imagined an exhibition space that was accessible and welcoming. How many artists did I know personally who would be happy to donate a painting for a cause so unquestionably noble? Which of many wealthy friends could be tapped for a contribution?

By the time we arrived home, I had the skeleton of a plan in place. Abol listened thoughtfully and made some suggestions. I called the cultural center at the Iran-America Society. It was a wonderful idea, the director agreed, and he offered a permanent gallery space for the project. Hoping for some top-drawer support, I invited the American ambassador, Richard Helms, to dinner to discuss the plan. Helms's wife, Cynthia, was knowledgeable about American art and well connected. She embraced the project enthusiastically and gave me introductions to several collectors in Washington and to Carter Brown, who was director of the National Gallery.

I traveled to the United States as soon as I could make arrangements. Nima had recently moved to New York after graduating from college in Geneva. She had found a job writing for *Interview,* my old Bonwit colleague Andy Warhol's new magazine, and was herself as plugged in to the art scene as anyone could be. I figured it would be a good time to visit with her and brainstorm together.

I headed for Washington first. The meetings went well enough, at least in that bland, gracious, and expertly inscrutable way that Washington affects in its dealings with potentially useful foreigners of no particularly urgent interest. Carter Brown said that if he could find any extra paintings that weren't needed at the National Gallery, he would send them over. I wondered what he had in mind. A Rauschenberg lying around gathering dust? A Rothko that some curator had a personal vendetta against?

At Helms's bidding I also paid a visit to Kermit Roosevelt, who likewise promised to help in a very noncommittal way. I wasn't really sure what he had to offer. At the time I didn't have a clue about his role in the CIA's meddling in Iran in 1953, when he competed with Donald Wilber for the title of über-spy in the Mossadegh affair. Even with hindsight it's hard to figure why Helms had sent me to meet him unless it was just to busy me, or for Roosevelt's nostalgic amusement.

A luncheon at the Georgetown home of another ambassador and collector was a little more productive. One approached the mansion through a park of huge magnolias, then went past the scrutiny of the primmest of secretaries, continued through rooms hung with a museum's worth of modern art, and finally entered the formal dining room, where my hostess and I, just the two of us, were served by a waiter in white gloves. I was starving. The small stuffed artichoke on my plate was sufficient only to leave me wondering how people could live so magnificently on so little food.

My hostess was eager to introduce me to Frank Stella, whose paintings were a highlight of her collection. We set up an appointment. He lived in New York, which suited me fine. I had had enough of Washington. I was eager to see Nima and to reconnect with the artists I knew.

When the taxi reached the Jones Street address in the Village, I thought I must have written it down wrong: it was a run-down garage front, its peeling paint barely adhering to the walls by the grace of several layers of graffiti. I rang the bell; nobody answered. I waited, then rang again. I was thinking how badly the building needed a new coat of paint when a man appeared beside me on the sidewalk wearing sneakers and a baseball hat, all smeared with paint. He had a couple of teeth missing as well as three fingers. A sad case, I thought, but at least there's no lack of work for a painter around here. He opened the door and let himself in. "I'm here to see Mr. Stella," I told him.

"Come on in," he said. He led me down a narrow hallway, then up two flights of very steep stairs and into a huge studio, probably one whole floor of the building. There was a round table the size of a helicopter pad, and everywhere there were paintings, huge paintings on a scale that fitted that hangar of a room. I recognized one by Stella and a Noland, but the rest were unfamiliar. The man had disappeared while I was getting my bearings in front of the vast canvases. I found my way to a chair, sat down, and waited. And waited. That nasal voice came through a doorway from what I supposed was the kitchen. "Would you like a coffee?"

"Coffee would be nice." When he came out again about five minutes later with a cup of coffee, I asked him, "When is Mr. Stella coming?"

"I'm Stella myself," he said very softly. When I recovered from my embarrassment, it occurred to me that I had been spending far too much of my time in the United States with patrons and not enough time with artists.

We hit it off very well. He seemed to have some reservations about my project, however, and said he would give me an answer soon. A few days later he asked if I would like to join him that evening for an opening at the Museum of Modern Art. I was delighted—so much so that I forgot to ask whose opening it was. He picked me up at Nima's later, but when we arrived at the museum, the attendant at the door wouldn't let us in. Frank had forgotten his invitation.

"I'm Stella," he said.

"So what?"

He looked as though he was ready to shrug the whole thing off and come up with a better way to spend the evening. It seemed an afterthought when he mentioned the name of a curator and asked the attendant to call her. That did the trick, and we took the elevator up, then walked through several galleries and arrived at a dining room with some thirty tables set for a formal dinner. We were a little bit late; the room was full of glittery women and men in black tie. As we wove through the tables to our assigned place, many of them rose from their seats to greet Frank and say a few words to him. There was an awkward tension in these encounters, as if he was not eager to introduce me but also reluctant to seem rude. We made it to our table and through dinner well enough. As dessert was being served, the director of the museum made a speech and several others followed, paeans to the accomplishment of the evening's honoree, who, it turned out, was Frank himself. As everyone clapped, he just sat there with head bowed and a slightly hangdog expression. When it was his turn to speak, he stood up and mumbled succinctly, "Thank you so much, everybody, for coming. I'm very happy and honored." That introduction to the modest Mr. Stella was the beginning of a long friendship.

A few days later a friend invited me to another opening. Two floors of the old Whitney Museum were given over to an exhibition of huge abstract paintings by Joan Mitchell. I was very impressed by the work, though I didn't recognize the artist's name. I was standing in the crowd in the main lobby at the foot of the stairs when a flutter of voices echoed, "Joan is coming down, Joan is coming . . ." I looked up and saw a tall, thin woman with salt-and-pepper curls framing a very familiar face. For a moment I was back in the smoke-hung Cedar Tavern, listening to a passionate disquisition as Joan punched emphatic holes in the air with her cigarette.

"Monir!" She danced down the stairs and landed with a big hug. "Where have you been all these years?"

"In Iran . . . ," I started, but there was no way to say it all on our feet in the middle of a crowd that was eager to greet her. Obviously she also had tales to tell. I could hardly wrap my mind around the happy fact that one of the old gang was now firmly installed on two whole floors of the Whitney. We made a plan to meet the next night.

Before dinner we sat in her hotel room and compared notes on art and life and husbands and more. She had actually made it to Paris and was living near Monet's garden. Eventually I got around to the purpose of my trip. I told her about the children of Shah Abdolazim, about the effects of Pollock and homemade finger paints, and the idea for a collection of contemporary American art on the children's own turf. I asked if she would be willing to contribute a painting.

"Are you serious?" The rant that exploded blindsided me. "Give *my* art to *that* damn country? To that dictator, that crook, that . . . *Shah*?!"

"But Ambassador Helms said—"

"Monir, your 'Ambassador' Helms was the head of the CIA. They're all in bed together. I don't know how you can even live there!"

I was shocked to learn how nasty our national reputation had become, and my gut told me to listen to Joan—an artist, a friend— just as it had told me that I was wasting my time in Washington. I was ready to concede any political point she had the confidence to make. (Obviously I was naïve and uninformed—hadn't that always been the case?) But was I guilty just for living in my own country? And what did any of this have to do with the children? Were they to blame for what the Shah was doing? Was it wrong to try to help them? It was all very depressing.

We managed somehow to finish dinner on a lighter note. Joan invited me to visit her in Paris and said that if I came, she would give me a painting personally, as long as I didn't give it to my country. Another meeting with a collector went well enough, but it didn't matter. Joan's words were echoing doom in my head, and I knew the project was dead in the water if the artists themselves would not get behind it. Frank Stella confirmed my fears a few days later when he voiced the same sentiments, though more calmly. He too offered me a painting as a personal gift but refused to support the project.

When I got back to Tehran, I was deeply torn. I was reluctant to admit defeat so easily and to turn my back on a vision that had seemed so worthwhile. At the same time I felt ashamed. It was as if I had shit on my shoes: the stink of corruption and despotism that surrounded me was obvious halfway around the world, and yet I had hardly noticed. But that wasn't true either. Of course I was aware that corruption infested high places and low, but it struck me as a failure of character on the part of the individuals involved rather than something inherently wrong with my country. I knew very well that we had a few honest politicians too. Yes, the Shah was stepping farther beyond the bounds of good governance each day. His refusal to tolerate any dissent smacked of hubris and paranoia. But as my father had so often said, there was no quick fix, no hero waiting in the wings. Change would take time, education . . .

Which brought me back full circle to my students and the less rational question that squeezed my heart: Why was I made to feel foolish for wanting to do good? Weary of arguing with myself, I decided to trust instinct and aim one last shot blindly at the belly of the beast. I phoned the queen's office and asked for a meeting with her. I wasn't so important that I could get a meeting without explaining my business to her aide. He called me back a little later to say that the queen was willing to meet me. Indeed, she had been working on a similar plan independently. Cynthia Helms was somehow involved. An entire new museum was going to be created, dedicated to contemporary art, and the queen was hoping that I would come work for her.

If it was closure I was looking for, that did the trick. I said that I would call back to confirm a date for our meeting, but I never did. I figured that one way or another some good modern art was about to find its way to Tehran. It didn't matter whether I had anything to do with it or not, as long as it happened. I told myself that when the queen's new museum opened, I would take my students there for a field trip.

CHAPTER THIRTY

Monir *joon*, I'm off to New York for business in a few days," Abol's brother told me, "and I'm meeting with David Rockefeller. Why don't you let me take one of your art pieces to show him? You know he's an art lover and a big collector. I'm sure he could arrange for you to have an exhibition at a good gallery in New York."

Abol's brother was indeed well connected, and it was kind of him to make the offer. Or perhaps he owed me a favor. After all, I had built two spectacular mirror mosaic installations for his dining room wall and fireplace (at no cost to him, of course—but how could one even think of setting a price among family?). I didn't have the self-confidence to assume that he simply believed the art deserved to be seen.

Mindful of the hassle of carrying a heavy, fragile work of art, I chose a small piece. It was one of my earlier mirror mosaics, using long slivers of mirror cut on a curve in a composition that swirled with energy, accented with small fragments of flowers and nightingales that I had rescued from a broken Qajar painting behind glass. When he returned to Tehran, Abol's brother reported that Rockefeller had indeed liked the piece and had shown it to Dorothy Miller at the Museum of Modern Art, who also thought it was interesting. End of story. Rather than lugging the thing back, he had left it behind at Nima's apartment in New York.

But connections can be slow-climbing vines, putting out shoots when you've given up tending them, bearing fruit when you least expect. It was Nima's efforts that first made the difference. She showed the piece to Jacques Kaplan, and on the strength of that one view, he offered me an exhibit at his gallery on East 71st Street.

For the show, I selected more of the early mirror mosaics—spontaneous compositions of swirling shards of reflections: wild seas where fragments of the past bobbed half-submerged, wild skies where folk-memory glinted like guiding stars. Something new, something old. The opening at Jacques Kaplan Gallery was a New York fairy tale, the guest list as sparkling as the art. I greeted old friends and new

from the art world: Sally Avery (Milton
had passed away by then), Frank Stella,
Louise Nevelson, Richard Linden, Salvador Dalí, Saul Steinberg, Larry Rivers,
and Robert Indiana (who invited me later
to his loft, which was so big he used roller
skates to get around). Andy Warhol came,
tape recorder in hand, and I asked him
for the record, "Do you remember when
you used to draw shoes at Bonwit Teller
and they paid you twenty-five dollars
a piece?"

ANDY WARHOL AND
SALVADOR DALÍ AT THE
JACQUES KAPLAN OPENING.

"But, Monir," came the wide-eyed, nasal response, "it was so much
money then!"

The director of the Guggenheim Museum showed up, and Ted
Sorenson, who had been John Kennedy's right-hand man, and Lily
Auchincloss, the arts philanthropist. Dorothy Miller came, with Mrs.
Whitney in tow. Dorothy bought a piece for the Chase Manhattan
collection; we would become very close friends. After the opening
the Iranian ambassador to the United Nations gave a dinner for the
guests, so the party continued. And all through the evening Abol
beamed proudly, his smile like a beacon in the crowd.

It was 1975. The Shah and Queen Farah were coming to Washington for an official visit. It was decided that the show at the Jacques
Kaplan Gallery would move to Washington, to the Kennedy Center,
where the royal couple were scheduled to see the ballet: an Iranian
artist honoring their presence, or some such thinking. And so there
was another opening, this time very exclusive indeed, where I introduced the work to the Shah and his guests, including Nelson and
Happy Rockefeller. Andy came too, the celebrity weight being irresistible, and in any case he was busy cultivating a relationship with
Farah.

After the ballet, which was actually a private rehearsal, the Iranian
embassy hosted a dinner party for more than a hundred people. I
was on my own that night—Abol had returned to Iran by then, and
I was staying outside Washington at the home of an art collector who
was eager to be part of the scene. (I had met her when she came to
Tehran trying to sell a very large Chagall to the queen's new museum.)
The route between the Kennedy Center and the embassy party was

chaos—Iranian student groups were demonstrating against the Shah, barriers and police were everywhere, and traffic was detoured for security. When I finally got to the very elegantly appointed dining room, the crowd of milling guests was thinning quickly as people found their name cards at the dinner tables. I asked an aide where I should sit and waited as lists were checked and rechecked.

"Khanom, there has been some mistake. If you would like to stand at the side here with the staff, we can eat after the guests have finished." I wasn't *that* hungry. I decided to call it a night and catch a cab back to the collector's home in the suburbs where I was staying. I could see she was chatting very happily with the other guests at her table, and I didn't want to disturb her, so I sneaked out.

I had dressed for the event with a certain flamboyance—after all, I was supposed to be "the Iranian artist," not some diplomat's wife. I was wearing an embroidered Baluchi tribal dress and heavy Turkoman silver jewelry, and my hair was long then, flowing freely—all very well for art gallery, ballet, and embassy dinner. But I felt more than a little foolish wandering through the picket line of enraged young Iranians (who had more than a small portion of my sympathy), weaving around police barriers, and hiking down the avenue in search of a nonexistent cab. When I finally got to the house, it was locked and dark, so I sat on the stoop listening to the crickets until my hostess returned home from the party.

"Monir! The embassy just phoned—you've been invited to tea with Joan Kennedy! At her home!" I didn't see what the fuss was all about, and I already had a full schedule for the remaining days in Washington.

"I'll have to pass. I don't see how I can fit in another appointment."

My hostess was outraged. "Monir, don't be stupid! Drop everything! How can anyone be too busy for Joan Kennedy?"

It turned out that Joan had seen the exhibition, though I hadn't noticed her at the opening. She liked it very much and was curious to meet the artist. She had tracked me down through the Iranian embassy.

Another suburb of Washington, another mansion. We sat in the living room, drinking tea and talking for a long time, while her son—afflicted with cancer in the most recent episode of the continuing family tragedy—played with a pet gerbil. Joan projected an instant intimacy: she was artistic too, she confessed, and played the piano seriously. She asked how I spent vacations, and I told her a little bit about our cottage at the Caspian Sea. She was enthralled.

"If I come to Iran one day, would you take me there?"

"Of course. We would love to have you. Friends often come to stay there. I'm sure you would enjoy it." Iranian hospitality is offered freely and, when the guest appears at the door, delivered lavishly. But one hardly expects that every earnestly pressed invitation will be accepted. The subtext is often *I would lay my life at your feet if it came to that, but* inshallah *it won't be necessary.*

She asked for my address and wrote several long letters to me after I returned home. So I was not entirely surprised when I received a call from the American embassy saying that Joan was in Tehran, along with her husband, Ted, and two sisters. I threw a big luncheon party for them and invited all the artists I knew, a few members of the family, and a few people from the diplomatic community. Vida helped me decorate the garden beautifully, and it turned out to be a really lovely party. Joan brought up the question of a trip to the Caspian, and we set a date. Her husband and sisters were traveling on to Israel, but she would stay behind in Iran for a few days at Dozdak. I

THE PARTY PLANNED FOR THE KENNEDYS.

told her I'd like to bring along my niece and a few friends who would be interesting company.

"Please, Monir, don't. Let it be just us two. We'll go for long walks, enjoy nature, and talk about art . . ."

Oh dear, I thought. *She's not going to let me off the hook.* We met again at another party hosted by the embassy, and once again she insisted that she wanted to spend the time at Dozdak alone with me. At the same party gossip buzzed among embassy staffers about my prospective guest's drinking habits, and I began to get very cold feet. I called Ambassador Helms the next morning and did something I had never done before: I recorded our conversation. If anything happened, I wanted it on record that I had given him fair warning and that the trip was not at my instigation.

"Richard, I'm worried. There's no security. The cottage is isolated. We're at the end of a dirt road. If anything happens to her, what can I do by myself?"

"Nothing will happen. She really wants to do this."

I thought up all kinds of strategies. I would take her to one of the luxurious villas at Farmansara instead of my humble cottage. I would hire a private plane to get us there. But no, she wanted the cottage, she wanted the drive, she wanted the whole authentic experience.

I sent the cook up in advance with a carload of groceries and a menu plan. I sent the housekeeper up to clean the place and change the sheets. I sent Vida along with a couple of friends to my sister's place nearby as a backup crew in case of emergencies.

One day left to go. My sister-in-law phoned: "Monir, there's a bulldozer and a team of workers wandering around Farmansara, looking for a dirt road that needs leveling. They say they're here because Kennedy is coming. Shall I send them over to Dozdak?" I had to laugh. Obviously Helms had informed SAVAK that my dirt road was a security risk. Could I ever explain to my guest that this kind of interference was as authentic as anything else she might experience in Iran?

We drove up to the hotel at ten sharp, the car freshly washed and full of gas, the oil and tires checked, and Sasha looking even more dignified than usual. I had filled an icebox with drinks, fruit, and snacks for the road and wrapped up a kilim that Ted Kennedy had admired in my garden to offer as a gift, following the custom of *pishkesh.* When I asked the front desk to ring the room, a man came down who introduced himself as Joan's brother-in-law. He said that she was terribly sick, could not make the trip, and would be flying home immediately.

In spite of myself I blurted out, "I don't believe it!" With all the anticipation and preparation, I couldn't process this news. He took me up to the room and showed me Joan, sprawled unconscious on the bed. The party was over. I heaved a sigh of relief that disaster had been averted, at least on my turf. I left the kilim with the brother-in-law and asked him to give it, with my condolences, to Joan. It wasn't the end of our friendship—not yet. She continued to write me long letters and insisted that I must come visit her when I came to America.

CHAPTER THIRTY-ONE

No, no, no! Not there! Don't put it there!"

Hajji Ostad teetered at the top of a ladder, clutching the spherical, mirror-encrusted sculpture with both hands, and looked across the room at me with pleading eyes. *Enough is enough,* I thought.

"Yes, put it right there," I confirmed, and then turned to the little tornado of hysteria who was acting director for the cultural center of the Iran-America Society: "Khanom, if you set foot in this room again, I will throw you out, physically, right in front of Hajji and these workers. I don't want you in here until opening night. I made this art, and I know how to hang it." She stomped out. I was trembling, as much from the weird novelty of my own outburst as from anger at her incessant interference. I had started out conceding every point, assuming she knew best, but it didn't take long to figure out that I had a much better eye for the visual task at hand and that she was creating drama for drama's sake. When the adrenaline subsided, I found that I was pleased with myself. I had never before stood my ground in such a direct confrontation, and it felt significant that I had done it in defense of my art.

In spite of the headaches of hanging the show, the opening went smoothly. Soon afterward I received a call saying that a certain Denise René, who owned galleries in Paris and New York, was in town. She wanted to see the exhibition. Could I come show her around? Most certainly.

It turned out that Dorothy Miller at the Museum of Modern Art in New York had recommended my work to her. At the time, Denise was representing Max Bill and Victor Vasarely and was especially interested in abstract op art. What I had to show her seemed to resonate. The exhibition was my most recent work: minimalist explorations of geometric themes distilled from Islamic mosaics—straight lines and clean surfaces—mirror, stainless steel, pure white plaster, and single brilliant colors behind glass. After half an hour of walking with Denise through the gallery, with some silent contemplation in spite of my nervous patter, she turned to me.

"I'd be happy to give you an exhibition in Paris, if you like."

My heart stopped. When the beat resumed, I reached to give her a big hug, and before I knew what I was doing, I had lifted her off the ground—she was a very petite angel—and was whirling her in circles around the gallery, screaming, "Thank you! Thank you! Thank you!" This was not the cooler-than-thou behavior appropriate for high-level art world encounters. This was sheer, unapologetic joy. The centrifugal force of our spinning dance seemed to pull from my heart all the

TRIUMPHANT, WITH ABOL,
AT MY OPENING IN PARIS.

weight of dead hope that Paris had ever meant to me: the impossible wartime destination, the bitterness of Manou's sojourn there, the disappointment of the Galerie de France debacle . . . Yes, I'd had a great show in New York, but New York was home turf, with all the advantages that entailed. Paris was the real thing. Thank you!

Abol understood what this meant to me, as no one else could. He pulled out all the stops. We stayed in St. Germain at L'Hôtel, a small, nineteenth-century fantasia of a hotel, laden with luxury, history, and high culture. After the opening Abol arranged for a dinner party for sixty people at the hotel, with champagne and kilos of caviar. Even the two ducks splashing in the fountain seemed magically set there for me. There was one thing more I could have wished for, and it appeared: Zahra was living in Paris just for that one year, studying at the Sorbonne, and Nima flew in from New York. Their presence was the icing on the cake.

The exhibition in Paris led to a place that I never would have expected. It happened to be a bedroom. Two American interior designers saw the show and invited me to their home—a watermill on the outskirts of Paris—to discuss a "highly confidential" project. I was so stunned by the extraordinary beauty of their home, not to mention their collection of Iranian antiques, that I had a hard time focusing on the conversation at first. When I actually listened, I was no less surprised. They had been hired to decorate the queen's new

MY PHOTO ON THE GALERIE DENISE RENÉ CATALOG, 1977.

office and living quarters at Niavaran Palace in Tehran, and they wanted me to cover the walls and ceiling of her bedroom with mirror mosaics.

Frankly, what popped into my mind first was not the politics of the job, or what my mirrors might reflect, but the materials. "I want to use antique mirror," I said instantly. In the end, it wasn't actually antique but a good copy. They sent me to a factory outside Paris where glass, in myriad colors, was blown by mouth into huge spheres that were cut with scissors, flattened, and then coated with silvering. The glass was rich with texture—molten cracks and ripples, thicker areas where the color deepened, thinner spots of sheer, translucent candy. I chose earth tones and pastels, shades of red, brown, olive green, pale blue, and amber . . . I was greedy. I chose far more than I needed. No doubt I would find a use for the surplus.

I worked on that room all through the summer of 1977. I went back to the spontaneous compositions I had done earlier—the austere geometric forms seemed too hard-edged for a queen's bedroom—and created a cascading waterfall of broken light and shimmering colors, now deep, now soft, here and there an accent of painting behind glass. I built a maquette and samples; Hajji set up camp in the palace, and I went daily to check on the installation and make adjustments.

The queen, of course, was not hanging around while we worked, having moved to the summer palace at Saadabad. But when she appeared at a gallery opening not long after the job was finished, she singled me out of the crowd. ("She's recognized you! Go to her!" insisted a friend who was standing beside me.) In a very quiet voice she complimented me on the work and asked several questions about how it had been done, while everyone around us bowed and scraped even as they pressed forward and elbowed neighbors for a better position. When the moment was over and she had moved on, the crowd pressed in on her wake, every face a question mark. Prime Minister Amir Abbas Hoveyda sidled up to me and asked, "What was the queen talking to you about?"

"Just a private matter," I smiled. "Bedroom business."

Joking aside, I had always carefully avoided being drawn into the life of the court, and I kept my relationship with Farah strictly confined to matters of art. Not that I had anything against her personally at all; I just didn't want the package deal, with its dubious politics and high-stress socializing. But I invited her to my openings, and on several occasions I went to her to complain about the appalling condition of national treasures that I had witnessed on my travels.

Each time I'd be ushered through her office suite at Niavaran Palace, with its display cases of Iranian antiquities side by side with contemporary sculpture (I remember Arman's pieces of a broken piano in Plexiglas) and into her study, a living room–size affair with magnificent Persian carpets and antique French furniture. After five or ten minutes' wait, she would appear, a picture of businesslike elegance. I'd manage a little bow over the handshake; we would sit, tea would be served, and we would talk. She was always agreeable and relaxed, really very pleasant. I liked her husky voice; it was rather like my own. I would try to make my case briefly, emphatically, but without getting too emotional, though I'd cried over what I'd witnessed: the oldest known fire temple, hidden for millennia, the ash and charcoal still on the altar when it was buried to conceal it from the enemy armies approaching, now exposed, half excavated, and melting to mud in the rains while sheep and goats sheltered there.

"How on earth can the government give someone a permit to excavate without ensuring that they protect the site once it's opened?"

"I'll ask the minister of culture to check on it."

Or the fortress at Bam, a whole ancient city dissolving slowly under the elements: "Talk to the scientists. There are ways to preserve these things. Maybe they could coat the mud walls with fiberglass—"

"A whole city dressed in a fiberglass raincoat! You have quite an imagination!"

Nothing ever came of my complaints. Archaeologists continued to dig without care for what happened to the sites once their papers were published. Bam would continue to dissolve until the earthquake of 2003 finished the job. Even if she'd had the best of intentions, I don't know that she had the power to shift the deadweight of bureaucracy with a single command.

In any case, she was a busy woman, and many more people besides me were vying for her attention. In those years Tehran was the honey pot of the art world. Aside from redecorating her bedroom, the queen was shopping for art—enough to fill a museum or two. If her budget had a limit, it was beyond the imagination of the gallery owners, museum curators, private collectors, and artists who were converging on Mehrabad airport and hovering in hotel lobbies. Every deal was hush-hush, of course, though gossip bubbled constantly.

Andy Warhol couldn't have missed a scene like this. He came to Tehran to photograph the queen for a silkscreen portrait series. Nima arranged the trip for him and acted as hostess throughout, shuttling him back and forth between his hotel and the palace and ensuring a steady supply of caviar. I did my part, throwing a big garden party that turned into a press event, complete with television crews. Andy brought me one of his Marilyn Monroe silkscreen prints as a gift; I gave him one of my mirrored balls, which lived on his desk until he died. He was still, as ever, a man of few words: "Oh, wow!" or sometimes "Oh, please!" But there was no question that he was having a very good time indeed.

The opening of Tehran's new Museum of Contemporary Art was celebrated with a three-day gala. This was the big prize, the culmination of several years of frenzied wheeling and dealing for the art world and, I noted quietly to myself, the destination I had silently promised my young students at Shah Abdolazim. Eventually Tehran's young art students would indeed fill those halls, but for now it was all big shots. Henry Kissinger and Nelson Rockefeller came, along with art critics, museum directors, and collectors from around the world.

Of course, I also threw a party for the opening. I decorated the garden with even more care than usual, hanging Bokhara tapestries from the second-floor terrace and spreading fine carpets and kilims over the grass. I don't know if anyone recognized these tributes to the garden within the garden, the soul of the country they had come to visit. It seemed to me they were too busy angling for introductions,

YEARS AFTER ANDY WARHOL LET ME KEEP HIS
DISCARDED DRAWINGS OF SHOES, I GAVE HIM ONE OF
THESE MIRROR BALLS AND IT SAT ON A TABLE
IN HIS MADISON AVENUE APARTMENT.

too busy jockeying for the right seat next to the right person, the right ear to bend, to even notice that they had come all the way to Iran. I was glad that I had decided to serve peasant food. The cook ladled up a hearty soup of *aash* from a huge pot on a makeshift stove in the garden. I informed the honored guests they would have to pay a few coins for their dish, and they seemed happy to play the game.

We are driving in the mountains behind Tehran, leaving all the fuss behind. In the convertible with the top down are a couple of old friends, one of them the actress Shohreh Aghdashlou, her hair whipping in the clean, dry wind. We're somewhere between Jajerud and Galandarak, the rhythm of the village names singing in my head. Another beat comes faint on the wind. An oil can serves for a drum, surrounded by a half-circle of seven or eight men singing, dancing, arms flung high and feet pounding. The words and the beat have an

Afghan lilt. They are refugees, no doubt, but they are laborers too, and they need this break. It shows in the release that flies from their hands, the abandon of their voices. We stop, of course, and before we can think, we're dancing too, the arc now a little bit bigger. Shohreh is a great dancer, and the men respond as if an angel has dropped down to visit. The beat is relentless, the smiles broad and beaming. We're ready to collapse, exhausted and laughing, when we realize that we have an audience. A dozen cars have stopped on the highway to watch. I know what to do with an audience. Joining hands with the dancers, I lead the line up to the cars and pass the hat, moving from window to window. People empty their pockets happily, generously. I leave the pile of cash with the men, we say our goodbyes very formally, and we're off again into the wind. I'm happy to be alive, happy that this is my country.

CHAPTER THIRTY-TWO

I was in the pool, giving a swimming lesson to the cook's daughter, while the nymphs and the devil undulated under us. Yasmin was making good progress, her little arms plowing through the water with determination as she covered the scary, short distance from the pool's edge to my waiting arms. When she realized she'd made it, she gave me a big, dripping smile. *"Afarin!"* Bravo! I congratulated her.

"Can I do it again?"

But just then her elder brother called from the shadow of the doorway, "Yasmin! Come here at once!" She scrambled out of the pool and ran to the house. I caught the first sounds of a fierce scolding before the door closed. I got out, dried off, threw on a wrap, and followed in my own good time.

The scene in the kitchen was not happy. Yasmin was in tears and ran from the room the instant I appeared. Her brother Hamid glowered darkly as only a teenage boy can and followed her out. Their father apologized, embarrassed by the scene.

"I'm sorry, Khanom. The boy went to Mashhad for a pilgrimage this year and came back completely changed. I hardly know him. He spends all his time at the mosque. And now he insists that Yasmin shouldn't swim. I don't know what to say to him."

"Don't worry, it will pass," I said.

That evening, sitting on my glass island, I looked at the painting on the bottom of the pool. The devil leering at the rippling naked flesh seemed profoundly tired; the paint was peeling off due to the effects of the chlorine. It was time for something new, something a little more sober perhaps, now that teenagers no longer partied poolside through the summer. Perhaps a geometric pattern, pure and precise. A trail of hexagons, starting small and exploding in size, appeared in my mind.

I did the painting myself this time, clambering up and down the ladder a hundred times with my cardboard templates and buckets of paint. It was physically very hard work but well repaid in personal satisfaction.

Hamid's getting religion was not my only run-in with Islam that year. Kamran Diba, the architect who had designed the new Museum of Contemporary Art, decided to create a minimalist mosque in the grounds of the park adjacent to the museum. It consisted of four blank walls with no ceiling, open to the heavens above. A vertical crack split the center of one wall for the *qibla,* to show the direction of Mecca. That was the sum total of it. Or it would have been, except that Kamran asked me and Parviz Tanavoli each to do a sculpture for the site. Parviz came up with a very down-to-earth response to the challenge. He made a pair of bronze stands for people to leave their shoes at the door. I decided to make a *panj-tan,* the symbolic hand representing the five members of the prophet's family at the roots of the Shi'ite faith. It's a common motif in Iranian folk art, one that often tops the dome of a shrine. I made it of stainless steel and mirror, a meter and a half high, with the familiar flat shape doubled in rotation on a central axis, visible from four directions. I envisioned it at eye level, right in front of the *qibla* crack, but Kamran said no. He didn't want it to distract from the austere purity of his design. He set a tall pole, actually the base of a streetlight, near the building and placed my sculpture at the very top.

I was grumbling to myself, walking in a straight line through the park as I tried to get enough distance to even see the damn thing in the context of the building, when I overheard a couple of the park's groundsmen grumbling too.

"Disgraceful!"

"How can they call this a mosque? It's an insult."

"It's not a mosque at all. It smells like something a Baha'i would build."

They had a point. It was obvious enough that we were playing with ideas and forms more than creating a space for a community to gather in worship. And the structure did have a certain Unitarian flavor that might suggest Baha'i ideals, although that was not at all the point that this conservative critic was making. To most Iranians, Baha'i was a label for the foulest of heresies.

It wasn't immediately obvious that these religious rumblings were portents of something bigger, or that they had any connection at all with the demonstrations. In January of that year, 1978, the police in

Qom had opened fire on a group of protesting seminary students. The protesters were angry about a newspaper article denouncing a cleric who had long been a thorn in the Shah's side, a certain Ayatollah Khomeini. Seventy of the unarmed protesters were killed in cold blood. Shi'ite custom calls for a memorial gathering on the fortieth day after a person's death. Forty days after the killings in Qom, people gathered to honor the dead at mosques in several cities, then marched into the streets. In Tabriz the demonstrations turned violent. The police opened fire again, killing more than a hundred. Forty more days, and this time Yazd exploded. Forty more days . . . by summer demonstrations were happening constantly, all over the country.

The press, controlled by the Shah's watchful censors, barely acknowledged the religious fervor that fueled the demonstrations. According to the papers, the protesters were leftists, communists, troublemakers, rabble under the nefarious direction of foreign powers . . . which naturally was an invitation to real leftists, intellectuals, and the generally alienated and disaffected populace to join the fray. In retrospect it seems obvious where this was all leading, but at the time nothing was clear. It wasn't that the revolution came out of nowhere—the causes and conditions had been right there for many years. Political oppression, long tolerated, had become a familiar, well-worn fact of life that faded into the background for anyone unwilling to risk his life to challenge it. As for the pious complaints that the Shah was rushing headlong toward the West and its immoral ways—well, my crowd and I were among the worst offenders.

I spent a couple of months in New York that summer. Zahra was headed to Bennington College in Vermont; Nima had married the year before and was expecting her first child. I wanted more than anything to be there with her. Aziz, my dear Aziz, was born on August 7. The hospital corridors glowed with unreasonable joy. The nurses stared in disbelief at the gold Pahlavi coins I handed to each of them in gratitude for bringing this boy healthy into the world. I didn't care what they thought. I was a grandmother now. Grandmothers are entitled to indulge themselves with quaint traditions from the old country.

The old country, though, was clearly in trouble. Watching events in Iran through the doomsday filter of American television news, it was hard not to panic. The relentless demonstrations continued, and now an epidemic of arson was spreading. Fires were being set at cinemas and nightclubs—symbols of Western decadence—at banks and police stations, at offices connected to the Shah. The crowds were calling explicitly for the Shah to go, and Khomeini was now a real force, calling the shots from exile in Iraq.

The events unfolding worried me terribly. I was anxious, restless, and helpless, stuck halfway around the world. I wanted to get home, but Abol kept asking me to wait, reasoning with me over phone connections that became more and more difficult as the weeks passed. (Were the operators all out marching in the streets? Or were the lines overloaded by countless others as worried as I was?)

"Khanom, what difference does it make if you're here or there? What can you do?"

"It's not about what I can do. It's about where I belong. I can't stand being here when everything is happening there."

"Khanom, please, wait just a little bit longer. I have to come to New York in a couple of weeks for meetings with clients. Just hold on till I get there."

I waited, glued to the television. When the news broke of the Cinema Rex fire and how the doors were locked, I could wait no longer. Dialing long distance for Tehran over and over and over again, the numbers ran an endless mantra in my brain. On the hundredth-and-some try, the distant ring seemed miraculous.

"Abol, to hell with it. I'm coming home. I can't stand it here a moment longer. How could they burn four hundred people alive?"

It was a couple of days after September 8—Black Friday—that I got home. The end of Ramadan had triggered four days of massive demonstrations in Tehran, martial law was declared, and the troops fired into the crowd at Jaleh Square, killing perhaps hundreds. I arrived to find my worst fears realized and the city in shock.

Every time I ventured out of our gates—to visit my mother, or for some necessary shopping—I entered a war zone. There were tanks in the streets and truckloads of soldiers everywhere, cars overturned, piles of garbage, and tires burning where demonstrators had set up roadblocks. Soldiers stopped us at checkpoints, waving guns, and peering into the car, looking for God knows what.

Because of the curfew social life shrank to embrace only family and the closest of friends: anyone who came to dinner would have to sleep over. Every conversation turned to speculation about body counts. Word of mouth became strangely precise: what exactly was witnessed, what was heard from whom, and whom they in turn had heard it from, as if people felt a responsibility to pass the truth as far as possible without distortion. And yet at the same time conspiracy theories ran rampant. The rise of religion was just a tactic, some said, to harness the people's will; in the end the communists would have their day. Or the Americans were behind it all; the French were behind it; and of course, the British. After all, to Iranian eyes there was not a moment since the dawn of history that had not been manipulated by the British—why should it be any different now? We tuned in nightly to the BBC anyway, because only the British could tell us what was going on, especially once the local press had joined in the antigovernment strikes.

Around eleven o'clock each night an eerie noise would begin and continue into the early hours of the morning: cries of *Allah o akbar!*— God is great!—echoing from rooftop to rooftop. The nightly chorus unnerved me profoundly and brought me to tears again and again. I had visions of the parents of students who had been killed or arrested in the demonstrations, standing on the rooftops and screaming their grief to the sky; visions of hellish bloody chaos in the darkened city that spread below us, with only these distillations of anguish rising up to our privileged enclave.

Abol took a more sanguine view and tried to reassure me. He had seen far more than I had of what was happening in the streets on his daily trip to his law office. The excitement of the crowds had rubbed off on him, planting a guarded optimism that change—and change was inevitable at this point—might bring real reforms. "Khanom, nobody's killing anybody out there tonight. The soldiers have put flowers in their guns. They're siding with the people."

"Then what's all this screaming *Allah o akbar?*"

"I don't know what it is, but I don't think those voices are real people." When we learned that the voices were in fact cassette recorders blasting from the rooftops, it wasn't much comfort. The wailing still struck terror in my heart. Now I just felt mocked as well.

October passed. The demonstrations continued sporadically, but now there were strikes everywhere: the oil workers, the civil servants. Without fuel, and with nothing moving through customs, factories closed. The country was grinding to a standstill.

November arrived, and with it an incongruous problem. Before I left for New York in the summer, I had been busy preparing for an exhibition of my Turkoman collection. It was supposed to open in

November at the Negarestan Museum, another of the queen's new art museums located within the old palace complex on Kakh Avenue. For a few months the curator, Barbara Schmidt, had spent almost every day at my home, sorting and selecting the pieces to include in the show. A thick catalog was proofed and ready to print; Souren Melikian had came from Paris and stayed at our home for two weeks to photograph the collection. I had put a lot of energy into designing the exhibit. To show how the pieces were worn, I'd commissioned several sculptures by an extraordinary artist named Mash Esmail. A janitor at the School of Fine Arts at Tehran University, he would come into the studio there on weekends and evenings to build his own sculptures. Using thick wire soldered together, he made three-dimensional figures that breathed character. For the exhibition he created life-size human figures that we dressed in Turkoman robes and jewelry and a kneeling camel that wore magnificent trappings of cutaway patchwork decorated with large silver buttons, as if it were ready to be sacrificed for *'eid-e ghorban*.

All this had been meticulously prepared in what seemed now like another universe. Still, the date for the opening approached. Five

OUR EXHIBITION CAMEL IN TURKOMAN TRAPPINGS.

days in advance I phoned Leila Diba, the director of the museum. "Leila, I don't see how we can do this now. As if the queen has nothing more pressing to do than open an art show when fires are burning in the streets and the whole country is screaming *Allah o akbar*—and there we stand like fools in our elegant dresses. It's not right."

They canceled the opening. Three days later the crowds set fire to the palace next door to the museum. Leila called, her voice sharp with urgency. "You've got to get the collection out of here. I can't be responsible. There's nothing to stop them burning this place too. We've taken everything out of the cases and packed it all up. Please, Monir, send your driver down to come and get the boxes."

"Leila, I didn't gather this stuff for myself. I want it in the museum. Put it in the basement, hide it somewhere, but don't send it back to me." She insisted, but so did I. She insisted again, and so did I. "I'm not going to take it. That's final," I said.

But it wasn't. When I made it home the next evening after running some errands, I found boxes and more boxes stacked in the entrance hall, each one labeled with the display case number. I sighed. So much for my gift to the nation. It would have to wait till the nation knew where it was going.

That year the beginning of December coincided with the start of Moharram, the Shi'ite month of mourning for the martyrdom of Hossein. Even at the best of times Moharram is a dark period that culminates in an outpouring of communal grief, when processions of mourners surge from the mosques onto the city streets, pounding their chests or flailing themselves with chains to the hypnotic beat of their chanting. At Moharram time folds on itself, and the events on the battlefield at Kerbala centuries ago become immediately present. Martyrs then, martyrs now: it's all one. Everyone knew what was coming.

Hundreds of thousands of people took to the streets; some said millions. People of all ages and every political bent, and those who had never dared think such a thought before, were all chanting *Marg bar shah!* Death to the Shah!

By then I was a nervous wreck, startling at every strange noise, tears welling up at each random piece of news that reached us and in between times for no reason at all. I was past logic. Politics seemed to me almost irrelevant, with so many competing versions of the truth and so little certainty as to where it all would lead. I felt for the people who marched toward the tanks, I felt for the frightened young soldiers who faced them, and I felt not least for the terrified parents of all these young men. I could identify no enemy, only the looming threat of bloodshed and unthinkable violence, right here on these streets that I knew like the back of my hand.

Finally Abol suggested that we spend Christmas in New York with Zahra and Nima. It was to be just a brief vacation. The possibility that we might not return, that it might not be a matter of choice, was something I avoided thinking about. I knew, of course, that if the Shah fell, the name *Farmanfarmaian* would become a curse. But denial works in strange ways. This was my country, regardless of who my in-laws were. Then a practical thought crossed my mind.

"Abol, let's send something out, something we could sell if we had to. If worse comes to worst and we can't come back, we have nothing at all outside of Iran." He agreed. We chose several pieces that were small but exceptionally valuable—several antique rugs from his father's collection, and three pieces of Russian needlework from the Caucasus that I had bought at Sotheby's for a small fortune each—and packed them into a bundle. Sasha went to the airport, along with a clerk from Abol's office, to send the package to New York by airfreight. Not surprisingly, the man at the counter expected a bribe. I don't know whether the revolution had instilled in Sasha and his companion a freshly patriotic sense of ethics, or whether the man's demand was simply too outrageous to swallow, but for whatever reason they decided not to pay the bribe and brought the bundle back to the house. It went down to the storage room, along with all the boxes from the museum.

Then it was back to denial. I packed clothes enough for a few weeks and Christmas presents, nothing more. Abol had more foresight. He packed a small but valuable antique rug in one of the suitcases and a stack of books in his hand luggage. They were the cream of his calligraphy collection—he had caught the collecting bug from me some years before—antique Qorans, including one that had belonged to Fathali Shah. And finally, before we headed for the airport, he took several tins of caviar out of the fridge and placed them on top of the books in his hand luggage. "For Christmas, maybe," he said.

Mehrabad airport is chaotic at the best of times, but that morning it was mobbed by people desperate to get on one of the few flights leaving the country. By some miracle we had managed to get tickets to Paris; once there we could get to New York. Traffic was at a standstill, backed up to the square, and we feared we would still be sitting there when the plane took off. Two porters were recruited, and they dove into the melee with our suitcases high on their shoulders. Abol and I followed, saying only the quickest of goodbyes to Sasha, left in the car. We had no need for emotional farewells, we would be back, this was really just a Christmas vacation.

At customs the officer spotted the caviar immediately. It hadn't been bought legally at the government outlet, he noted: there was no official seal. Normally this would have led to a bribe or at the very least an argument. But Abol just dumped all the tins out on the table and swung the bag onto his shoulder. "I guess I'll have to leave them behind." The officer waved us through.

"What was that about?" I asked. "You could have tried—"

"He has the caviar, Khanom. I have the books."

At Orly airport in Paris, our suitcases didn't show up. We stayed for an unplanned two weeks in Paris, waiting until our luggage was finally found. It was a delightful interlude and a much-needed relief from the relentless tension in Tehran. We especially appreciated the opportunity to spend time alone together. We slept late, walked the streets of St. Germain for hours, browsed in antique shops, and bought some clothes to wear.

But the mess we had left behind caught up with us. One morning over coffee and croissants, Abol looked up from his usual stack of newspapers and said to me bleakly, "Khanom, the story is over."

He showed me a page in *Time* magazine. The article that so disturbed him was a series of profiles of Iranians from all walks of life and their reflections on the revolution. Included among them was one Abolbashar Farmanfarmaian. I couldn't believe what I was seeing.

A few days before we left Tehran a friend who worked for an international press agency had called me. "I have a couple of American friends who are visiting Iran," Parviz said. "I've told them so much about your home, and you being an artist and Abol a lawyer—I'd like to bring them over to meet you." They showed up that same evening. We had a drink sitting by the fireplace and talked. Naturally the conversation turned to the revolution, and Abol spoke very frankly. They left early so that they could get back to their hotel before curfew, and we thought nothing more of it at the time. Now Abol's words from that evening were laid out in black and white for all the world to see:

"Both sides have made mistakes," he says. "The Shah's was to modernize too rapidly without considering fundamentalist views. The mullahs, on the other hand, have no concept of what a modern state ought to be. The issue is not the Shah or Khomeini," says Farmanfarmaian, munching on caviar before a crackling fire in his Tehran home.

There was more, but already I felt naked and nauseous. Abol looked at me, forlorn. "If the Shah stays, we can't go home. If Khomeini comes, we can't go home."

CHAPTER THIRTY-THREE

We arrived in New York the day before Christmas Eve and drove to Long Island to spend the holidays with Nima's family. Her in-laws were gracious and welcoming and Aziz, now six months old, was a perpetual delight. The picture was completed when Zahra joined us from Vermont—a perfect Christmas picture of comfort and plenty, hanging on a very flimsy wall while the storm still howled outside.

Back in the city we nursed the illusion of a temporary visit. We stayed for a week in the hotel where Abol usually stayed on business trips, then moved to another hotel closer to Nima's apartment. Our days and nights were spent tracking the news from Iran—through stacks of newspapers, nonstop television, and endless phone calls to family, to friends, to Abol's office. "Maybe it will quiet down," Abol kept saying. "Maybe something good will come out of all this, a government that answers to the people. Maybe then we can go home again." But the news only seemed to get worse. Whenever it all became too dark—when the hotel room seemed to be suddenly shrinking and the same news segment kept repeating like a hammer to the brain—I did the one thing I knew to keep sane. I packed up Aziz in the stroller and went for a walk in the park. Baby talk was a blessed relief, and his innocence was unfazed by my stream-of-consciousness chatter: "Stupid Shah! Nobody checked his diaper!" Breathing, open space, one foot in front of the other.

By the time the Shah left Iran in the middle of January, I had had enough of hotels. We rented an apartment, the first of a succession of month-to-month, furnished sublets that were memorable only for their disturbing smells, reminding us constantly of their rightful owners.

At the beginning of February, Khomeini returned to Iran in triumph, welcomed by hysterical crowds. Immediately the executions began. These "corrupters of the earth," the generals and politicians who had held power under the Shah, were no strangers to us. Their faces in the gruesome photographs were still burning holes in my mind when the news reached us, one by one, of the arrests of several of Abol's brothers and sisters. The stories trickled in over time: battles fought on legal grounds that were shifting like quicksand as the country redefined itself, heart-wrenching betrayals, miraculous interventions, and dramatic escapes. The old order had been turned upside down by machine guns in the hands of neighborhood "committees." Your gardener might now hold your life in his hands, and God help you if you had not treated him well. In the end, no one in Abol's family was executed, thank God, but some remained long years in prison.

I fretted over my mother and the daily trials of an elderly, disabled woman amid this chaotic new order. I felt I had abandoned her. And I grieved all over again for my father's death.

During this time Abol's sister Leila came from Paris to stay with us for a month. She was good company in misery. We worshipped together at the altar of the television with offerings of whiskey. I had quit smoking long before, but now I was begging "just one cigarette" after another from her until I admitted defeat and bought a pack. "This is crazy, Leila," I said finally. "I've got to do something constructive." I bought some wool to knit a scarf for Zahra. I knitted through chanting crowds, through the endlessly repeated scene of Khomeini's arrival, through a hundred pundits telling me in a thousand different ways that I couldn't go home. I knitted blindly, my eyes glued to the television, extruding inch after inch of scarf into a shopping bag on the floor, buying more wool as soon as I ran out.

"If you keep that up, Madame Defarge," said Leila, "the guillotine will come next." When I pulled the scarf out of the bag, it snaked around the room for more than ten yards. I unraveled it, then turned instead to pen and paper. Sitting in front of the television, I filled page after page after page of spontaneous compositions of calligraphy: stream-of-consciousness ramblings, phrases repeated obsessively, prayers and cries for help, all in wild colors snaking tortuous paths around the page. I made more than a hundred of these testaments, my hand moving compulsively, almost unconsciously.

At night, sleep was elusive. I gave up chasing it and instead took myself on trips elsewhere. Lying in bed, I would tell myself: now I am going to Gorgan . . . now I am going to Dozdak . . . I would conjure up every detail on the screen of my eyelids, every turn of the road and each unfolding of the landscape. A carpet of tulips . . . the shadow of a cloud bank trailing purple across the mountains . . . rain dripping from thatched eaves . . . shiny fish in a basket, a bucket of cucumbers . . . the wrinkles of a stranger's smile, now a long-lost friend. More than anything else, it was these nightly journeys that kept me going from day to day, secure in the knowledge that memories couldn't be stolen.

Financially we survived by selling off the few things we were able to bring out of Iran. Unlike so many wealthy Iranians who had jumped ship at the earliest signs of trouble, we really had no investments outside the country. When it became clear that we wouldn't be returning anytime soon, my brother Hassan had gone to the house in Elahieh and packed up a few boxes, which he managed to send out through a connection at the Belgian embassy. He found a way also to send a few carpets from my father's workshop, paying the huge guarantees that were demanded of merchants in order to prevent people from using that route to take capital out of the country. Finally, he arranged to rent our house to the French chargé d'affaires. We hoped that diplomatic immunity might protect the place, but the neighborhood revolutionary committee came to take inventory, and later, when the French eventually closed their embassy in Iran, they confiscated everything. But in the meantime the rental at least meant that we could continue to pay Sasha's salary for a couple of years.

We sold the carpets one by one, and we sold Abol's collection of antique Qorans—the ones he had carried under the caviar, and more in the boxes that Hassan had sent. I couldn't bear to sell the Turkoman collection, or rather the small fragment of it that Hassan had managed to save. Deep down it seemed wrong even to take the stuff out of Iran, especially after all I had spent to repatriate pieces from antique dealers abroad. In the end I gave several pieces each to half a dozen different museums in the United States. I only wish that it had all remained in the museum in Tehran, regardless of who came to power.

As far as we knew, everything that had been confiscated was gone for good. We heard stories of many homes abandoned by people fleeing the country. They were taken by the government, dismantled, and split into apartments as housing for the poor or for those with solid revolutionary credentials. The best antiques and carpets found their way into the mullahs' homes, and the leftovers were sold off in shops that the government set up specially for this purpose. I did my own inventory of the losses, walking through imagined rooms: the bulk of the Turkoman collection, the coffeehouse paintings, all of the paintings behind glass from the Gulf; contemporary art, gifts from American artists who were friends and from the many young Iranian artists I had collected as a gesture of encouragement; not to mention all the treasures I had woven into the fabric of the house itself. And the garden. I didn't give a damn about the closets full of Dior, Chanel, Hermès—I would have traded them all for one of the Turkoman coats. And my personal photographs.

When my mental inventory was complete, I sat down and had a good talk with myself. Where was the loss in all this, really? I had experienced the pleasure of collecting: the joy of discovery, the adventures of the road, and the satisfaction of seeing dusty, discarded objects restored to their beauty and of sharing these long-ignored treasures with the world. It was a pity, perhaps, that my children would not inherit it all. But we were alive and safe, healthy, and living in relative comfort. Many had not escaped so lightly, and those who had rarely counted their blessings. The last thing I wanted to do was to whine like friends I knew who mourned the loss of every knickknack, every silver ashtray.

Then, of course, there was my own art. Bits and pieces that I had given to friends, and several pieces bought by collectors, were scattered around the world. I could track down some photographs here and there that were taken for exhibitions. But for the most part it was gone, a lifetime's work vanished.

A small voice inside me still echoed after all these years: if it was mine, then it was obviously no big deal. Besides, I had been so prolific. Where would I put all that stuff if I had it? In a rented storage room in Queens, most likely. Were my mirror mosaics hanging now on some mullah's wall, or had they trashed it all? Let it go, Monir, let it go. And yet I often wished that I had just one of my paintings behind glass. Just one of so many things . . . More than anything else, I regretted the loss of my drawings, not just because those sketchbooks had followed me all through my life, but damn it, they were really good.

If I ever felt a wave of self-pity approaching, I had only to remind myself of Abol's steadfast example. A couple of times, very briefly, he mentioned the loss of two particular items—family heirlooms that had personal meaning for him as well as historical value. But all he said was "*Heif,* it's a pity." About everything else—the factories he had built from the ground up, his precious sailboat, his library, his law practice, his land—he never said a word. And if I said anything, he laughed it off. "Your drawings? Khanom, they've given them to the grocer, and he's wrapping cheese in them right now. What's past is past. Forget about it. It's enough that we have each other."

For almost two years—all through the mind-numbing TV images of blindfolded hostages and angry crowds at the American embassy in Tehran, the endless numbered days, and the annoying yellow ribbons—we lived an uncertain existence, moving every few months from one temporary apartment to another. Finally, in 1981, we were able to buy our own place, thanks to a stroke of luck. Many years before, Abol had sued the British oil consortium over its meddling in the business of the chlorine factory in Abadan. The case had shuffled through the international legal system for so long that I'd forgotten about it, but finally Abol won the suit. I gave a prayer of thanks; if the settlement had come sooner, when we were still in Iran, it would have been lost now along with everything else.

After a long search we settled on a Fifth Avenue penthouse of such extraordinary character that it more than made up for its impracticality. Never mind that it had only one bedroom and we'd have to improvise whenever Zahra came home from college. (I also chose to ignore the fact that the previous owner was linked to a famous murder case, and I turned a blind eye when the real estate agent who showed us the place opened and quickly closed the door on a closet full of whips.) It was an art deco gem with spectacular views of Central Park, built in 1923, with elaborate wood carving, a long terrace enclosed in stained glass, a dining room of black lacquered panels etched with gold, marble columns, and its own gold dome. There was even an open terrace where I could begin a roof garden. It wasn't the grand canvas of Elahieh, but miniatures have their appeal.

Soon after we moved in, the maintenance problems started. The terrace was leaking and had to be resurfaced. I was calling the workmen in to lunch (yes, clinging to old ways—should American workers be treated less kindly than Iranians? God forbid one day there will be a revolution here!) when I noticed the white net they were using as a base for the tar. Something in me sparked. I asked if I could have

MY ART DECO GEM ON FIFTH AVENUE.

a piece of the net. Fair trade for lunch. I gathered odds and ends: cardboard from the packing boxes, newspapers, some crayons that Nima's kids had left. I made a small collage and stapled the net over it. That, quite simply, is how I started over.

A few days later the phone rang: an agent from Boston was arranging artists' commissions for a new airport in Saudi Arabia. She was familiar with my work, she said, and thought it would suit. "Can I come and see your studio?" I told her I had nothing to show her. No studio, no art. Maybe I could dig up a brochure from an old exhibit, a photo or two. It was hardly worth a trip from Boston.

She insisted on coming anyway, so I showed her the only thing I had: cardboard, crayons, and roofer's net. "I love it!" she said. "Can you do something like this, eleven by seven feet?"

"What? In this apartment?"

"I'll send you the contract. It's up to you."

It was the first time that I was properly paid for a commission, and I was very pleased that I could make a real difference to our finances. God bless New York, I thought; it was almost like being back at Bonwit Teller. I bought sawhorses and a couple of doors at a lumber-yard and made them into a work table in the dining room. When the piece was finished, they had to hoist it down from the roof with a crane.

I needed a studio, and luck was with me. A suite of what had once been servants' quarters was available for a reasonable price on the ground floor of the same building. We knocked out some walls and turned a bathroom into a kitchenette to make not just a studio for me but also a tiny apartment for Zahra. The place had disadvantages too. New York had its own ancien régime, and I had to dress up to the standard required by a Fifth Avenue condo association just to go downstairs through the lobby and out to the old servants' entrance before changing into my work clothes. Even worse, for a time I couldn't bring myself to set foot in the place, having been mugged there by a pair of intruders. One choked me till I passed out. When I revived, I tried to bite the hand at my throat but only managed to bloody my own mouth. They got away with the cash in my purse and the jewelry I happened to be wearing, but more important, the peace of mind I had found working down there was shattered. I worried terribly every night that Zahra stayed down there alone.

Once I got started, I did a lot of commercial work. I did textile designs, just like in the old days, only now the pay was much better. Several commissions came to me, from people who had seen my work in Tehran, for mirror mosaic installations. The first was a wall for a reception lobby in a building on Park Avenue. I didn't know how I would pull it off without Hajji Ostad. An architect labored for days at the computer to figure out how to fit my pattern to the space, where Hajji would have done it with his piece of string in a few minutes. The finest mirror available was double the thickness of what we used in Iran and very slow to cut. I hired a man who charged by the piece and gave me only a fraction of what I needed each week. I had to "kill" the plaster myself, kneading the stiff mass till I was sore, so I abandoned that and used acrylic modeling paste instead. In the end it all worked out, but I had a new appreciation of the old craft.

Of all the commissions I did, the most ambitious was a huge stained-glass window, over twenty feet high and nine feet wide, on the thirty-sixth floor of the Dag Hammarskjöld building. The challenge was exactly the reverse of the windows I had done so long ago in the Senate building: they wanted stained glass, but they didn't want to lose the spectacular view. I kept an open square at the top

INSTALLING THE WINDOW AT THE DAG HAMMARSKJÖLD BUILDING.

THE RESULT.

with geometric motifs descending in a narrow panel. I was very pleased with how it came out, and Abol was ever so proud. He came to the site every morning to watch our progress as the scaffolding shifted down step by step and the image was revealed.

Eventually the cost of maintaining my art deco gem was more trouble than it was worth, and we decided to sell the place. For months I kept it company-ready, clean and polished, flowers arranged, as real estate agents trooped in and out with clients. "One in a hundred will love it," they said, "and pay any price." I gave up counting; I didn't need a hundred strangers in my home, just the right one. Paul Newman was a neighbor, and though we hadn't met, I wrote him a note. Perhaps he had a friend who would appreciate the dramatic flair of the place. Not long afterward the agent brought a tall, good-looking man who kept his dark glasses on the whole time he looked around. We chatted, and he was charming, but he seemed far more interested in the photos of Zahra on my refrigerator door than in the apartment itself. It wasn't till after he left and I spelled out to Nima over the phone the odd name that the agent had scribbled on a card that I realized I had been talking to Warren Beatty. I was sorry to be so clueless, but even more sorry a few days later that I wasn't home when Robert Redford came to look. In the end we sold it to someone whose name I didn't recognize, though that's no guarantee that I shouldn't have.

MY FIRST GRANDCHILD, NIMA'S SON AZIZ, HELPED ME ENJOY
OUR LAST DAYS PERCHED HIGH ABOVE FIFTH AVENUE.

We moved to a much more modest apartment, where I sectioned off an area of the living room to make a tiny working studio. I continued making collages from fabric scraps, sequins, beads, and glitter. The images were flights of nostalgia on jeweled wings, glimpses from childhood, the windows of old Qazvin, lovelorn nightingales, clouds lifted from miniature paintings . . . but all this was barely seen. I finished each piece with a veil of net as if telling myself: *Wrap it up. Wrap it up and forget about it.*

We spent some time in Long Island, and I started drawing again as soon as the flowers bloomed. But whenever I worked from imagination, instead of going straight from eye to hand, memories of Iran loomed over the page. I did a series of pastels, desert landscapes emerging unconsciously in all their subtle play of color. In each was the suggestion of a village, adobe melting into the colors of the earth. And in every one of them a woman stood: dark, alone, isolated.

CHAPTER THIRTY-FOUR

One morning I set breakfast out on the terrace and called to Abol to join me.

"Yes, I'm coming." He didn't come. I called again.

"I'm coming, Khanom." The coffee and toast were getting cold. I went to the bedroom. Abol was standing there half dressed, staring at the shirt in his hands.

"Abol *joon*, breakfast is ready." I went back out and waited. He still didn't come. I went back to the bedroom and found him frozen in the same position, shirt in hand.

"Abol *joon*, let me help you." I held the shirt, and he put it on. Breakfast passed normally. Afterward I brought him *The New York Times*, and he settled in his chair to read. I cleared the breakfast things, tidied the kitchen, and puttered around. Every time I came back to the terrace, Abol was sitting like a statue, the same page unturned.

Something is wrong. I phoned the doctor. *Something is terribly wrong.* An address, a laboratory, blood tests, then finally the safe haven of Dr. Samii's office. Abol seemed cheerful, happy to see an old friend. Everything looked normal. Then Dr. Samii asked, "Can you tell me your name?"

Abol smiled and shrugged. "I don't understand what you're asking."

"What day is it today?"

Abol laughed. "You know better than I do."

A small stroke had affected his memory, the doctor said. "Take him home and watch him. We'll see what happens."

The day passed almost normally, except for the terror in my gut and the dead-end conversations that Abol brushed off with good humor. I called Zahra and Nima and told them what had happened, and they both came over. Nima was several months' pregnant with her third child, which had been the focus of much happy anticipation.

"Look, Abol, see how much Nima's belly has grown."

"Yes. Is she pregnant?"

I went out to pick up a prescription. I was so distraught that I ran across the avenue without looking at the light. Brakes screeched as a car narrowly missed me, then a loud crash as a second car rear-ended it.

Later that night, as we were getting ready for bed, something shifted in Abol's expression. As we talked, it became clear that his memory had returned. All that was missing were the events of the day that had just passed.

That was the beginning. Dr. Samii called for more tests, a special diet, and monthly tests. Everything was under control and stayed that way for six years, as far as I knew.

In 1988 something changed. I had come down with pneumonia. One night I realized through my feverish half-sleep that Abol was in more distress than I was, waking up many times in the night. In the morning when he brought me breakfast, he was ashen pale. He agreed to get himself to the doctor.

Dr. Samii phoned me. "I'm admitting him to the hospital. He's lost a lot of blood."

I called a friend and asked her to bring Abol's slippers to him. "They've given him three pints of blood," she reported back. Nima and Zahra came. They knew then what I didn't know.

Abol was home from the hospital in a couple of days, but he needed constant blood tests. Then he made a visit to his sister-in-law, who was a hematologist at Princeton. I wanted to come along, but he made excuses—a long ride, other business on the way, he said.

He was getting dramatically weaker, and any small wound refused to heal. A bump against the corner of a table had him off his feet for weeks. I bought an album and arranged a table for him to work on sorting his collection of Persian calligraphy. I sat nearby and worked on drawings, pointillist sketches of flowers. Each dot I placed on the paper was a mark of foreboding, a surrogate tear.

Finally, in late October 1991, Nima and I accompanied him to yet another doctor who had done a bone marrow test. It was impossible for him to hide the truth from me any longer. I sat numb with shock as the doctor spelled it out. It was leukemia, and very advanced. The only remedy was constant blood transfusions; chemotherapy threatened dire complications, and he was far too old for a bone marrow transplant. Abol hugged me, weeping. Nima embraced the both of us together, and the three of us stood there crying.

For three or four weeks he was in and out of the hospital for transfusions. I sat with him for long days, watching the bags of blood empty slowly into his vein, willing my prayers into that thin, dark tube. I brought caviar and gifts for the doctors and nurses, desperate gestures. One of them recommended I join a support group that met at the hospital. *The hell with them,* I thought. *How will that help Abol?*

At home he had terrible night sweats. I bought T-shirts by the dozen and helped him change five or six times each night. Leila came to stay with us, flying in from Mallorca where she had settled after the revolution, and other members of the clan converged on New York. Nima gave a dinner party for the family; Abol looked so good that night with the color returned to his cheeks that I dared to hope he might live for years with the help of the transfusions.

The next night he complained of a headache so extreme that the doctor sent him to the hospital in the morning. It was Thanksgiving Day. A crowd of siblings, nephews, and nieces gathered at the hospital, some twenty people spilling out into the hallway from his room.

Playing hostess was more than I could handle at that point. Nima saw my distress and dosed me up with tranquilizers. The next morning, between fixing breakfast and buying a camp bed and sheets for the siblings who were still arriving, I phoned Abol's room at the hospital again and again. He didn't answer. I called Nima, and she went over to check on him. She called me from his room. "He's sleeping, Mommy, that's why he doesn't answer."

I went down to the hospital a couple of hours later, and Abol was still asleep. I shook his arm. "Abol *joon,* wake up, please!" The doctors couldn't wake him either; they realized his brain was hemorrhaging, and they moved him to intensive care. It was almost midnight by the time I got home.

At four in the morning the doctor phoned: "He is going." I went back to the hospital, the taxi floating in slow motion through the deserted streets. Abol was awake, his eyes alight with recognition under the big plastic mask that enclosed his head. I held his hand. He picked up my hand in both of his and lifted it toward his lips as if to kiss it from under the mask. Before my eyes the spirit left him.

I don't know how much time passed. I was paralyzed, completely empty and alone in the universe. Finally the room returned. I asked the doctor if he could cut a lock of Abol's hair for me. He handed me the white curl, and I found my way to the door.

It was daylight when I left the room, though I could hardly see through the blackness that squeezed my head. A faceless crowd was waiting outside the intensive care unit. I don't remember how I got home, or how we fed lunch to the crowd. Nima took charge with a calm grace. I sat in a corner, blind and dazed. Nima's husband made arrangements for the burial at Sag Harbor, where Abol had loved to sail, the announcements in the papers, a breakfast served in the lobby of our apartment building, and a bus to ferry the mourners from New York.

At the graveside Nima and Zahra each spoke very briefly. There were long speeches from others and a poem. I carried the beautiful patchwork, all gold lamé and velvets, that Sasha's wife had sewn from my mother's antique dresses, and asked Nima to spread it over the coffin before Abol's nephews lowered it into the earth. Nima arranged lunch for seventy-five people at the hotel in Sag Harbor, and the crowd followed us home. The next several days were no less blurred: visitors filing into the apartment to pay their respects, Zahra and her school friends serving round after round of tea and cakes, friends laying out a buffet lunch . . . I sat like a zombie, just a few words here and there reaching my ears through the fog.

Then it was over. The endless arrivals stopped; the houseguests packed up and left. I was well and truly alone. I went to the bathroom and cried, releasing all control. I climbed into the tub and screamed, pouring water over my head from a copper pot, beating myself on the head with the pot. It didn't matter that I was in an apartment on the Upper West Side of New York. I was an old woman in a village at the edge of the desert, pouring dust on her head, beating her breast, and wailing for God's pity.

I cried for hours each day for weeks on end. Nima rescued me briefly. She was writing a book about traveling with children and asked me to join her and her kids on a couple of short trips to Mexico and New Orleans. We were tourists, seeing the sights, going for walks on the beach. It was a sweet relief not to be alone for a while. Still, I cried every night, and young Aziz would hold my hand.

THANK GOODNESS FOR GRANDCHILDREN.

I filled the days by sorting Abol's papers and arranging the artifacts of the funeral—telegrams, letters, cards, newspaper clippings, pressed flowers—in a large scrapbook. It grew into page after page of collage, the papers and cuttings surrounded by sketches and miles of calligraphy like the tracks of a small bird wandering lost, phrases repeated obsessively. All in the clear, bright colors that have nothing to do with happiness but are simply the colors that my heart speaks with.

I sat in the bedroom and worked on that scrapbook and nothing else for two years and more. I ate breakfast standing in the kitchen and brought my lunch and dinner on a tray to the bedroom. I couldn't bear to sit at the dining room table without Abol. I couldn't bear to be alone in the living room, and I couldn't enter the room that had been his office without bursting into tears. To other people's eyes, everything was normal. I went out to shop, visit friends, and see galleries. I spent time with Nima's children, grateful for their unquestioning affection. But inside I couldn't lift myself out of the desolation of Abol's absence.

Working on the collages, cutting and pasting snatches of a lifetime, my hand tracing words and phrases over and over, I gave myself up to memories . . .

Abol reciting poetry in the car . . . It was a ritual on the drive to school, when Nima and Zahra were still very young. Sa'adi, Hafez, Shakespeare, and many more . . . *"How do I love thee? Let me count the ways."* The first time we visited the ruins at Persepolis, Zahra was just five. She shuffled through the gravel, her skinny legs covered in dust. Delight and surprise shone on Abol's face when she announced, as if discovering Sa'adi's words herself, *"Rig-e hamun o doroshtiha-ye oon mesle pariya mimanad."* The river's sands and rough banks are like feathers of an angel's wings.

ABOL *JOON.*

Abol and his precious Shakespeare. He had played Othello in a costume I improvised from a bedspread when it was his turn to entertain the other guests at the Shah's brother's private resort at the Caspian. He knew the part by heart, knew vast portions of Shakespeare by heart, as someone else might pride themselves on knowing the Qoran by heart. But his Desdemona barely spoke English, and we died laughing as he coached her through the scene. He so much enjoyed playing a role that another time we dressed him as an Arab sheikh. He arrived complete with motorcycle escort and fooled everyone, not least the many money-dazzled women who flirted outrageously with him for hours right in front of me.

Abol sitting on the deck of his sailboat, meditating patiently on a perfectly calm Caspian Sea. Just the faintest breath of a breeze carried the smell of rice from the ripening fields.

"Mmmm . . . I smell lunch." No answer; I could see by his pallor he was seasick. How could someone be seasick when nothing moved? "Abol, you really should put a motor in this thing."

"It's a sailboat. Why should it have a motor?"

"Abol *joon,* we've been sitting here for four hours!"

"Khanom, that's the advantage. We have plenty of time to think and absorb nature."

"What nature? There's nothing here but water and sky. It's like sitting in an empty parking lot." But he was happy, and I wish I hadn't spoken so sharply.

Abol speeding through Central Park on his racing bike—his surrogate sailboat after the revolution—bending low over the handlebars with his white hair wild in the wind. Startled kids shouted as he sailed by, "Hey, old man, slow down!"

Our evening walks through the chlorine factory, when Abol would feel the machinery with his hands, or stand at the edge of the mercury lake . . . Was that what had caused the leukemia?

Piecing together the afterwords of family and friends, the epilogues of doctors, the date of the red-pen corrections in his will, I understood that Abol had hidden his diagnosis from me for more than two years. How could he face that alone? How could he not confide in me? It was kindness, I knew, to spare me the pain for as long as possible. There was more that he never told me. Acts of quiet charity surfaced in stories that friends and strangers shared with me after his death. These surprises still unfold many years later. It wasn't secrecy that kept these stories from me for so long, but Abol's simple modesty.

There was one thing that he told me again and again, as if it explained all there was to know about the two of us: "*Khoda najar nist.*" God is not a carpenter, but he knows how to make the door fit the frame.

CHAPTER THIRTY-FIVE

I n the winter of 1992, a year after Abol's death, I returned to Iran. It was not an easy trip.

A few years before Abol died, in a random encounter on the subway, we had run into a young Iranian who had once been his student at the law school in Tehran. Abol took him under his wing and helped him to find work with a law firm in New York, and he remained a devoted friend. When he came to pay his respects after Abol's death, he told me that one of his relatives had been a minister in Khomeini's government and might be able to help me reclaim some of Abol's property.

Fourteen years had passed since the doors had closed behind us at Elahieh that winter morning. I wasn't too optimistic about claiming Abol's property; nor was I all that concerned about it. We had managed this far and made a new life without it. Still, it was Nima and Zahra's inheritance, and I shouldn't turn my back on it. Nima had married very well, but I still had a mother's normal worry for Zahra's future—and to be honest, for my own future, although not financially. I was well off enough, but I didn't fancy the prospect of growing old in America. My vision of a happy old age was to be respectfully cosseted in the warm embrace of an Iranian extended family—notwithstanding the tangled dramas and nosy busybodies that came with the generic package. Revolution or no, I was determined not to end up in an American nursing home, fading into lonely, grumpy oblivion under the watchful eye of a television. But I wasn't doddering yet, and I needed to see for myself what Tehran might offer in the way of a gracious transition. Could I live under the Islamic regime as an artist? As a woman? Was there anything left of a cultural life in the city, or had the mullahs squeezed its soul dry? Was I indulging myself with a nostalgic fantasy? It was worth a trip to find out.

I would have to travel under my maiden name. Although the fervor of the revolution had faded somewhat, or so said friends who traveled back and forth, the Farmanfarmaian name was still a red flag that I didn't want to wave unnecessarily. My Iranian passport had expired years ago, and its worn pages still bore the Pahlavi emblem of the lion and sun. Fixing it required a trip to Washington, to a corner of the Pakistani embassy that served as a makeshift consular office for the Islamic Republic of Iran after diplomatic relations with the United States were severed during the hostage crisis.

The scene that met me in Washington seemed an ominous preview of life on the other side. Surly officials wore three-day-old stubble as a mark of piety and shirts buttoned right up to the neck as if to advertise the defiant absence of a tie—symbol of all things Western. They barked impatiently at the cowed applicants, every one of them dressed as if they had come to bury a loved one rather than chase documents. The women looked most miserable of all, as if their unaccustomed headscarves were knotted with hundred-pound weights. I wrestled with a photocopy machine in a windowless, blank-walled room, then jumped out of my skin when a voice informed me over a loudspeaker that it was out of order. Obviously they had mastered the technology to observe my every move on closed-circuit television, but not to fix the photocopy machine.

Finally Monir Shahroudy was the bearer of a passport of the Islamic Republic of Iran. A stranger's face peered at me from the passport photo: black scarf pulled low on her forehead, not a wisp of hair showing, no makeup. She looked grim as a death mask.

Direct flights between the Great Satan and the Islamic bogeyland had been suspended years ago, so I flew via Paris, where I was joined by my nephew's wife, Sudabeh, who traveled often to Europe. The Air France hostesses who served us after Paris were shockingly rude, slamming the meals down on the tray tables and making it very clear that passengers were presumed guilty until proven innocent on any point of dispute. I learned that the route was considered a hardship assignment and given to employees with the least seniority: the air hostesses refused to wear the headscarves required to disembark in Tehran, so they stayed on board the grounded plane for six or seven hours waiting for the return flight to Paris. Good grief, I thought, wiggling my flight-swollen ankles. How bad could it be?

My headscarf was the least of my worries as we circled Mehrabad airport. Mehrabad—"place of kindness"—was a potential black hole that led straight to jail if the name in your passport found a match on the dreaded blacklist. The crowd of relatives who squeezed against the barriers could wait forever, hoping that the worst that had happened was a delay, a missed flight, or a change of plans. I could only pray that the bureaucracy now was no more efficient than it had ever been, that any new computer system could not search back far enough to link my name to Abol's family.

"Just do whatever I do," Sudabeh said. "Don't say a word more than you have to." Luck was with me. The questions were perfunctory, my answers no less so. I kept my trembling hands in my pockets, and my wobbling knees were hidden under my long coat. I had no argument against the Islamic dress code in that moment. At the thud of the stamp in my passport, I breathed a long sigh of relief.

Once past that hurdle I was struck by the dilapidated state of the building and by the darkness of the crowd milling in the large hall. My first impression was that I happened to arrive on one of the religious holidays mourning the Shi'a martyrs; but no, every day was a day of mourning now. The black chadors or low scarves had become routine, universal. But all that blackness paled in the explosion of bright, teary smiles and warm hugs that welcomed me past the barriers. We laughed and cried and screeched and giggled and cried some more. Faces wore a few more wrinkles and some fresh gray, but there they were: the arc of a smile, the angle of an eyebrow, the myriad shades of expression that had replayed in dim versions of memory for so many years, now gloriously alive and present.

I barely recognized the city that we drove through from the airport. Tehran had doubled in size during my absence. New freeways crisscrossed the landscape; buildings that had once been tall landmarks were now dwarfed by their neighbors; and to complete my confusion, virtually all of the streets had been renamed to honor the heroes of the revolution and erase any memory of monarchy.

Home for now was the house that my brother Ali had built in the foothills at the northern edge of the city, a fond fragment of the life I remembered. My niece Vida and her brother still had their same upstairs apartments in the old house, although Ali and his wife had both passed away. My mother had died here too, ten years before. (She had been ailing for a long time, and Ali had brought her to live in his own home when her cook and housekeeper decided that the revolution entitled them to ownership of a portion of her house and no further obligation to work, though they still expected their salaries.) Vida had nursed each one of them through their last days in the same bed I occupied now, and much of my first few days there was filled with the details of their illnesses and passing.

Sasha too had died several years before. At home in New York I had opened the letter from his son Varoush, now a successful architect in Los Angeles, to find the sad news written in the most beautifully expressed Persian and exquisite calligraphy. At the end, Varoush said, Sasha had asked again and again for Zahra, hoping till the last moment to see her one more time. I brought gifts for his wife Emma Khanom and went to visit her at home—the same house we had helped them to buy, which she shared now with her sister. The whole extended family showed up, eager to see how Khanom Doctor had fared since the revolution. Emma Khanom served cognac she had made herself, a rare treat in the Islamic Republic, and we drank to Sasha's memory.

Logically I knew that all these deaths, and many more that I learned of from the constant stream of visitors who came to greet me at Vida's, were simply the work of time. For the most part they had nothing to do with the revolution. It was only my own absence and belated return that conflated all these losses with the fact that the world outside had turned upside down so suddenly. In the winter-bare garden at Ali's home, the trees had grown much bigger and the vines matured, now thick as my wrist. The truth was that time had passed in the slow, steady way that time does pass, regardless of where I had been.

Still, when I caught a bad cold and found a crowd of nieces, nephews, cousins, and more all hanging out in my bedroom to keep me company (and reminding me how much Iranians value companionship above privacy), I couldn't help joking with Vida: "I know you've buried three people from this bedroom, but if you think I'm going to be the fourth corpse that's carried out through that door, you're mistaken. I have no intention of dying before I get back to my own bedroom in New York!"

Venturing out beyond the safe haven of home, every random encounter with strangers was a measure of how much had changed, and then, under the surface, how much remained the same.

"That comes to five thousand *toman*, sister." Never mind that inflation had brought the price of a few kilos of fruit to what once was a respectable month's salary; I couldn't stomach the casual intimacy of these revolutionary "brothers."

"Excuse me, I'm not your sister."

"Yes, mother," he responded, unfazed.

"I'm not your mother either!"

He stared at me. "What should I call you?"

"Khanom," I said, quietly but with all the dignity I could muster.

He raised an eyebrow. "Oh?" But having submitted my request for a little respect, I had no desire to end the exchange on that note. It didn't take me long to learn that if I persisted gently at the semblance of a friendly conversation—"The grapes aren't bad, but of course they're nothing like the grapes we grew in Qazvin when I was a child . . . And of course the price was different in those days. How can a family survive now, with the cost of food what it is?"—within moments my victim would shed his prickly skin and warm to the exchange. It would take more than a revolution, I realized, to kill the profoundly sociable soul of the Iranian people.

The Shah's palaces at Niavaran and Saadatabad had been thrown open to the public as museums, so I decided to play tourist for a day, half hoping that I might stumble on some of my own art. As I paid for my ticket, I was very surprised to be greeted by one of the guards:

"Monir Khanom, *salam!*"

"Esmail! Is it you?" Esmail had been one of the gardeners at the palace. I knew him because he also moonlighted at my brother's house. I suppose the Shah had not paid his gardeners very well. In any case, Esmail had been one of the first men in when the palace was claimed by the people during the revolution, and after that he was promoted from gardener to guard. Now he was proud to give me a private tour, including sections that were closed to the public and anecdotes about his own personal encounters with the royal family during the twenty-some years he had worked there.

The objects on display were a very odd mix: a few clothes and personal effects of the royal family that supposedly were proof of their decadent lifestyle but only looked pathetically out of fashion at this late date; some genuinely beautiful antiques of museum quality that they had owned; and artifacts of the revolution, including a smashed-up helicopter from the failed Eagle's Claw operation to rescue the American hostages. I laughed out loud to find a display of the soldiers' costumes from the celebration of twenty-five hundred years of monarchy. They looked even more ridiculous now, like clown suits in brightly colored synthetic satin and hats of cardboard and papier-mâché.

"Khanom, don't even bother looking at this junk," Esmail told me. "When the revolution came, we took everything! The really good stuff is all stashed in the basement now." I didn't find any of my own art among the "junk" on display, so I could only hope that it was somewhere in the basement. But Esmail's considerable authority did not extend far enough, he claimed, to allow me down there to search for it.

I realized that although the revolution hung like a black cloud over my own experience of Iran on this trip, it was actually stale news. The eight-year-long war with Iraq, only recently ended in stalemate, was a far fresher trauma. With a million dead on our side alone, there was hardly a family untouched by tragedy. When I went to visit the graves of Ali and his wife at Behesht-Zahra, Tehran's vast cemetery, it was easy enough to pass quickly by the grandiose mausoleum that housed Khomeini's angry old bones. But I could not ignore the surreal fountain that gushed fake blood as a memorial to the war dead, or the row after row of tiny, heart-wrenching shrines to the memory of sons, brothers, husbands lost. These "martyrs" peered out from formal photos with rigid earnestness, or laughed in fading snapshots from a happier time, surrounded by vases of flowers and pathetic mementos: a doll, a poem, a drawing, a wallet encased in plastic. Most were still in their teens when they died, and all too often brothers lay side by side.

I paid a visit to the home of a man who had worked at our house for many years as a gardener and whose wife now helped Vida with housekeeping. The address surprised me: the city had renamed their little street to honor their son as a martyr. Memwar had given up gardening, but he was quite active and had learned to drive with his two wooden legs. He had lost them on the battlefield, in the same explosion that killed his only son.

Most of Abol's family had left the country by then, but I paid my respects to two of his siblings who had stayed behind. Alinaghi had been arrested after Khomeini came to power and was kept in prison for five or six years. Almost all of the homes that belonged to the family, many of them in a single large compound, had been confiscated and were either boarded up or inhabited by new residents. Ironically, the law allowed those imprisoned to reclaim a small piece of their property on their release. Alinaghi and his wife were confined now to the top floor of their old home. They had turned one of the bathrooms into a small kitchen, and bedrooms now served as living room and study. He showed me a collection of watercolors he had painted while he was in prison. There were portraits, flowers, landscapes—all from memory, all very colorful and primitive. He was a banker, not an artist, after all; but the paintings had an innocent beauty, and they had kept him sane under the daily threat of execution. Now he no longer had time to paint: he spent all of every working day in the offices of the *komiteh,* the local revolutionary committee, devoting himself calmly, patiently, and single-mindedly to the Sisyphean task of reclaiming his confiscated properties.

Maryam, Abol's eldest sister, had an even sadder story. An ardent communist, she had married the leader of Iran's communist Tudeh party, which was outlawed by the Shah. They had fled to East Germany, where they lived in exile for twenty-five years. Maryam and her husband returned to Iran in the early days of the revolution, fired by the heady optimism of the moment. The Tudeh party was instrumental in installing Khomeini, and they fully expected to share that power, an expectation that was thoroughly and brutally betrayed. Maryam, her husband, their daughter, and even some of their household staff were arrested. Tortured. Mother and daughter had no choice but to listen to each other's screams.

By the time I arrived in 1992, Maryam's daughter had been released. Every other week Maryam and her husband were allowed out for a few hours, under guard, for a visit to their daughter's home. I joined them twice on these occasions: somber lunches under the disdainful eye of a bearded soldier. We kept our headscarves on as if we were in a public place. Our small talk made no reference to the past or to anything of substance in the present; the future likewise did not exist. After lunch they loaded the car with groceries that their daughter had shopped for and headed back to prison.

What had become of our home in Elahieh? That question of course had haunted me for years, but now I dared to allow myself to look for an answer. My friend Ghasem Hajizadeh, who came to visit almost every evening while I stayed at Vida's, reported that shortly after the revolution it had served as the personal office of the minister for information and culture. (Better that, I supposed, than a *komiteh* office or an interrogation center. Did the minister realize how much culture had been nurtured in that house?) Ghasem had found reason to go there several times when he was working on arrangements for an exhibition of his own paintings. A dozen or so desks filled the living room and dining room, he said. The mirror mosaics on the ceiling and fireplace still remained when he last visited. He was not allowed to go upstairs, though he asked several times. But all this had happened years before.

I learned that a seamstress who worked for my cousin was living in one of the new apartment buildings that had gone up on the adjacent property. I gathered my courage and called on her. She was happy enough to tell me as much as she knew: the ministry had moved out years ago. Some important mullah lived there now. We stepped out onto her tiny balcony, and as I looked down over what had been my garden, a wave of nausea came over me. One small patch of green remained at the bottom of the garden, and the trees still stood, unmoved by the desolation around them. The pool was dry and cracked, portions of lawn were paved over, and dusty patches of desert were all that was left of the Japanese pond and the rock garden where flowers had filled every crevice.

I thanked her and said goodbye, then took a chance and knocked at the door of the house opposite ours. The neighbor who answered the door filled in a few details: she had watched truck after truck driving away, loaded with all our possessions. Yes, it was true that a mullah lived there now. There had been an accident in the driveway recently and three people were killed, she told me: a gas leak . . . a welding torch . . . a car loaded with machine guns. "We thought at first that the Iraqis were bombing again, that the war had somehow started over."

I swallowed it all. Though I told myself to turn my back and walk away, it would be a lie to say that it wasn't painful. The worst of it came in the form not of new information but of the irony of sad contrasts. Once I had made it safely into Iran, Zahra had decided to come too and explore the possibility of living here herself. She hoped to stay for a year or two, so I helped her to find a furnished apartment in the same neighborhood where we had lived. The best we could find was a dark little place with tacky furnishings and a gruesome, flowered wall-to-wall carpet. Whenever I went to visit her there, the taxi drove past our old home on the way. A chill went down my spine every time at the sight of the garden wall, the suggestion of lights behind it, and the sad prospect of Zahra's new home. Each time I was tempted to ask the driver to take another route, but a stubborn pride kept the words inside me. It would have felt too much like defeat or denial.

I begged Vida to come with me on a trip up to the Caspian Sea. I wanted desperately to see Dozdak one more time and to find out what had become of our land there. Staying unchaperoned in a hotel was not an option for two women in the Islamic Republic at that time, so we recruited a friend who had a house at the beach nearby and hired a car and driver for the trip. Three women sitting unchaperoned in a restaurant was not an option either, so we invited the driver to join us when we stopped for lunch on the way. We pretended he was my son, and I couldn't have wished for a sweeter, more polite young man in the role.

I had expected changes, of course, but I was shocked to find the sea itself transformed. The water level had been rising gradually over several years. On segments of the coast the waves had washed away houses, and owners had tried to protect those that remained by planting huge boulders on the shore, making it impossible to walk the beach. The orange trees that edged the strand were dying slowly as the soil turned salty. No one really knew the reason behind this mysterious, creeping disaster, except in the vaguest sense that the sea was rebelling against environmental abuse.

Before facing Dozdak, we drove first to the hilltop land where Abol and I had hoped to retire one day. It was just as I remembered, a landscape by Cézanne: the orange orchards, the rice fields, the hillsides planted with tea, the snow-covered mountains in the distance. Here time had stood still, more or less. The only change was a brand-new school building, and asphalt laid on our dirt road. Who could argue with that? A man appeared on the road, so I stopped to ask what he knew of the land.

"It belongs to a doctor who lives abroad. He hasn't been here in many years. Why do you want to know?"

"I might like to buy it."

He answered my lie with one of his own: "Then you'd better move fast. A lot of people are interested. They come from Tehran all the time to look at it. The price is going up."

We left him to his story and drove on to Dozdak. The cottage was completely boarded up, and a small factory producing cement blocks had been built next to it. The land was enclosed with a high wire fence, with a sign on the locked gate announcing that it belonged to "all the workers and staff of the Central Bank." Except for these surreal incursions, it was as beautiful as it had ever been.

Once the constant rounds of visiting and my sentimental detective work had slowed a bit, I faced up to the business portion of my trip. I called the contact that Abol's student had offered to introduce me to and set up a meeting. He suggested that we meet at what had once been the Intercontinental Hotel. (It was now renamed Hotel Laleh— Tulip Hotel—a reference to the tulip-red blood of our martyrs again, but veiled so as not to offend the few remaining tourists?) I agreed immediately. I was eager to see if the mirror mosaic walls I had done there years before were still standing.

"How will I know you?"

"I'll carry a newspaper and stand at the front of the lobby. How about you?"

I paused. The whole point of *hejab* was anonymity; it wasn't that easy to distinguish myself from any other shrouded woman. "I'll wear a gray headscarf and sunglasses."

I arrived early to look for my mirror mosaics. The columns were gone, but the two walls remained, one just a little worse for wear where a computer desk had been pushed up against it. A waiter approached and asked if I wanted anything.

"No, I'm just looking at the art."

"Oh, yes. All of the guests come to look at it. The Japanese especially admire it. They like to touch it."

"Is that so? Do you know who made it?"

"No, but I've heard it was a woman."

I peered at my signature. "Yes, it looks like it must have been a woman."

The game ended. I spotted my contact, and we sat down to talk. I sketched out what I understood of the situation and showed him the documents I had gathered. He said there was a slim chance of success, and no longer any real danger in trying. His assistant would escort me to the *komiteh* offices and guide me through the labyrinth of paperwork.

I had to dress for my visits to the *komiteh* as if I were going to the mosque, wearing not just a headscarf and overcoat but a chador on top of it all. It seemed totally appropriate: bureaucracy was its own religion here. On my first visit I got past the police barrier and the security check before I had to show my documents to a bearded man in a camouflage jacket carrying a machine gun. I didn't protest when he called me "sister." He leafed through my papers. On one page my name was written Monir Kamkar Shahroudy, followed by Farman-farmaian in parentheses.

"What connection do you have to the Farmanfarmaians?" His exact words were less than polite, his tone aggressive.

"I *had* a connection." Past tense. I said it with a tight-lipped finality that I hoped would signify that any further questions were unnecessary and inappropriate.

He asked more questions, many more, poring carefully over the papers. He asked enough questions—and I answered at length—that soon enough we were no longer strangers. His tone softened and warmed as those old, deeply ingrained habits of politeness and human connection proved stronger than the thin veneer of angry revolutionary bravado. In the end I felt confident enough to ask him frankly, "*Agha,* what do you have against the Farmanfarmaians? Why were you so angry when you asked about my connection to them?"

"They were evil and decadent," he said. "They had orgies, big parties with dancing and drinking and gambling."

"I never saw anything like that myself as long as I knew them," I said. He didn't answer, and we left it at that.

After weeks of trekking from one office to the next, I had a moment of optimism when a clerk admitted there was nothing in Abol's file to indicate that he was one of the "bad" Farmanfarmaians, and the fact that he had taught at the university was definitely in our favor. But that wasn't enough to get the wheels turning, and greasing them with bribes seemed to make no difference. In the end I got nowhere at all and decided to stop wasting my time.

Before I left, I visited Valiollah's shop, the antique dealer who had helped me collect the paintings behind glass from the Gulf and so much more. It was an emotional meeting. We couldn't even shake hands in public, so we went to the back of the shop for a big hug. Tears were pouring down his stubbly, wrinkled face, and my own knees were trembling. His son Reza, the little boy I had surprised once with a gift of a bicycle, was a grown man now. He kissed my hand and then surprised me with the news I least expected:

"Monir Khanom, I have found a storage room on the Karaj Road that belongs to the government. I saw your art there, hundreds of pieces!" I assumed he meant my collections, or some portion of them. I doubt he would have recognized my own work.

"Agha Reza, can you take me there? I would love to see them again. And if you can arrange it, I'd like to buy three pieces. For my children, for the memories. I'll pay any price they ask." He agreed to make the arrangements and call me.

The phone rang early the next day. "Khanom, they refuse to give permission. They say that women are not allowed in the storeroom." The disappointment hit me like a slap in the face.

"That's crazy," my nephew told me when I shared the news. "I've never heard such a thing. He's lying." Odd as it was, he was right. I could hear the lie in Reza's voice. But I had no idea why he would do such a thing, and there wasn't much I could do about it. I had reached the end of my stay.

Leaving Iran through Mehrabad airport was only a shade less frightening than arriving had been. Once again my name was checked against blacklists. Had my paper chase alerted the powers that be to the presence of a Farmanfarmaian on the loose? Once again hands dug through every corner of my overstuffed luggage. No, I had no gold, rugs, antiques, opium, or anything else that was prohibited to carry out. I had hoped to travel light and refused to take a second suitcase, which meant that all the gifts I was asked to carry for others, including a ridiculously large quilt, refused to go back in the suitcase until I asked a friendly tourist to sit on it. Finally, every last hurdle passed, I stood at the glass wall and waved my stamped passport with a big smile, as if waving goodbye but really to let Vida and family waiting on the other side know that I had made it through safely.

CHAPTER THIRTY-SIX

A few months after I got back to New York, I had a phone call from Tehran. It was Reza, Valiollah's son. I was surprised by the call but glad to hear from him, until I heard his news. He told me that he had sold six hundred of the paintings behind glass from my collection that he had found in the government storage room. The purpose of his call was to ask me to write a letter saying that the deal was done with my knowledge and agreement. I was furious, but I laughed as I told him, "Agha Reza, what the hell do you think you're doing? I bought those paintings once from your father, and he made a good profit on them. Now you've sold them a second time, for a second profit, after they were stolen from me. And you want me to say I'm happy about this? *Inshallah,* one day you'll sell them a third time and profit a third time, but no, I am not at all happy about it." I understood now his reluctance to let me see the paintings, and I understood even better when they started to show up at art auctions in the West. His buyer wanted a document that would protect him against the possibility of my suing. Although I recognized the paintings quite clearly, I didn't bother to pursue the matter. Nothing I could do would restore the trust and honor that Reza had squandered, and that mattered to me infinitely more than the monetary value of the paintings.

Although the trip to Iran was a turning point, a huge step toward acceptance of the fact that I would somehow have to get on with my life without Abol, actually doing it was a geologically slow process that had little to do with my conscious mind. I still lived every moment as if it served no purpose other than as a story I could recount to Abol in my mind, the actions encrusted with descriptions even as they happened. His absence was a dragging weight, a heavy stone of desolation that I carried everywhere. Its sharp edges cut my insides with every unaccustomed move—each "first" that happened without him. Then, ever so slowly, the patches of time between these lonely firsts began to stretch and they visited more randomly. As their rhythm slowed, anniversaries became a heavier beat: the calendar dates we had marked together, the turning of seasons that each time opened a flood of memories, and most of all, the deep season of darkness that surrounded the anniversary of his death every year. Every winter arrived with mythically barren proportions, and Thanksgiving weekends had forever changed their meaning.

Even now I still carry the stone of his absence, though its load has lightened and its sharp edges have worn down under the drip of time. Over the years a moss of new memories (grandchildren: babies grown into real people!) first gained a microscopic foothold on its surface, then slowly thickened into a vague resemblance of something softer, green and growing.

It was a very long time before I could focus on work more substantial than drawings and occasional small projects, but once I began working on my memory boxes, they became all-consuming. They were invitations, perhaps, to a sense of closure; like the collages under net, a wrapping up of a life. But once I placed myself inside their little compartments (they had to be small, not much larger than shoeboxes; I was working in a miniature studio in a corner of my living room), windows opened onto vast views that stretched inward for many decades. Corners turned in surprising ways, insides became outsides, doorways became reasons unto themselves, and gardens flourished in closets. Within these complex, nested chambers I arranged fragments of a life: snippets of the few old photographs I had of myself, my home, and my family, remnants of my mother's dresses, jewelry that she wore, suggestions of the stained-glass windows of Qazvin, flowers and nightingales, fragments of poetry . . . Mirrors appear in every one of my memory boxes, and there are reflections, of course, of a life in art: the eyes of artists I wish to honor, the landscapes of old miniature paintings with their roiling rocks alive with hidden creatures, and hexagons tunneling through time with their codes for infinite space and pure order. Sometimes a woman appears: here a tiny doll with arms raised in startled surprise, there a figure clipped from a miniature painting with finger to mouth, again a gesture of surprise. She is asking, "*Chi shod?*" What happened? What happened to my past?

As soon as I finished one memory box, I started another, until I had created about thirty of these self-portraits in collage over a period of two years. In the meantime some friends had started a small nonprofit gallery promoting Iranian art, and they asked me to show some of the boxes as well as some of my drawings in an exhibition. I appreciated their efforts for a good cause and did my best to help make the show a success. When the possibility came up of inviting Queen Farah to a party at their loft gallery, I offered to call her myself and encourage her to accept.

A few phone calls passed between us—she was concerned to know who would be at the party, and I promised to keep it to a small group that she would be comfortable with. The last time she happened to call, when I picked up the phone and recognized her voice, the words popped out of my mouth for the very first time: "I bow to you." It had taken almost thirty years for the expression to gel in my mind, and even now I couldn't say it without giggling.

The event went smoothly. Farah was as gracious as I remembered, attentive both to the art and to the comfort of others. "Monir," she said to me at one point, "Frank Stella is sitting by himself." I followed her gaze. There he was, parked alone on the windowsill. "Perhaps someone should keep him company?"

When it was time for her to leave, I walked with her downstairs to her car. As we said our goodbyes, she handed me a bouquet of lilies of the valley that she had picked from her own garden in Westchester. "*Bagh-e-moon sabz bud,*" she said as she gave me the flowers. Our garden was green. I was very touched by that bittersweet note, knowing that whatever loss I had experienced, her own must have been more painful.

WITH DORIS HALABY AND QUEEN FARAH.

I went back to Iran in 2002. In the ten years that had passed since my first return, much had changed. The mood of the country had lightened altogether. The high moral fervor of the revolution was fading, rubbed thin by people's mundane concerns: finding a job, supporting a family, muddling through the end of the twentieth century. It was not unusual to see young men and women walking together in the park holding hands, or fashions that pushed the boundaries of the Islamic dress code. A whole generation had no memory of the revolution, viewed the rule of religion with a profound cynicism, and waited impatiently for a freer future. I allowed myself to drift again to thoughts of a graceful twilight and the possibility of living again in my homeland. It was beginning to look less like a leap of faith and more like a logical conclusion. I started to explore practical considerations, like finding an apartment that matched the general outline of my daydreams.

While I was there, I tried to make an appointment to meet with the director of the Tehran Museum of Contemporary Art. I wanted to make it known to someone who cared about art that pieces from the confiscated collections were finding their way into the hands of dealers abroad. After many unreturned phone calls, a chance encounter with his assistant got me in the door. The director, Dr. Samii Azar, listened to my concerns—that I didn't want this art to be taken from the country and our heritage lost, regardless of whether it belonged to me or not—and he promised to look into the matter.

When I got back to New York, I sent him the few old brochures and exhibition catalogs I had been able to gather over the years, and messages trickled back that this piece or that had been found. Then, early in 2004, he sent a message of a different sort altogether, a message that took my breath away. I sat down, speechless. Was I dreaming? No. The Tehran Museum of Contemporary Art was offering me a major retrospective exhibition. They would help me to locate whatever could be found in storage of my own work that had been confiscated, and to ship my newer work from New York.

I had been rehabilitated. The wheel had turned again. I was going home, and in the best of all possible ways.

I went back to Iran that summer to begin preparing for the exhibition, which was scheduled for the fall of 2005. When I unrolled the plans for the exhibition space, the reality hit me again. Gallery after gallery would be mine to fill, nine in all. Two additional galleries were included, and I was asked to invite two artists of my own choosing from America to exhibit with me. (Frank Stella popped immediately into mind—what a treat it would be to show him around!) Oh yes, and in the meantime would I accept a commission for another exhibition opening very soon, on the theme of Iranian gardens? Of course I would!

It was not all cake. I still had a mountain of bureaucracy to scale and a lot of hard work ahead of me. The confiscated art was scattered around Tehran. The Museum of Contemporary Art had nine pieces of my work in its storage, and there was one more in the basement of the Saadatabad Palace Museum, the same basement that Esmail had not been willing to show me. There was more, I was told, in the Dafineh, a government storehouse for confiscated goods.

The director of the Saadatabad Palace Museum offered to guide me on an inspection of the storerooms. But first he led me through the museum with much fanfare, introducing me proudly to all the staff and dropping the Farmanfarmaian name at every opportunity, as if we had just arrived from some parallel universe. One surreal moment followed another. We stood in the Dafineh, which I had half imagined as a dank dungeon with dusty antiques and paintings stacked every which way. Instead we faced a modern storage system to rival that of any museum in the West. The first of the huge panels that the director slid out from its hangar included three pieces that I recognized from my collections: two Qajar portraits and a large coffeehouse painting. They had been well cared for, with new stretchers and some skillful restoration work. But these details I noticed only afterward.

The fourth painting on the panel had sent me into shock: it was my life-size nude portrait of Abol, lifted out of a playful weekend so many years ago and staring me now boldly in the face. Aside from the shock of the time warp and Abol's unexpected presence in these surroundings, I was profoundly embarrassed to be caught like this in front of the museum director and his staff who, whatever else they might be, were still civil servants employed by the Islamic Republic. I opened my mouth, and a spontaneous fib escaped from it, a half-baked detour of an excuse: "It was the gardener's son." Even as the words slipped out, I knew I had only made things worse. My face was a deep shade of red by the time I mumbled, "No, I lied. It's my husband."

We found several more of my paintings there, as well as several of the coffeehouse paintings and a few of the antiques that had been in Abol's family for generations. We passed through rooms full of crystal chandeliers hanging thick from the ceiling, tables with hundreds of candlesticks lined up, and shelves full of antiquities, some of them millennia old. Every single piece had been confiscated from homes abandoned by people fleeing the revolution. Later it became clear that if I wanted to claim any of my own possessions, I was expected to buy them back at market value. The museum might fish out pieces for the exhibition, but nobody was going to give them back to me.

On that same trip I made a final visit to the house in Elahieh. I learned that it had been taken over by another government ministry. It wanted to tear the house down and build a high-rise apartment building on the land, a fate that had already transformed many of the old homes and huge gardens of the neighborhood. The development demon had been so greedy that the city was finally reacting: a new law prohibited any new building that would involve cutting down trees. And so they had simply stopped watering the garden and were waiting for the trees to die a slow death.

For the first time since the morning we left in the winter of 1978, I entered the house itself. The stone steps to the threshold were deeply cracked; they had obviously not been cleared of ice in the winter. All the mirror mosaics, all the antique woodwork had been stripped from the walls and ceilings. Looking out onto the dying garden from the window of Nima's bedroom, that fine room she had chosen with Abol's blessing almost half a century ago, I felt like I was witnessing an ancient ruin melting back into the desert. A lone caretaker had his living quarters now in Abol's office. When he saw me, he must have realized from the expression on my face, the trembling of my hands, that this was once my home. His eyes refused to meet mine, but he mumbled, "I'm sorry, Khanom."

CHAPTER THIRTY-SEVEN

I knew that the only cure for the sadness I carried home with me that day was work. I had promised to create an installation piece for the next exhibition at the Tehran Museum of Contemporary Art, a celebration of the Iranian garden. It was time to roll up my sleeves and get down to business. Images hovered over the blank page of my sketchbook like projections on a movie screen: the dying garden in Elahieh; bare branches of murdered trees reaching out to me like beggars' hands. Broken stone and parched earth, riddled with cracks. The same cracks mirrored in the soles of Uncle Dervish's feet, confused cracks like a map of long journeys. The spring at Abdolabad, with promises dangling from the old tree. Water oozing from a crack in the mountain, tumbling down rocky steps and careful channels . . . My long, long thirst for this land. And then, beyond images, an idea bubbled up. I would build a fountain. Water sculpted into flowing liquid light, the pool that lies at the heart of the fantasia of roses and nightingales, blossoming, singing, and dying, that fill the garden—the very source of its life. The lines, the material would have to be absolutely clean, pure, abstract. I pictured terraced slabs of glass, each a pure geometric form, and the water sliding smoothly down their stepped sides. Water, light, life.

The idea for the fountain gave me a surge of optimism, but I was worried about the big exhibition looming ahead. So little of my old work was turning up. How would I fill the space? Besides, I was eager to forge ahead with something new. Retrospective or no, I wasn't dead yet. I had some ideas for a new series of mirror work, a progression of simple shapes, increasing in complexity, that would honor the Sufi symbolism that is expressed in geometry.

But I needed help. Could I track down Hajji Ostad? Was he still alive? Tehran had grown to a vast metropolis of twenty million people. All I had was a name, a photograph taken more than thirty years ago, and a vague memory of the neighborhood where he had lived in the old part of the city, below the bazaar. I headed south and cruised the streets, looking for glass and mirror shops, flashing my photo like a detective.

"Do you know this man? Hajji Ostad Mohammad Navid. He was a master mirror worker, lived here a long time ago." Negative, but at each shop I asked if they knew of an older shop. Finally there was a glimmer of recognition, a phone number scribbled on a piece of paper.

I dialed and heard a hello out of the distant past. When we got past the initial surprise and the second stage of flowery expressions of praise and gratitude, I made an appointment to visit him at home. Hajji Ostad had done well for himself. His beaming wife served us tea in a well-appointed room spread with fine carpets. He was a busy man, much in demand for decorating the many new mosques under construction, but he agreed to carve out ten days from his schedule for me. He also helped me locate a small studio for rent and recruited two assistants. One was an opium addict and the other half blind, but they worked well enough. Still, it wasn't like the old days. Hajji Ostad had become ostentatiously pious and spent most of the time praying loudly in the next room, which annoyed me beyond reason. I was managing well enough with the assistants, so I didn't press him for more when the ten days were up.

We had made good progress, finishing the first two pieces of the series before I had to return to New York. I was very pleased with them. The original concept had found its form in a progression of bold mandalas, each unfolding from a grounded center into an explosion of brilliant color and fractured light. Back in New York, I fine-tuned the plans for my fountain, deciding eventually on stainless steel instead of glass. With a friend's help, I played with designs on a computer for the first time—to be honest, she performed the technical magic while I watched and made suggestions. But trying to supervise the fabrication long distance from New York to Tehran was a headache, and I was eager to get back.

I returned to Iran again later that same year, 2004. Traveling back and forth was exhausting, but at least I had managed to set up my own apartment in Tehran. The building was brand new and well designed, built by my nephew Kayhan who lived next door, so I was able to add my own touches to the design. After endless construction delays I finally moved in. The day that I first lit a fire in the fireplace, Tehran had a record snowfall. From my little balcony I could look down on my niece's roof and my nephew's garden, and on pine branches heavy with sparkling snow. Off in the distance, beyond the city muffled in white, four separate mountain ranges dissolved into a clear blue sky. Yes, I could grow old comfortably here. I wasn't quite ready to give up my foothold in New York, but it slipped a little further when I found that my health insurance in the United States was canceled, all my payments vanished arbitrarily into thin air.

Around the time of Iran's elections in the summer of 2005, plans for my big exhibition began to come unglued. The uncertainty surrounding the election had thrown the whole country into a state of suspended animation. No one could foresee exactly what our dark horse, Ahmadinejad, had in store for us, but the museum director knew he would soon be out of a job. My show was postponed so that he could end his tenure with a bang: a spectacular exhibit of Queen Farah's collection that had been seized in the revolution. I couldn't blame him—he was sitting on a vast trove of important paintings that had been hidden for decades and would now draw world attention. But I was uncomfortable sitting on a back burner, and I had my own doubts about the prospect of dealing with a new administration at the museum. Meanwhile the money they had promised to cover my expenses had not yet materialized, and Frank Stella had declined my invitation to share the exhibition space with me. No show was worth the possibility of being beheaded by terrorists, he said, genuinely worried. "It's Iran," I said. "It's nothing at all like Iraq. You have to come see for yourself." He wouldn't budge.

There's a saying in Persian: "When one door closes, another opens." The Farhangsara cultural center in Niavaran offered to host the exhibition late the next year, 2006, and the plans shifted with little trouble from one venue to another. Set in a beautiful park not far from my home, it was a far more pleasant and convenient place. By that time, however, my tiny studio was stacked to the ceiling with new work, and I was desperate for a bigger space. I looked all over without luck. One landlord wouldn't rent to a woman alone. "*Agha*, I'm an old woman!" I pleaded. "You find me a husband, and I'll sign the lease on my wedding day!" Finally, on the edge of despair, I found my new studio. More perfect than I could have imagined, it was close to home and spacious, with beautiful light and easy garage access. It even had a small courtyard with a venerable old mulberry tree and rosebushes. A sprinkle of rain on the dry earth and dusty branches released a scent that twined around deep-rooted memories. It would be a very good place to work.

I was making steady progress on the new pieces when something even bigger appeared on the horizon. The Victoria and Albert Museum in London was launching a new gallery dedicated to Islamic art, and they were interested in my mirror work. Seriously interested: it was a huge commission, a whole wall to fill. Every trip between New York and Tehran now included a stop in London for meetings, more meetings, measurements. My luggage was stuffed with drawings, rolls of tape, and cans of special paint. My sketches evolved into six panels, each seven feet high, that played with geometry and perspective to hint at magic portals. I wanted them to reflect the viewers and at the same time surround them, pull them in. In deference to the Islamic theme, I narrowed the palette of colors to the blues of mosque dome and sky, and to nature's green.

I was permanently groggy with jet lag. I kept my assistants going by fueling them with kebab, cookies, tea, and the promise of a big bonus if we finished on time. But they bickered among themselves and argued constantly with my driver, whom I had assigned to keep track of expenses. I told them to take their fight elsewhere, but I didn't really want them to go. Finally I came up with a generic solution: whichever antagonist was the younger, he had to apologize first, and the elder had to forgive. This family logic seemed to make sense to them, and we got back to work.

The race continued right up to the opening. There was not just the art to complete but designs for the catalog; photographs had to be taken, and the massive panels had to be professionally packed for shipping. Then I was off to London once more to get them out of customs and supervise the installation. We finished just in time for the press conference, the speakers arrayed in front of my wall.

I was staying only a couple of blocks from the museum, but my room was up five flights of stairs. The final sprint back from the hotel between the press conference and the opening was too much for me. I hailed a cab. "You're right there," he argued, ready to pass up the fare.

"I'm an old woman, I'm wearing high heels, and I'm willing to pay you. Just get me there!"

Security at the museum was heavy, and not just because the exhi-

PRINCE CHARLES ASKS ME TO TEACH AT HIS SCHOOL.

bition was focused on Islamic art. Prince Charles was there for the opening, along with the foreign minister, Jack Straw. After their speeches—again, in front of my very proud wall—the museum director steered me over to meet the prince. We chatted a bit about the design and mirror technique, and then he surprised me:

"Would you teach at my school?" He had founded a college in London to teach traditional Islamic arts and crafts. Interesting, I thought, but my plate was already full.

"I'm honored, but I don't think my English is up to it."

"You're doing fine," he said, patting me on the arm.

"But I'm an old lady," I demurred. "You know, I'm the same age as your mother." He seemed royally amused.

On the flight home (Which home? In my exhausted daze, I hardly knew if I was headed for New York or Tehran) I tried to digest it all. The opening was a great success—no, it was downright dazzling, the sun on a snowy pinnacle, served with a fine champagne of praise that made my head spin. Every bit of self-doubt that had ever crossed my mind, every slight that I'd ever imagined, was wiped away in those few hours of glory. My only unfulfilled wish was that Abol might have been there to witness, with his smile, that his long faith in me had indeed been well placed.

But success, I realized, is a temporary state of mind. There was so much work still to be done for the exhibition at Farhangsara, the final stretch . . . An old lady, indeed! Only when it suits me. I thought of friends who are fading now into senility. When I'm with them, I catch myself reacting with impatient judgment, as if it's their fault. It's not rational or fair, I know, and certainly not kind, but I fear that fading. Still, if they're entitled to repeat themselves and dither, then I'm entitled to be a little selfish with the time that remains to me. I have work to do. And I think it will suit me to do it in Iran, where the earth smells so good after a rain.